INSIGHT AND VISION
The Problem of Communism in Marx's Thought

INSIGHT AND VISION

The Problem of Communism in Marx's Thought

R.N. Berki
Reader in Politics, University of Hull

J.M. Dent & Sons Ltd
London and Melbourne

First published 1983
© R.N. Berki, 1983

All rights reserved
Phototypeset in 10/12 VIP Times by
Inforum Ltd, Portsmouth
Made in Great Britain by
Biddles Ltd, Guildford, Surrey, for
J.M. Dent & Sons Ltd
Aldine House, 33 Welbeck Street, London W1M 8LX

This book if bound as a paperback is subject to the
condition that it may not be issued on loan or otherwise
except in its original binding

British Library Cataloguing in Publication Data

Berki, R.N.
  Insight and vision: the problem of Communism in
Marx's thought.
  1. Marx, Karl   2. Ideology—History
  I. Title
  193   B3305.M74

  ISBN 0-460-10172-2
  ISBN 0-460-11172-8 Pbk

Contents

Acknowledgments vii
Foreword ix

1 Communism and Marx's Thought 1
2 Full Vision 26
3 Strengthening Insight 58
4 Fusion 87
5 Receding Vision 124
6 Heaven and Hellas 162

Notes 188
Index of Names 205

Acknowledgments

The author and publishers are grateful for permission to quote from the following copyright translations:

Karl Marx and Friedrich Engels, *Collected Works*, 1975 and following (the collection will comprise 50 volumes, of which 20 have so far appeared), and Karl Marx and Friedrich Engels, *Selected Works in One Volume*, 1980, reprinted by permission of Lawrence and Wishart, London.

Karl Marx, *Grundrisse: Foundations of the Critique of Political Economy*, translated by Martin Nicolaus, reprinted by permission of Penguin Books Ltd (The Pelican Marx Library, 1973) and of Random House Inc. Translation and Foreword copyright © Martin Nicolaus, 1973.

Karl Marx, *Capital, Volume 1: A Critique of Political Economy*, translated by Ben Fowkes, reprinted by permission of Penguin Books Ltd (The Pelican Marx Library, 1976) and of Random House Inc. Translation copyright © Ben Fowkes, 1976.

Foreword

The original inspiration to write this book came from two doctoral theses with which I have had the privilege of being associated in recent years, in one case as external examiner and in the other as supervisor. From the first (on Plato) I learnt the value for interpretation of probing beyond the immediate, ostensive meaning of an author's actual utterances. From the second (on Hegel) I learnt to appreciate the distinctive character of the classical Hellenic ideal, so often confused with modern radical utopias and eschatologies. With what success these influences have been able to bear fruit in the present effort is of course not for me to judge. For the most part, my intention was to concentrate on Marx's writings and to derive the substantive aspect of my interpretation from these writings alone; composing the book became a confrontation or grappling with the texts, an individual and solitary hermeneutical exercise. Hence the somewhat heavy documentation from Marx's texts and the corresponding relative unconcern with the vast secondary literature (with which I cannot claim complete familiarity anyway). Three further remarks concerning sources. Firstly, following academic orthodoxy I have confined my attention to Marx's writings, including those jointly authored with Engels, but excluding Engels' independent works, except for the odd marginal comment. Secondly, I did my actual research for this book on the English translation of Marx's writings, except for two small instances. My German is tolerable and in fact I am familiar with the basic texts in the original; I have, for instance, vivid recollection of the headache and sweat accompanying my reading of the *Grundrisse* in the mid-1960s, before it was translated. However, since my German is far from perfect and since the available translations are of excellent quality, it would have been both unnecessarily pedantic and irritatingly time-consuming to resort to the original texts here. At the same time, I thought it advisable to give the original of certain key terms and phrases in the text and corresponding references in the Notes. Thirdly, italics in direct quotes are invariably in the original. Here I might add that in retrospect I feel somewhat uneasy about my own overabundant italicization; partly, I suppose, it is a result of being

Foreword

concerned with Marx's emphasis-saturated writings and partly a personal stylistic peculiarity which I have not been able to overcome. All in all, I must say I have had a great deal of fun writing this book and I hope that at least some of my enjoyment will be communicated to the reader.

Hull, March 1983   R.N.B.

1 Communism and Marx's Thought

Communism is not just a fascinating aspect of Marx's thought, albeit without doubt it does provide uncommon fascination, intellectual delectation for the student. But there is a great deal more to it than that. The point we have to grasp right at the beginning is that communism is the most important thing about Marx or the most central and crucial concept in his entire literary output viewed as a unity; nay, I shall go even further and put forward the contention, as the starting-point of this study, that ultimately communism is the *only thing* that is important about Marx's thought. A number, perhaps the majority, of commentators on Marx have failed to see this and accordingly devoted their attention to the sundry details of Marx's analysis of the capitalist mode of production, his 'critique' of political economy, his minute historical investigations, abstruse 'scientific' categories and deductions, his political and journalistic harangues, endless fratricidal denunciations and polemics, or perhaps his organizational suggestions and schemata, while neglecting the only thing, viz. communism, that bestows on all these particular aspects of Marx's lifework their meaning, their unity and their significance. There are, of course, intelligible reasons for this relative neglect over the decades, and it is very far from my intention here simply and abstractly (and thus unfairly) to debunk and dismiss other interpreters of Marx – especially since my debt to a good number of them is pretty obvious (as the sequel will show). The underplaying or missing the importance of communism for Marx's thought is not, in the main, the consequence of misdirected scholarship or a too shallow conceptual interpretive apparatus or a too ready, too submissive, too committed hagiographical acceptance (or a simplistic demonological reading of Marx's doctrine), though these have also often played their part. An example of what we might call insufficient philosophical penetration is provided by the recent (and in other respects most competent and lucid) study by A.W. Wood, *Karl Marx*, in which it is argued: 'Marx's critique of capitalism is based on some familiar philosophical value conceptions, such as self-actualization and positive freedom. But it is wrong to conclude from this, as some writers on Marx appear to do, that his denunciations of capitalist alienation invoke or presuppose a conception of a future communist lifestyle or future social arrangements . . . Marx never describes future social arrangements in detail . . .'[1] And: 'Marx's desire to overthrow capitalist society is not motivated by any ideal picture of communist society, but by the real alienation and deprivation of people in capitalist society . . .'[2] It is, of course, true that Marx never describes communism 'in detail', but surely the point is that concepts like 'real alienation' and 'deprivation' are only rendered intelligible by virtue of a substantive, i.e. another concept which refers to 'arrangements' and 'lifestyle' where these features are *absent*.

The mistake, it seems to me, lies in identifying Marx's *concept* of communism with an 'ideal picture of communist society' or what is commonly called the 'vision' of communism. This ideal picture is assuredly and demonstrably present in Marx's writings but it does not exhaust the meaning of communism for him – which itself, the heterogeneity, the ambiguity, the tensions of his concept of communism, accounts both for its central importance in his thought and for its being the source of major problems. We get much nearer the mark in another recent work, a collection of essays entitled *Marxism and the Good Society*, where it is rightly said in the editors' introduction: 'The centrality of the good society – as a conception, as a historically plausible aim, and as a program of human action – is hardly to be doubted in the context of Marx's theory.'[3] Nearer the mark, but this is still too circumstantial, inaccurate and misleading, since Marx's concept of communism cannot entirely be subsumed under the category of the 'good society' either. Richard T. De George, in the same collection, helpfully suggests that communism in Marx (and Engels) refers to three interrelated entities, viz. a doctrine, a movement, and 'a stage of historical development'. De George correctly intimates that communism *qua* doctrine and *qua* movement derive their meaning from the third referent, communism *qua* 'stage of historical development'. But is this the same as the 'good society'? Not necessarily, as De George's further analysis seems to imply, though again we might argue that here there is another instance of insufficient conceptual penetration, in that De George does not follow out his suggestion. He lists four components of communism *qua* 'good society':[4] it is the stage of development after capitalism; it means the abolition of private ownership of the means of production; it signifies the absence of evils associated with capitalism (i.e. alienation, exploitation and oppression); and it contains human 'emancipation' and 'all-round development' as its central values. He adds that it is these last two components or 'second-order' characteristics that make communism (for Marx and in general) 'worthwhile'.[5] Two points must be noted, indeed stressed. First, it is clear that the first two components in De George's list do not have any *obvious* value connotations or meanings; by themselves they have only a formal and ethically *indifferent* meaning, and do not as such constitute the 'good society'. Secondly, it is also abundantly clear that there is no *necessary* (logical or even commonsensical) relationship between these formal components on the one hand, and the substantive, ethically super-charged components on the other. And here we have the underlying *problem* of communism in Marx's thought in a nutshell, for as we shall see later Marx's concept of communism unites, or attempts to unite, these two distinct kinds of components.

At this point, however, we have to introduce and initially define the two ideas around which this study is organized, and which, in their polarity as well as interpenetration, appear to lend a poignant expression to the problem of communism in Marx. Vision and insight refer, in the first instance, respectively to the value-laden (substantive) and indifferent (formal) components of communism as suggested by De George's analysis; together they make up Marx's *concept* of communism; in that, as has been noted above, vision and insight do not easily, smoothly, automatically and comfortably cohere in Marx's thought, we also have a succinct presentation of Marx's problem. Now insight and vision, as they will be used in this study, do not refer to two sharply opposed and neatly separated principles or elements in Marx's thought, and, initial resemblance notwithstanding, even less to the often drawn, and somewhat vulgar, distinction between Marx's 'values' and his 'science', or his 'humanism' and his 'materialism', or his 'libertarian' and 'determinist' arguments, or 'philosophical' and 'proletarian' communism in Marxist thought, or the views of the 'young' and the 'mature' Marx. Such distinctions, though heuristically acceptable, cannot be seriously sustained or if they *are* insisted upon they merely succeed in distorting the subject matter they are supposed to explain. Here we need to draw a more subtle, wispier kind of distinction but one that makes a significant point; a distinction not between disparate elements but overlapping shades or colours or tones, a distinction between two parallel – alternating, converging, interpenetrating but ultimately also *diverging* – Marxist moods, attitudes, idioms, approaches. The two terms were deliberately chosen to suggest the close proximity of the two basic idioms in Marx's understanding of communism between which we wish to distinguish here. Both 'vision' and 'insight' refer to the faculty of *seeing*, or in a more allegorical (but related) sense to the faculty of understanding or knowing. But they signify seeing or knowing in different *ways*. Let me illustrate by a simple example what I have in mind (and obviously I shall depart somewhat from customary usage): a person who stands on a hilltop or on a beach and looks to the distance, with erect head and, in order to enjoy and appreciate the infinite horizon in front of him, with his eyes suitably narrowed, has *vision*. He sees far, far ahead, and he sees large things: majestic peaks, undulating pastures, misty waves, in the distance while being relatively oblivious of, relatively 'blind' to, the details of objects and of things: pebbles, crags, bird-feathers, immediately around him. He now inclines his head a little, opens his eyes fully and even strains them, so as to take in his immediate surroundings, noting minute particulars and at the same time becoming (relatively) oblivious of large vistas; he loses the clarity of his vision but gains a clear, articulated, vivid *insight* instead.

The analogy does not fit our subject perfectly, but nevertheless it will be useful to interpret Marx's understanding of communism as a kind of alternating-coalescing gaze, now large-scale and perhaps more aesthetic in inspiration, now small-scale concentrated on actual details and displaying a more pronouncedly cognitive interest. Yet both vision and insight connote both knowledge and a definite attitude, an emotive stance, in both cases we are dealing with 'facts' as well as 'values'. Of the two partially overlapping, partially distinct stances it is, without doubt, the Marxist *vision* of communism that is easier to comprehend. It signifies Marx's understanding of communism as, so to speak, a large and distant and somewhat blurred entity, a proper object of knowledge and reflection, but only as an internally undifferentiated *category* or a *dimension* which, though continuous with the world of the observer, is yet seen as being essentially *different*. The observer is in this world, communism is in another world. Going beyond the optical analogy, we can extend our definition of the Marxist vision of communism by identifying it with Marx's *absolute* value-position, his ultimate moral touchstone, his norm or ideal: communism in this visionary understanding is defined essentially by its purity, its transcendent distance and untroubled totality, its moral quality and its *ideality*; communism is another world but it is that which this world *should* become.

Marx's *insight* into communism, on the other hand, is rather more difficult to conceptualize, but in my view it is by far the more important and more interesting of the two components that make up his concept (which is why it figures as the first word in our title). The Marxist vision might appeal to our moral or aesthetic sense and might turn us into followers of Marx; but it is Marx's insight that we shall find the more fascinating if we want to become Marx's *students*. Now 'insight' in our interpretation, as noted above, is not intended to refer *simply* to Marx's 'scientific' theories of history and political economy (these, to be sure, have a heavy visionary content as well), but rather to Marx's discernible 'down-to-earth' attitude and attention (as optically illustrated in the above example), his absorbing interest in the world immediately surrounding him, his hard and intense glance relentlessly directed at 'pebbles, crags, bird-feathers' or their equivalents in the social human world. In this clearer but more confined perspective communism appears also as a proper object of valuation, but now instead of a pure, firm, absolute value-position we find Marx being somewhat ambiguous, somewhat hesitant and indecisive, even indifferent to the value that communism presents to him. And so this communism, as revealed by insight, is characterized by its details rather than its totality, its vicinity rather than its dimensional difference and distance, its uneven, multi-coloured, rough surface rather than its purity and depth; this communism is *almost* here and now, it is not another world but this world which not merely should be but *will* be, the present world as it is *becoming*. This communism is highly structured, an assemblage rather than a totality, consisting of forms, not colours, empirical features rather than a moral content. The communism of vision has or is *ideality*, the communism of insight has or is, above all, *reality*.

The dominant message in Marx's thought is that the vision of communism and the insight into communism ultimately coincide, that they are essentially one and the same thing, real and ideal fused together. It is as a *fused* concept that communism provides the intellectual starting-point and central motive force of Marx's doctrines. Communism in the Marxist scheme of things is thus somewhat analogous to God in the main Western transcendental religions. Note that the analogy is with God, and not with 'heaven' or 'salvation' which at first sight could have appeared more obvious candidates for making the relevant comparison. But heaven and salvation, in any intelligible or pictorial shape and form, are not logically necessary for religious belief, for the reasonableness of religious consciousness, although they are undoubtedly important as psychological props for the religiosity of the adolescent or simple-minded believer. Communism also has its aspects of 'heaven' and its not-too-sophisticated, though suitably secularized, references to 'salvation', but these are secondary in importance to its central character as God presented also in a suitably desacralized, demystified and terrestrial manner. The only ultimately meaningful question to be posed in the context of religious controversy, and cutting through the maze of successive layers of theological refinements and well-intentioned evasions, is this: does God exist? Is it meaningful at all to conceive of, and to accept as the guiding principle of one's life-conduct, some figure or shape or entity or image or notion in the universe that is both *distinct* from one's own life and consciousness, and at the same time relevantly, intelligibly and benevolently *superior* to them? Is there, as Max Eastman once formulated the question in the context of a study of Marxism, something in the universe that cares for me? The rationality of religious belief turns on the answer we give to this question. And religion fades away and ceases to be a distinct form of consciousness and experience, once the question and answer are fudged and either the distinctness (as in certain kinds of idealist philosophy or modern theology, e.g. when God is conceived as 'our innermost being') or the benevolent superiority of God (as in modern witch-craft and devil-worship) are denied, whether explicitly in the manner of militant atheism or implicitly in timid accommodation to secular fashions.

And just as there is absolutely no point in being religious if we deny the existence of God (though we may still profess ignorance of, and indifference to, heaven and personal salvation), there is no point and no meaning to being a Marxist, to accept Marx's theory of history, account of alienation and exploitation in the modern bourgeois world, the notion of the class struggle and the proletarian revolution, as being true, if at the same time we deny the reality of communism. To be a Marxist, not only in the crude everyday sense of being an activist adherent to a political party or movement bearing Marx's name on its banner, but also in the more rarefied, profounder sense of taking a positive, favourable intellectual and emotional attitude towards Marx's doctrine and accepting its basic tenets as 'sensible', 'reasonable' and/or 'basically valid', means *eo ipso* to be a communist. Otherwise Marxism as a doctrine or system of thought has no coherence, no identity, no meaning. Similarly to the case of religion, the acceptance and profession of communism for a Marxist would not necessarily, logically entail (although, and especially for the mass of ordinary adherents, it would usually be accompanied by) the belief in communism as a veritable heaven, as salvation; what it does entail is a belief in communism as an historical, philosophical, ethical and social-scientific *vantage-point*, as depersonalized deity, as ultimate reality, as the distinct and superior warranty that present tribulations, uncertainties, doubts, struggles, sacrifices and commitment are not wholly useless and meaningless. Communism as the fused product of insight and vision is that something in the Marxist mundane, secular universe that 'cares', or, to put it in the more germane, humanistic idiom, that which ensures and guarantees that *our* caring, committed attitude in the face of what here has the shape of merely superficial, contorted, undesirable social reality, i.e. capitalism, bourgeois civilization, our opposition to it and endeavour to change it, amounts to more than self-deceptive mockery. God as communism is not directly, immediately and representationally the warranty of a particular and distinct mode of life contrasted to the present, i.e. heaven contrasted to earth, salvation contrasted to suffering and heterogeneity; it is rather the supreme *conceptual warranty* of the historical limitation, finiteness of the heterogeneous present, and thus the indirect, mediate promise of a different mode of being and consciousness. Now the analogy with God and religion should not be pursued to its absurd limits; quite apart from its being offensive to both religious sensibility and Marxist humanistic *amour propre* (and with equally valid reasons), it would obscure the very telling and relevant differences between these two approaches. As regards the similarity of Marx's thought and religion, what one has to bear in mind is the god-like quality of communism having a *distinct* identity (vision) and being the supreme principle (insight) guaranteeing the *finality* of the present. And as regards the basic difference of religion and Marx's thought, for the moment let us just note that the very explicit, very emphatically asserted non-religious or anti-religious character of Marxism renders the concept of communism deeply embedded in it decidedly more problematic than it would be otherwise. To wit, and to express it crudely, God in religion need only be believed in, intuitively or with childlike innocence. But communism needs also to be *understood*.

Insight and Vision

Let us here clarify another point. The argument of this study is that Marx's thought ought to be approached through his concept of communism and not from any external or derivative angle, that it is communism, rather than any other notion, like alienation, historical materialism, revolution, surplus-value or class consciousness, that provides the ultimate key to a proper understanding of Marx's thought as an – *ex hypothesi* – coherent *unity*. This is not to say that there could be no valid academic reason for taking a more selective approach to Marx, isolating one or another freely chosen aspect of his doctrine – to be sure, Marx's literary output is vast and complex enough to cater for any kind of taste! We all do find Marx's particular arguments and observations 'useful' and 'stimulating', and obviously we will continue so to do. But it is important to understand clearly what one is doing when one employs this 'scissors and paste' approach. It may present unexpected dangers for the interpreter. One instance of this is found in self-professedly 'non-Marxist' attempts to deal with Marx, those in particular which seek to draw a sharp distinction between Marx's 'critique' of capitalism, which they find congenial and valid, on the one hand, and his 'vision' of communism on the other, which they dismiss as starry-eyed and utopian. (In parentheses: had the author not in the past been a victim to this unfortunate self-delusion himself, he would not have the force of his present convictions – may we at least sometimes realize our own mistakes!) The point here is, of course, and once stated it does appear obvious enough, that Marx's critique of capitalism has no sense whatever in the absence of his fundamental belief in communism. What sympathetic but sceptical commentators are apt to overlook is that a critical, or even hostile, attitude to certain features of modern Western industrial society, such as its plutocratic elements, its endemic poverty and vast distinctions of wealth, its crass materialism and egoism, its hypocrisy, its anarchy coupled with waste and bureaucratism, etc., etc., and a critical approach to 'capitalism', are essentially different things, even though they run a parallel course, and even though it is not possible to detect, let alone prevent, linguistic cross-fertilization and some degree of interpenetration between them. However, it is still one thing to object to certain features of modern industrial society, on the basis of some sundry philosophical or ethical conviction, and another thing to ascribe these features to an agency called 'capitalism' or, which is really the prior step taken towards confusion, to *see* them, collectively and integrally, as so many features *of* capitalism. Capitalism is a term of art, not invented by Marx and not confined exclusively to the Marxist vocabulary; however, since the time of Marx's working out his own theory of political economy and particularly since the worldwide spread of its fame and influence, its employment in discourse has inevitably involved the tacit and often unwitting acceptance of Marxist assumptions, Marxist logic and Marxist values.

Capitalism is a particular conceptualization of a collection of phenomena, and for Marx certainly it presupposes a certain view of what is good and what is evil, what is normal and abnormal in social relations and historical development. The evils of the modern age are squarely ascribed by him to this, the capitalist mode of production, and the term 'capitalism' is employed by him interchangeably with the more expressive phrase, 'rule of capital', which in turn is logically tied up with the notion, more freely used in the early writings, of the 'alienation of labour'. Now the point is that for Marx the only way out of capitalism, the only effective way to destroy the rule of capital, the alienated productive capacity and social productive relations of human beings, the only way to end human slavery and unhappiness and to institute real freedom and genuine human relations, is by organizing society along communist lines. The real, as contrasted to the sham and partial, destruction of capitalism amounts *eo ipso* to communism (whether or not the latter is to be introduced gradually – this detail is not relevant just here). Marx indeed has a field-day showing, from his own seemingly unassailable position, that the rule of capital is *not* destroyed, only made more pernicious by attempts to mollify it or 'humanize' it; all endeavours short of communism simply amount to the continuation of slavery, dependence, poverty, conflict and degradation. And as the destruction of capital is unintelligible without the introduction of communist society, so the very understanding, comprehension of capitalism as a distinct mode of production depends on our adopting a communist point of view. To understand modern society *qua* capitalism means of necessity to want to move towards communism, even though this simple desire and yearning may not in given instances be accompanied by a clear and full comprehension. As the negation of capitalism is communism, nothing else, communism and capitalism in Marx's thought furthermore compose a logical, dialectical unity – but this is to anticipate my ensuing argument, the climax of which will be reached in Chapter 4, presenting what I take to be the highest point of development of Marx's thought. For the

Insight and Vision

moment let us just note, by way of concluding this slight digression, the degree of irony, in part comic and in part lamentable, attaching to conservative, liberal or Christian strictures on the 'evils of capitalism', combined with forlorn and confused endeavours to baptize or academicize Marx, to make him look a 'respectable' commentator and philanthropist, i.e. to deny the communism which in truth alone defines his thinking.

The fused concept of communism thus, to continue with the main theme of this introductory chapter, has reference above all to a superior standpoint which pronounces negatively on the finality, the historically finite character, of the present, and at the same time, by the same token, positively on the basic defining qualities of the future. (As will be seen, I have somewhat modified De George's 'components', while essentially building on his analysis.) These three aspects: present, future, and the intellectual cognitive link between them, at least *appear* to hang together, and in a way it would be correct to say, in the apt words of a contemporary Marxist philosopher, that 'the innermost essence and the deepest meaning of Marx's thought' is 'that the future is the point of departure and the essential dimension of the historical process and of historical movements'.[6] That Marx does argue from a definite, putatively higher, standpoint about present and future comes out very clearly from a preliminary perusal of the texts; we could briefly survey here a few characteristic examples, selected almost at random.

In 1845, in a draft article devoted to a criticism of Friedrich List's *The National System of Political Economy*, Marx mentions specifically a 'different point of view' of modern industry, this being higher than the view of 'sordid huckstering interest'. This standpoint, he goes on, 'is *not* from within the industrial epoch, but *above* it; industry is regarded not by what it is for *man* today: but by what present-day man is for *human* history, what he is historically; it is not its present-day existence (not industry as such) that is recognized, but rather the power which industry has without knowing or willing it and which *destroys* it and creates the basis for a *human* existence'.[7] Again, in a newspaper article published in 1853 he warns of a 'silent revolution' which society is undergoing and 'which must be submitted to', and he castigates those who do not see beyond the immediate present: 'But can there be anything more puerile, more shortsighted, than the views of those economists who believe in all earnest that this woeful transitory state means nothing but adapting society to the acquisitive propensities of capitalists, both landlords and money-lords?'[8] In the *Grundrisse*, he defines communism, the free association of 'social individuals', as a standpoint or 'departure' even more clearly: 'The social relation of individuals to one another as a power over the individuals which has become autonomous, whether conceived as a natural force, as chance or in whatever other form, is a necessary result of the fact that the point of departure is not the free social individual.'[9] For Marx the inadequacy and error of 'bourgeois political economy' (and related views) lies in its conceiving the bourgeois system as 'natural' and 'eternal'.[10] To this he sharply opposes the 'correct view' which 'leads ... to the points at which the suspension of the present form of production relations gives signs of its becoming – foreshadowings of the future'. From this standpoint contemporary conditions 'appear as engaged in *suspending themselves* and hence in positing the *historic presuppositions* for a new state of society'.[11] Capitalism, which embodies the *'most extreme form of alienation'*, already contains in itself the dissolution of all *'limited presuppositions of production*, and moreover creates and produces the unconditional presuppositions of production, and therewith the full material conditions for the total, universal development of the productive forces of the individual'.[12] Capital, as Marx sees it, 'is posited as a mere point of transition', which, 'although limited by its very nature', 'strives towards the universal development of the forces of production, and thus becomes the presupposition of a new mode of production . . .'[13]

According to Marx, 'the participants in capitalist production live in a bewitched world and their own relationships appear to them as properties of things . . .'[14] Capitalism is 'the bewitched, distorted and upside-down world haunted by Monsieur le Capital and Madame la Terre, who are at the same time social characters and mere things'. Classical political economy, he concedes, has helped dissolve this false and 'bewitched' appearance of things, yet he argues 'even its best representatives remained more or less trapped in the world of illusion their criticism had dissolved, and nothing else is possible from the bourgeois standpoint'. This limited and erroneous standpoint 'also corresponds to the self-interest of the dominant classes, since it preaches the natural necessity and perpetual justification of their sources of income and erects this into a dogma'.[15] In truth, the 'historic mission and justification' of capital is only its 'development of the productive forces of social labour'. 'For that very reason, it unwittingly creates the material conditions for a higher form of production.' Political economists like Ricardo, in Marx's view, are visibly disturbed by such phenomena as the rate of profit in capitalist production, being its main motive force and yet at the same time endangered by the further development of this very mode. Of the 'underlying reason', however, Ricardo has 'no more than a suspicion'. 'What is visible here in a purely economic manner, i.e. from the bourgeois standpoint, within the limits of capitalist understanding, from the standpoint of capitalist production itself, are its barriers, its relativity, the fact that it is not an absolute but only an historical mode of production, corresponding to a specific and limited epoch in the development of the material conditions of production.'[16] The political economists' 'thoughts being entirely confined within the bounds of capitalist production, they assert that the *contradictory form* in which social labour manifests itself there, is just as necessary as labour itself freed from this contradiction'.[17] But: 'from the standpoint of a higher socio-economic formation, the private property of particular individuals in the earth will appear just as absurd as the private property of one man in other men'.[18] And so, 'from the moment that the bourgeois mode of production and the conditions of production and distribution which correspond to it are recognized as *historical*, the delusion of regarding them as natural laws vanishes and the prospect opens up of a new society, a new economic social formation, to which capitalism is only the transition'.[19] And who are in the position of seeing the bourgeois mode of production as 'historical' and are thus free of this 'delusion'? The 'communists' who, in terms of Marx's and Engels' *Manifesto*, are defined primarily in *theoretical* terms, as people who 'have over the great mass of the proletariat the advantage of clearly understanding the line of march'[20] of the proletarian movement.

Capital is Marx's great scientific *magnum opus* and here, it might be thought, the standpoint is *merely* the present, the world close-up as it were, as it reveals itself to the insight of the social scientist. But this is not the case. Marx here, in the process of analytically disentangling and explaining the 'mysterious' properties of the 'commodity', the microscopic essence of the capitalist mode of production, resorts to various analogical devices in order to make his arguments clear. What he is primarily looking for, and the procedure is without doubt conducive to a clearer understanding of the issues involved, is suitable *contrasts* to the subject he is investigating, counter-points or horizons or transcendent perspectives which would serve to illuminate the 'bewitched' world of capital, of commodity production. Having mentioned the hypothetical example of Robinson Crusoe producing, 'distributing' and consuming alone in an uninhabited island, his work and existence constituting a simple economic system (a device popular with classical political economists and adapted by Marx for that very reason), he enjoins us 'finally' to imagine, 'for a change, an association of free men, working with the means of production held in common, and expending their many different forms of labour-power in full self-awareness as one single social labour force. All the characteristics of Robinson's labour are repeated here, but with the difference that they are social instead of individual . . . The total product of our imagined association is a social product.'[21] Marx goes on: 'We shall assume, but only for the sake of a parallel with the production of commodities, that the share of each individual producer in the means of subsistence is determined by his labour-time.'[22]

Now here perhaps at first the impression might be that this imagined 'free association' of producers is *merely* an analogical device, with no substantive historical connotations or futuristic implications, entirely *at par* with the Robinson story, which, whether or not it has any past historical basis, is very clearly not regarded by Marx as in any way being part of the 'foreshadowings' (in the *Grundrisse* phrase) of the future. In his terms this would be absurd. But I think that it is quite clear from the sequel to the above in *Capital* that for Marx the notion of 'free association' has a much greater philosophical and methodological significance. In this 'imagined association', he continues his argument, 'the social relations of the individual producers, both towards their labour and the products of their labour, are here transparent in their simplicity, in production as well as in distribution'.[23] In other words here, in this form of production exclusively, and in diametrical contrast to the merely past and isolated and/or hypothetical experience of Robinson, human beings *know* and *understand* what production, the expenditure of labour-power, and social productive relations, are really about, and they organize their lives accordingly: things and processes and relations here are 'transparent' and producers are no longer 'bewitched' by 'fetishism', by the fantastic shape their *own* productive capacities have assumed in their present alienated form. Here Marx resorts to a specifically favoured equation of his, viz. the basic identity of religious belief and the view that present productive relations are 'natural' and 'eternal'; both are manifestations of delusion, bewitchment, and he concludes by saying that 'the religious reflections of the real world can, in any case, vanish only when the practical relations of everyday life between man and man, and man and nature, generally present themselves to him in a transparent and rational form. The veil is not removed from the countenance of the social life-processes, i.e. the process of material production, until it becomes production by freely associated men, and stands under their conscious and planned control.'[24] It is thus that communism – the standpoint of normality, of reason, freedom, perfection of knowledge and clarity of understanding, the standpoint of ultimate reality – serves as the organizing explanatory principle of Marxist science. And let us note that here communism contains *both* what has above been called Marx's insight and what has been called Marx's vision; as yet we have not attempted to sunder them apart.

So much, then, for the centrality of communism in Marx's thought. The next step will be to attempt – in the way, similarly to the foregoing section, of a preliminary sketch – a consideration of the *problem* of communism for Marx. Ultimately this problem, as I have already suggested, is to be defined in terms of the difficulty of reconciling Marx's vision and his insight, his 'big idea' of communism and his comprehension of the 'nitty-gritty' characterizing the nature of the present and its alleged 'movement' towards the future. But in the first instance the problem of communism would appear, as it has done to well-nigh every commentator (not all of whom, however, have grasped its proper significance), as the problem of the paucity of the explicit references to the 'good society' in Marx's writings. Here the first point to note though is that this is only a *relative* paucity, and it would be ridiculous to want to maintain that Marx says 'nothing' or 'little' about communism in absolute terms. At a rough estimate, it could be said that Marx's explicit references to communism as the good society of the future would fill a volume of at least fifty pages. What is true, of course, and in part the cause of our optical illusion is that Marx has a great deal more to say explicitly about capitalism than about communism; the absorbing object of his attention *qua* critical social scientist is the immediate, existing world – economics, politics, contemporary history, personal polemics, organizational matters, etc. – rather than the (from his point of view) useless preoccupation with defining and describing in any great detail either his distinctive standpoint or the new and desirable form of society suggested thereby. A related point to note here is that Marx's explicit references to communism *qua* good society themselves differ notably from pronouncements found in the works of other radical and communist writers (like Fourier or Morris) in that they are almost wholly devoid of pictorial, representational detail; we never find in Marx's works what at one point he derisively dismisses as 'recipes for the cook-shops of the future'.[25] But this by itself does not prove anything and least of all that Marx does *not* operate with, and from the basis of, a concept of communism in his critical and scientific studies. And to the point is the observation here that while Marx's references to communism tend to be lacking in representational content, they are often cast in extremely vivid, evocative language, full of visionary pronouncements concerning the different *quality* of communist society, its ethical basis contrasted to the immorality of capitalism, its rationality of organization contrasted to the overall waste and muddle and unconscious subjection to 'natural necessity' characterizing the bourgeois mode, etc. Yet when all this is said, it *is* significant that Marx has relatively little to say by way of explicitly *arguing* his standpoint and thereby rendering his assertion concerning the historical finality of the present and the beckoning of the new fully intelligible.

Yet another, albeit similarly indirect, indication of the problem of communism in Marx's thought lies in Marx's relentless and emphatic rejection of practically all those conceptions of the good society with which he achieved familiarity during his long and distinguished career as a publicist. Nothing, for him, was the real article and his angry denunciations, hitting out with equal venom right, left and centre, almost leave one in despair trying to find what remains – if anything. Starting with the rejection of 'immature' and 'crude' communism in the early 1840s, he had very little but ill-disguised ridicule to pour upon his contemporary radicals, avowed socialists and communists, from Hess, Weitling, Fourier, St Simon, Owen, Bray and Hodgskin, to Proudhon, Bakunin and Lassalle (to name but a few), on account of their, in Marx's view, erroneous understanding of the nature of the good society and its relationship to the existing world. Other schools of radical thought were denounced by him as either innocently playing the capitalist game and being duped by the high-sounding phrases of bourgeois apologetics, or deliberately endeavouring to obscure proletarian revolutionary communist consciousness, or a combination of both. Socialists were backward or utopian or doctrinaire or aristocratic or bourgeois or petty bourgeois, imbued with the relics of religious consciousness or not seeing beyond their noses, attempting merely to oppose the ideals of capitalism to its own reality. John Francis Bray, for example, is cashiered for failing to see that his communist ideal 'is itself nothing but the reflection of the actual world . . . it is totally impossible to reconstitute society on the basis of what is merely an embellished shadow of it'.[26] Similarly, 'doctrinaire Socialism' (the reference, I believe, is to Louis Blanc and his followers) is said to be merely 'idealizing' present-day society; it 'makes a shadowless picture of it and seeks to oppose its ideal to its reality . . .'[27] We are led on to drawing two interim conclusions here, both of some consequence for our overall interpretation. Firstly it appears that Marx's extended total concept of communism, containing both his insight and his vision, renders his own radical commitment somewhat problematic. He is totally opposed, hostile to capitalism and the 'existing world' in general, yet he is so conspicuously scathing and critical when confronted with radical, including communist, literature. As a thinker or as a *theorist* of communism (as distinguished from, though not necessarily opposed to, his being a practical revolutionary, a committed protagonist), Marx's position is almost *equidistant* from the two abstractly contrasted ideological stances of conservatism and radicalism. His vision pulls him one way and his insight pulls him another way, while the attempted synthesis of his insight and his vision, i.e. his full concept of communism, comes to appear as his endeavour to transcend this ideological opposition – with what success remains to be seen. Secondly, Marx's vehement opposition to 'ideals', including genuine communist ideals, lands him in a rather sticky dilemma which it will be advisable for us to appreciate here, although at this stage this can also be done in a preliminary manner only. It is obvious that Marx *needs* his ideal, his vision, in order not merely to define his oppositional, revolutionary attitude, but also to be able to explain, and indeed have a *concept* of, capitalism. As we argued above, on the basis of some telling documentary evidence, Marx clearly approaches capitalism from a definite standpoint, that of communism, with his 'big idea' of communism (i.e. 'free association of producers', 'transparent' relations, etc.) being especially relevant. It is certainly not the case that Marx derives communism from his study of capitalism. Rather it is the other way round: he *presupposes* communism from the very start, defines capitalism in terms of this presupposition, and *then* ostensibly reaches his communist conclusions (doing precisely what Engels, in *Ludwig Feuerbach*, accused Hegel of doing, i.e. deducing the 'Absolute Idea' from itself, circular fashion). Now it could be argued that a standpoint or an explanatory principle or a 'departure' needs to be *distinct* and have an identity separate from its subject matter in order for it to be intelligible at all, to be a conceivable principle of explanation (as well, of course, as an aim or a guide to action) – the same as God needs to be distinct for religion to have any meaning. *Something* must be opposed to the real, otherwise you have no standpoint, no departure, no resolution, no critique, nothing. The question is then: if Marx is so critical of 'shadowless ideals' of the real opposed to the real, what can he offer us as a credible alternative? What else can thus be opposed to the real? If communism is not to be defined in ideal, visionary terms, how can it be defined? Can it be made intelligible at all? Should we try thus to make it intelligible?

I think that there is some indication in the texts that Marx actually wanted to convey the message that communism was essentially unintelligible. Here I may just be reading a bit too much into certain selected passages, though I do not think so. Let the reader judge. The point concerns Marx's apparent view that the nature of communism both as a higher standpoint and as the basic defining quality of the good society cannot be adequately captured in terms of existing language. One such statement conveying this message can be found in Marx's manuscript notes (pre-dating the 1844 *Manuscripts*), commenting on James Mill's *Elements of Political Economy*. Marx here says this: 'We are to such an extent estranged from man's essential nature that the direct language of this essential nature seems to us a *violation of human dignity*, whereas the estranged language of material values seems to be well-justified assertion of human dignity that is self-confident and conscious of itself.'[28] Man's 'essential nature' here can be taken to refer to the same substantial future ideal as gains a more rounded expression in terms of 'genuine resolution' in the 1844 *Manuscripts*. The 'language' of transcendence is thus diametrically opposed by Marx to the 'language' of estrangement, of material values; but it is a language that we cannot even begin to understand, as it were, from 'this side'. We have to 'move' in order to understand this 'direct language' of our own 'essential being', but then this movement must inevitably be a mighty leap into the *dark* which thus *shiningly* beckons us. However, this message of essential uncommunicability is by no means confined to statements found in Marx's earlier period, perhaps ostensively more 'visionary' than the mature years. Consider also the following few sentences, taken from one of Marx's most incisive, most clear-headed, most intensely political tracts, the famous *Eighteenth Brumaire of Louis Bonaparte*. Here Marx, very interestingly, talks about past social revolutions of the modern age whose self-consciousness usually involved what he calls ideological 'necromancy', e.g. Cromwell invoking the Old Testament, the Jacobins in the French Revolution fancying themselves as Tribunes of the ancient Roman Republic, etc. Marx is far from simply, one-sidedly dismissing these revolutionary evocations of the past, but his view is that 'the social revolution of the nineteenth century cannot draw its poetry from the past, but only from the future. It cannot begin with itself before it has stripped off all superstitions about the past. Earlier revolutions required recollections of past world history in order to dull themselves to their own content. In order to arrive at its own content, the revolution of the nineteenth century must let the dead bury their dead. There the words went beyond the content; here the content goes beyond the words.'[29] I won't attempt to paraphrase here, just give rhetorical emphasis to the point Marx seems to be making: is communism then the 'poetry of the future', is it just 'content beyond words'? Where do we go from here? Yet in another place, in fact in a short speech delivered by him in London in 1856, Marx enigmatically refers to 'the shape of the shrewd spirit' that marks the present contradictions of capitalism, and it is here that he makes one of his more memorable Shakespearean allusions to 'the old mole that can work in the earth so fast, that worthy pioneer – the Revolution'.[30] In *Theories of Surplus-Value* again Marx has nothing but disdain for 'vulgarians' who are unable to '*conceive* the social productive forces and the social character of labour developed within the framework of capital as something separate from the capitalist form, from the form of alienation, from the antagonism and contradiction of its aspects, from its inversion and *quid pro quo*. (And this is precisely what we say.)'[31] 'Say', indeed: how can you?

These immediately perceptible problems: Marx's paucity on communism, his scepticism concerning other radical views, and his suggestion that communism is inexpressible in words, lead us to a consideration of his *distinctive* contribution to radical thought, i.e. his understanding of communism as reality or his *insight*. It is, to say the least, exceedingly difficult to divine the actual substance, or content, of communism from Marx's texts, since Marx himself, increasingly as he develops his own distinctive approach, comes pretty close to arguing that communism has no substance, no content, no proper representational reference at all; yet he undoubtedly continues to believe in communism, continues to fight for it and employs the communist standpoint in his investigation of capitalism. On what basis? He seems to believe, and this is the core element of what we are calling here the Marxist insight, that in modern times 'science' itself supplies the basis of radical criticism and revolutionary aims. Looking at reality *properly*, he argues, means taking a revolutionary, communist attitude. Communists, as he makes the point in *Poverty of Philosophy*, see in existing poverty, the condition of the proletariat, the 'revolutionary, subversive side, which will overthrow the old society'. From now on science 'has ceased to be doctrinaire and has become revolutionary'.[32] In a letter dated 1881 (that is, written in his ripe old age), Marx pronounces critically on visionary elements in the proletarian movement, as he thinks that 'the doctrinaire and inevitably fantastic anticipation of the programme of action for a revolution only diverts one from the struggle of the present'. In the past vision, or 'fantastic anticipation', was apparently justified: 'The dream that the end of the world was near inspired the early Christians in their struggle with the Roman Empire and gave them confidence in victory.' The present, however, is essentially different. Now 'scientific insight into the inevitable disintegration of the dominant order of society', together with the proletarian movement and secular changes in production, is a 'sufficient guarantee' of a viable programme of revolutionary action which, Marx adds in parentheses, will 'certainly not be idyllic' in nature.[33]

Can Marx's scientific insight, however, his materialist conception of history and his theory of political economy, properly fulfil the task expected of it? Can you establish communism as a revolutionary critical departure on the basis of insight alone, without recourse to visionary elements, as a kind of 'revelation within the bounds of reason alone'? And if you do succeed in working out such an insightful understanding, does it really lead you in the *same* direction as your visionary expectations might have suggested? Such questions will provide the main preoccupation of this study and our attitude, basically, is one of scepticism. Even a preliminary reading of Marx's materialist view of history would indicate that Marx's 'scientific insight' must surely work havoc with any independent concept of communism, any *definite* idea of what the future might and ought to bring, any *definable* standpoint that is not squarely, straightforwardly, uncomplicatedly derived from the present. Our social being, Marx emphatically declares in 1859, 'determines' (or 'dominates') 'our consciousness',[34] and we cannot 'judge' of periods of transformation, like modern capitalist society, 'by its own consciousness'.[35] 'The phantoms formed in the brains of men are . . . necessarily, sublimates of their material life-process, which is empirically verifiable and bound to material premises.'[36] Morality, religion and 'all the rest of ideology', 'thus no longer retain the semblance of independence. They have no history, no development . . .'[37] 'The same men who establish their social relations in conformity with their material productivity, produce also principles, ideas and categories, in conformity with their social relations.' 'Thus these ideas, these categories, are as little eternal as the relations they express. They are *historical and transitory products*.'[38] If we take this view seriously, it seems to me, the only thing that can be validly said, communicated about communism is that it is part and parcel of the present world, it derives from its *own* 'movement', there is nothing else *to* communism except what is 'transitory' and 'historical', consequently communism cannot be the expression of a *new* society, or the good society, it cannot be a superior explanatory principle, cannot be the consciousness of a higher vantage-point. Marx himself, in the *German Ideology*, dismisses that conception of history which sees history as 'man's self-estrangement', this error being 'due to the fact that the average individual of the later stage was always foisted on to the earlier stage, and the consciousness of a later age on to the individuals of an earlier'.[39] It seems then that communism, in any sense *but* the strictly materialist one, and which must also include Marx's own vision of a 'free association of producers' and the like, must go by the board. Yet, on the other hand, this apparently purely processive, formal, indifferent conception itself *relies* on the vision of 'free assocation' and the like for its critical and revolutionary significance required by Marx. The dilemma is obvious, the problem of communism in Marx's thought is unquestionably a big problem.

At this point we shall bring this introductory chapter to a close, with a summary restatement of the most important results of the foregoing preliminary survey, and indicating the broad direction subsequent chapters are intended to take. The foregoing was a

Communism and Marx's Thought

rather sketchy presentation, it must be admitted, and not entirely free from some rhetorical flourish either. It was, however, paramountly necessary to begin our study by suggesting reasons why Marx's communism deserves serious examination, and why it ought to be – or to put it more tolerantly, could profitably be – examined along the lines we have suggested. The two points we wanted to bring home were, firstly, that communism is central to Marx's thought, and secondly that communism presents some tricky problems for Marx's thought. Concerning the first, it was suggested, on the basis of some documentary evidence, that Marx's scientific, empirical investigations into the nature of the capitalist mode of production, and the conclusions that he reached in respect of the future destiny of this mode, involved certain necessary assumptions or presuppositions, that he was in fact arguing from the visionary position of 'freely associated producers'. It is entirely meaningless to judge capitalism to be a 'bewitched' and 'distorted' world, unless your methodological position is that of a normal world, unbewitched and undistorted. We endeavoured to show also that Marx's substantive conclusion concerning capitalism was that it was merely an 'historical' mode of production, a 'transition point', driven by its very nature to destroy and transcend itself. And further we argued that Marx's understanding of the finality of capitalism was integrally connected to his rational (in his own terms) expectation of its being replaced in the future by a new mode of production, the basic quality of which is the free association of producers for whom the nature of production and social relations are 'transparent' and who exercise a joint and planned control over their productive forces. These three terms in Marx's fused concept of communism compose a seemingly coherent logical whole, a self-enclosed circle, leading to and at the same time being presupposed by one another. There is no higher vantage-point unless it is seen to issue out of a substantive view of real historical processes, no conception of finality unless it is seen from a firm, superior and substantive vantage-point, no rational expectation of the good society, or a new historical mode of being unless the present is judged finite, and so on. This 'circle' of communism then reveals itself as the innermost essence or hub of Marx's thought, the motor or spirit without which it would be merely a collection of unsystematic, scattered observations and inconsequential predictions and value-judgments.

But communism, as we had occasion to see further, instead of bestowing an untroubled identity on Marx's thought, illuminating it from the centre out, shows itself to be a somewhat dark, shadowy centre, itself in need of illumination. To express it in pithy colloquialism, communism appears to be 'neither here nor there'. If we accept – as I urged we should do – that communism constitutes the central motive force and core meaning of Marxist thought, then it will be only reasonable to move to interpret Marx's *project*, the in-built intention and direction of his thought, as an attempt to render communism credible, which means presenting communism as intelligible, historically warranted and also ethically desirable. Now the important point for us to grasp is that it would be ultimately senseless to argue that Marx's concept of communism is somehow weakened or contradicted by *other* aspects of his thought, e.g. his historical materialism or theory of surplus-value or theory of ideology, since we *already* argued (and I hope established) that these sundry parts themselves integrally relate to communism, that they have no meaning if abstracted from communism. It follows, therefore, that in so far as there is any problem, any tension in Marx's thought, it must in the last resort be recognized as the tension or difficulty *of* communism or *within* communism. The problem then lies in Marx's apparent inability (or reasoned reluctance at the least) to show that communism or indeed *anything* lies beyond the immediate, perceivable social present. Communism *ought* to be analytically distinct from the present, to have its own identity, own shape, own content. But communism, as Marx seems to argue, either has no content, or its content is 'beyond words'. In so far as it does have an identity, to the extent that it is intelligible, it *is* the present itself, existing society in 'movement' or its 'negation'. But of course this amounts to asserting, in plain words, that the present is not itself, that it has no firm identity either. Communism is neither here nor there, and capitalism likewise is neither here nor there; both capitalism and communism display the fascinating quality of the Cheshire cat. Is this a verbal conjuring-trick, an exercise in empty dialectical acrobatics? If it is, then it is Marx's, not mine; it is only by noting and emphasizing the duality of his concept of communism, I would contend, that we can do full justice to *all* that Marx is saying, can interpret him in such a way as to take *seriously* his claim to propounding 'revolutionary science'. Let sober philosophers explain precisely, and in disregard of the problems here discussed, what 'revolutionary science' means. They cannot. The immense bulk of Marx-scholarship accumulated over the years (with notable exceptions, of course) shows that interpretations of Marx tend to fall neatly into two categories. Marx is presented either in terms of insight, as a social scientist perhaps with an embarrassingly strong 'compassion' or 'sense of justice', or in terms of vision, as a revolutionary, a critical humanist or 'moralist' who unfortunately spends too much space and energy on matters empirical and mundane, who is strangely fascinated by the reality of capitalism, etc.

Marx attempts, in his revolutionary science organized around the fused concept of communism, to present vision and insight as one and united. His doctrine, Marxism, is an endeavour to offer a coherent, monistic explanation of human society, human history and human values. This means that Marx's revolutionary science has to contend with, and overcome, the given initial *duality* of the world and idea, of immediately existing social reality and a remote, ideal reality which effectively 'negates' the former but towards which the former is seen as nevertheless moving. Expressed in Hegelian terms (with which Marx's thought displays a remarkable degree of continuity), communism is Marx's way of demonstrating that 'substance' is 'subject', that spirit and Nature are intrinsically related, that 'the rational is the real and the real is the rational'. In more general terms, and highlighting now Marx's discontinuity with and opposition to Hegel, communism can also be presented as Marx's attempted resolution of philosophy as history, meaning the complete dissolution, annihilation of a mode of only illusory transcendence and sham victory over the heterogeneous external world, by showing that this heterogeneous, empirical world *itself* is moving, ideal, spiritual and self-transcendent. Changing the angle somewhat, the dualism which Marx's thought is intended to resolve also appears as that between human knowledge and understanding on the one hand, and human power and ability and conscious will actually to change things, on the other; this is the same, of course, as wanting to make 'science' 'revolutionary' and 'revolution' 'scientific', or the synthesis of 'theory' and 'practice'. (Somewhat facile juxtapositions these, the stock-in-trade of Marxist writing, equally incomprehensible to petrified anti-Marxist positivism which finds them totally absurd and to dogmatic and uncritical Marxism which sees them as totally unproblematic.) Marx said in 1844, in one of his most renowned and resounding statements, that 'the point is not to interpret the world but to change it'.[40] He did not, however, appear to argue this literally for this would signify dumb, fanatical, unthinking, destructive, puerile revolutionism, acting on pure vision, condemnable because ineffective. His real meaning was, as amply borne out by the subsequent development of his world-view, that the point is to interpret, comprehend the world *as changing*, and this in his terms connects up with our own will and conscious aims, with active human participation in this substantive process of worldly change.

All this depends on the success of Marx's 'fusing' his insight and his vision. I shall try in this study to examine and critically comment on the story of his attempt at conceptual fusion, which will obviously involve a consideration of numerous and perhaps seemingly unrelated problems and dualisms encountered in his writings. These *mediate* problems, however, such as the problem of communism as form and as content, the opposition of 'crude communism' and 'positive transcendence', freedom and determination in history, the human being as both subject and object of history, the proletariat as a social class and as the dissolution of all classes, the requirements of modern production and the free association of producers, victory over nature and the acceptance of the superiority of nature, the lower and the higher phase of communism, etc. will be interpreted as relevant sundry manifestations of the *big* problem, the duality of Marx's vision and his insight. We shall proceed in the ensuing chapters in a broadly conceived chronological manner (except for the last chapter which will offer a more general perspective to round off our exegetical conclusions): the study of the working out of Marx's concept of communism is really a *story*, with dramatic turns and changes, not entirely unconnected with the changing nature of Marx's own experience of the world. The story to be told, pictorially presented, has somewhat the shape of an hour-glass, wide and extended at two ends, concentrated in the middle. Marx starts with his full vision, a splendid idea of the good society, while his insight is at first intermittent, unrelated, seemingly far removed and in opposition to it. This initial stage culminates in Marx's fascinating antithesis of communisms in the 1844 *Manuscripts*. Thereafter Marx's insight visibly begins to gather strength and attain confidence and clarity, the result of which is a more rounded and more plausibly fused conception of communism, epitomized in such key terms as 'real movement', 'free development' and 'revolution'. But there is further development yet: Marx's thought in general, and his concept of communism in particular, reach the highest stage of theoretical excellence, a state of near-perfect *fusion* of insight and vision (the narrowest section of the hour-glass), in the groundwork of his science of political economy, displaying the dialectical unity of capitalism and communism. After this there is again weakening and decline in conceptual terms: Marx's vision is seen to be receding and his insight going in an unintended direction. At the end Marx the thinker appears to be acquiescing in the obdurate, recalcitrant duality of world and idea: here we might even detect the surfacing of a 'latent message' in his understanding of communism, contradicting his dominant message of triumphant conceptual fusion. All this makes a fascinating story and it may also be educational in some way, but perhaps I should make it clear here that except for a few passages in the last chapter this study, as such, does not concern itself with 'Marxism in the world' or indeed with the world, with reality, at all.

2 Full Vision

'From the idealism which, by the way, I had compared and nourished with the idealism of Kant and Fichte, I arrived at the point of seeking the idea in reality itself. If previously the gods had dwelt above the earth, now they became its centre.' Marx was not yet twenty when he wrote these sentences, in a letter to his father from Berlin, in November 1837.[1] They mark not only his burgeoning interest in Hegelianism (as noted by historians) but also, in an uncanny fashion, the main direction which his thinking was to take in the following years, indeed decades, almost right to the end. The search after the idea in reality, locating the gods in the centre of the earth, are youthful and, in point of language, somewhat romantic images, prefigurations, of Marx's fully fashioned concept of communism. The gods symbolize Marx's vision, the earth connects up with Marx's insight. Understandably, however, it took Marx a fairly long time, and some intricate conceptual manoeuvrings, to proceed from this brilliant but purely speculative projection to his mature and confident attempt at intellectual demonstration. Marx's vision of communism appears in its full splendour in 1844, in his *Economic-Philosophic Manuscripts*, expressed in highly flowing, almost ecstatic language; as regards the *substance* of communism as a visionary object, as the basic defining quality of the good society, Marx has nothing important to add later to this manuscript presentation; if anything, perhaps in subsequent years he dilutes it, takes away from it a little. However, it would be wrong to look upon the so-called 'philosophical' communism of the *Manuscripts* as representing Marx's vision of communism *only* (although it expresses his *full* vision). On the contrary, this philosophical concept of the *Manuscripts* also contains, though as yet only in an embryonic form, the first clearly recognizable contours of Marx's insight. But we shall come to this later, in the third and closing section of this chapter, having discussed two phases of Marx's development prior and leading up to the *Manuscripts*. These two phases are, in terms of a rough but perhaps not entirely fanciful categorization, firstly Marx's radical liberalism, political classicism and adherence to the natural law tradition, and secondly his philosophical critique of the state and modern 'civil society', the latter taking him to the very threshold of communism. Does Marx at that point – or ever – irrevocably, unequivocally cross this threshold and unreservedly embrace the communist ideal? This, indeed, is a serious question and we shall have to pay some attention to it as we go along; nomenclature notwithstanding, the answer is by no means obvious (the difficulty having already been alluded to in the previous chapter, in our remarking upon Marx's theoretical distance from other communist writers).

The importance of the period before the *Manuscripts* lies for us in the fact that here we see Marx already professing the very basic moral values that later enter into his communist vision, the sundry qualities of the good society before it is conceptualized as *the* good society, the content of Marxist communism before its form, inner substance before external, institutional expression. Looking at it from another angle, in this stage Marx has no conception yet of the historical finality of capitalism, and not even a notion of capitalism as such; even the concept of 'civil society' or 'bourgeois society', the immediate parent of the Marxist concept of capitalism, takes some time to mature and surface. However, the point is that Marx clearly notes, and resolutely condemns, a number of morally objectionable *features* of capitalism before designating them as features *of* capitalism, and of course this fundamental *moral* objection to the human (or rather: inhuman) quality of capitalism remains to the very end a central determining factor in Marx's *scientific* conceptualization of capitalism as a 'mode of production'. Thus we have the emerging substantive vision of communism built up, as it were, from two sides: positively, by Marx's adherence to certain basic moral values and advocacy of certain qualities of the good society, and negatively, by his branding certain features, qualities of the existing modern social world as undesirable. What is really significant in this early period from our point of view, however, is the perceptible discrepancy between the firmness, certainty and conviction with which Marx professes his basic values, his unambiguous adherence to *substance*, and his uncertainty, scepticism, hesitation and partial ambiguity concerning external *forms*. To put it somewhat simplistically, Marx is in no doubt about the 'good' but he does not (yet) see it as a definite kind of 'society'. It is this same tension or discrepancy which, through a number of terminological shifts and conceptual breakthroughs, will later take on a more enduring and more visible shape, defining the problem of communism in Marx's thought.

Let us then briefly note some interesting, and relevant, features of Marx's thinking in this earliest phase of his intellectual development, characterized by a certain kind of radical – democratic and egalitarian – liberalism. The first thing to be observed here is Marx's full and enthusiastic endorsement of the Enlightenment view concerning the overall superiority of the modern age over past ages in general, and the superiority of modern philosophy over ancient, classical philosophy in particular. Marx's departure is the teaching of the Enlightenment that it is possible as well as ethically imperative to change the human – social and political – world in accordance with the dictates of human reason. Of interest here, however, is Marx's combination of this view – clearly derived from the humanism of the Enlightenment, from the idea of moral and social progress, from Rousseau's doctrine of original goodness and basic moral equality, from the idea of the self-sufficiency of human reason, from Kant's system of ethics, etc. – with some older forms of expression. That is, Marx in this stage has frequent recourse to the language of natural law in his arguing the reasonableness of a human organization of society which would then lead to freedom, harmony and happiness (the language, but not the conviction underlying it, soon to be jettisoned). Furthermore, he also harks back to the ancient Greek state, the 'political' state, contrasting it to existing modern socio-political arrangements and the attendant modern servile, 'unpolitical' consciousness. Thus Marx detects as the fundamental defining characteristic of the modern age a discrepancy between its overall, philosophical superiority over the past and its inferiority concerning social and political arrangements and consciousness. In philosophy Marx is and, on the surface, remains a modernist. In politics he is now a classicist. As he says at one point: 'Antiquity was rooted in nature, in materiality. Its degradation and profanation means in the main the defeat of materiality, of solid life; the modern world is rooted in the spirit and it can be free, can release the other, nature, out of itself.'[2] But on the other hand, in the context of the debates on the freedom of the press, Marx contrasts 'a country which, like ancient Athens, regards lickspittles, parasites and flatterers as exceptions to the good sense of the people', and which he would therefore consider 'a country of independence and self-reliance', to 'a people without independence or personality'.[3] A short time later he writes: 'The self-confidence of the human being, freedom, has first of all to be aroused in the hearts of these people. Only this feeling, which vanished from the world with the Greeks, and under Christianity disappeared into the blue mist of the heavens, can again transform society into a community of human beings united for their highest aims, into a democratic state.' A modern, German Aristotle, Marx thinks, would define the human being as social but 'completely unpolitical'.[4] It is to be noted that, like the notion of natural law, the classical Greek political ideal (which, again, he obviously derives from the writings of the German classics like Goethe and Schiller, and some of his utterances here significantly recall Hegel's youthful preoccupation with the ancients), is explicitly rejected by Marx as early as the mid-1840s, Greek civilization being only regarded by him later (in the well-known passage of the *Grundrisse*) as the still admirable but irrevocably lost 'childhood' of mankind. But Marx's Hellenism cannot be overlooked here, and not for the obvious reason that the Enlightenment saw itself as the spiritual heir to classical humanism and secularism, Marx for example calling Epicurus the chief 'enlightener' of antiquity. The two not so obvious, but here more relevant, reasons are Marx's partial return to a conception of Greek 'substantiality' and Aristotelianism in his analysis of the capitalist mode of production (which will be commented on in our fourth chapter), and the *latently* Hellenic character of his mature understanding of communism, as derived from his insight (which will be elaborated on in the concluding chapter).

Central to Marx's early, emerging vision is the belief that there is a universal human nature, this recognition in his view being due to the correct stance of modern philosophy. 'Philosophy asks what is true, not what is held to be true. It asks what is true for all mankind, not what is true for some people.'[5] What is incontrovertibly true, for Marx now and later, is that the *essential* nature of the human being is to be free, independent, rational, moral and morally autonomous. As Marx puts it, again in connection with press freedom, 'freedom is so much the essence of man that even its opponents implement it while combating its reality ... No man combats freedom; at most he combats the freedom of others.'[6] Marx rejects press censorship on the same grounds as drive him towards an ever-hardening critique of religion, namely that both censorship and religion deny the innate and equal rationality and morality, or what he calls the 'good sense', of the people. The modern moralists whose teaching Marx still highly values at this time, like Spinoza, Kant and Fichte, according to him 'start out from a contradiction in principle between morality and religion, for *morality* is based on the autonomy of the human mind, *religion* on its heteronomy'.⁷ An interesting feature of Marx's radical liberalism here is his espousal of the essential *idea* of the modern state, seen by him as being basically similar to the 'political' state of ancient Greece, and he sharply opposes this political essence of the state to the heterogeneous mixture of the Germanic 'Christian' state and hereditary monarchy. The true state is now defined by Marx as 'a free association of moral human beings [*freie Vereinigung sittlicher Menschen*]', 'the realization of freedom', as contrasted to an 'association of believers' which has as its aim 'the realization of dogma'.⁸ The state, as Marx argues, 'itself educates its members by making them its members, by converting the aims of the individual into general aims, crude instinct into moral inclination, natural independence into spiritual freedom, by the individual finding his good in the life of the whole, and the whole in the frame of mind of the individual'.⁹ Again: 'In a true state there is no landed property, no industry, no material thing, which as a crude element of this kind could make a bargain with the state; in it there are only *spiritual forces*, and only in their state form of resurrection, in their political rebirth, are these natural forces entitled to a voice in the state. The state pervades the whole of nature with spiritual nerves, and at every point it must be apparent that what is dominant is not matter but form, not nature without the state, but the nature of the state, not the *unfree object*, but the *free human being*.'¹⁰ It will have been noted, of course, that here as yet particular institutions within the 'true state', like landed property, are not denounced *per se*; Marx's emerging vision of the good society is here still predominantly conceived in terms of inner, moral qualities, rather than external features. Marx begins, as it were, with a notion of communism of the spirit, to be, in part, supplemented as well as confounded later by his notion of communism of the flesh.

It will not come as a surprise that Marx indirectly defines his own political stance at this stage, in commenting on the failures of the liberal opposition in Hanover, as 'true liberalism' which 'must strive for a completely new form of state corresponding to a more profound, more thoroughly educated and *free* popular consciousness'.¹¹ His liberalism or libertarianism is in fact so 'true' as to spill over, almost immediately, into a view of radical, statist democracy, quite clearly derived from Rousseau's *Social Contract*. Marx sees, for example, the laws of the true state as essentially non-repressive, as 'the positive, clear, universal norms in which freedom has acquired an impersonal, theoretical existence independent of the arbitrariness of the individual'. 'Hence law withdraws into the background in the face of man's life as a life of freedom, and only when his actual behaviour has shown that he has ceased to obey the natural law of freedom [*Naturgesetz der Freiheit*] does law in the form of state law compel him to be free . . .'[12] However, Marx goes considerably further than Rousseau, and here we can glimpse an important ingredient of what soon gets crystallized as his communist vision, in clearly noting those particular aspects of modern social and political life which are chiefly instrumental in preventing laws becoming 'universal norms' and which concretely account for the 'arbitrariness' of some individuals who have the power thus to oppress others. In his famous article on the Prussian wood theft laws, Marx demands for the poor the 'customary right' to gather wood, a right that 'by its very nature can *only* be a right of this lowest, propertyless and elemental mass'.[13] Marx sees the private right of forest owners to be 'directly opposed to the sense of right and fairness in protecting the interests of those whose property consists of life, freedom, humanity, and citizenship of the state, who own nothing except themselves'.[14] Here then we see the vital link, in the form of a moral principle, between Marx's original democratic egalitarianism and radical liberalism on the one hand, and his vision of communism on the other, clearly displayed: the departure is the 'natural law of freedom' enjoining not only equal treatment of 'moral' human beings but specifically asserting the 'right' of those who 'own nothing except themselves' – we are within hailing distance of Marx's famous first, visionary, definition of the 'proletariat'.

Marx's notion of the 'true state', clearly an ideal, visionary representation, appears now in contrast to the existing state as spirit opposed to nature, or humanity opposed to animality – again, this contrast, though often muted, remains an underlying feature of Marx's thought. Marx looks upon existing forms of the modern state, with special reference to the Prussian 'Christian' state, as the 'spiritual animal kingdom' where, as distinguished from the natural animal kingdom, 'the drones kill the worker bees, and precisely by labour'.[15] Marx minces no words in condemning 'the petty, wooden, mean and selfish soul of interest'[16] represented by the forest owners as the visible embodiment of 'arbitrariness' and thus immorality. Clearly in Marx's view 'moral human beings' who obey the 'natural law of freedom' can have no real conflict of interests, since they recognize themselves as constituent parts of the public. But here 'private interest makes the one sphere in which a person comes into conflict with this interest into this person's whole sphere of life'. Private interest, Marx goes on, 'is always cowardly, for its heart, its soul, is an external object ... How could the selfish legislator be human when something inhuman, an alien material essence, is his supreme essence?'[17] It is of course easy to detect here in this contrast of the 'human' to the 'material', the initial gropings towards what soon becomes Marx's concept of 'alienation' in the *Manuscripts* and eventually his concept of 'fetishism' in *Capital*. The derivation of these later notions from the earlier idea of the 'true state' and 'moral human nature', and their logical dependence on the original philosophical context, is quite obvious and to be noted as being centrally relevant to our overall interpretation of Marx's thought. In the period under discussion here, to be sure, Marx's tone is much more explicitly emotive and 'moralizing' than later, and his writings are replete with emphatic denunciations of 'crass material interest' and 'utilitarian' interest,[18] generalizing from his criticism of the stand taken by the forest owners. The moral tone may be considerably subdued later on but Marx will continue for a long time with his morally based opposing of private interest to universality and morality, and with his imaginative contrast between the 'animal' nature of the existing state and the 'spiritual', genuinely human quality of the true state, even after abandoning his notion of the 'true state' and his humanism altogether.

But here we might want to pause for a brief moment. What have been presented so far, though admittedly in a somewhat truncated form, are as it were the dominant colours or themes in Marx's early substantive ideal, the embryonic appearance of his vision of communism. These dominant colours, conveying as they do Marx's impatient radical fervour and his seemingly naive belief in the direct presence of human morality and the effectiveness of human reason, will have indicated to us a *sublime* ideal, lofty in its aspirations, pure and appealing in its optimistic reading of human nature, inspired in its moral righteousness. The essence of this sublime ideal is Marx's belief in a 'free association of moral human beings' who have no conflicting interests. It is as well here to note the spiritual ancestry of this ideal, anticipating our concluding remarks in the final chapter, and what we cannot but clearly register is the deep and close affinity of Marx's stance to some fundamental motifs of Christian belief. Scathing and contemptuous as Marx's dismissal of the 'Christian' state in particular and religion in general might be, the ultimate origin and pedigree of his radical humanism are unmistakable; they clearly manifest their rootedness in the essential Judaeo-Christian belief concerning the superiority and ultimate triumph of 'spirit' over heterogeneous nature. The point to note here is that the very subjective, spiritual, humanist character of modern philosophy, which Marx contrasts and espouses in preference to the 'materiality' and substantiality of classical Greek thought, is itself but the last (in Marx's time) result of successive steps in the modern secularization of Christianity. The optimism and humanism of the Enlightenment themselves sit squarely, if not entirely comfortably, on the hunched shoulders of Christianity from whose conception of deity as benevolent and omnipotent spirit, of moral perfection, salvation, ultimate harmony and the super-natural kingdom of heaven, they derived their shape and content. To this extent then, in the sense that Marx's early emerging vision does contain some assimilated and transliterated motifs of Christianity, his communism can truly be described as 'millenarian' or 'eschatological', as indeed a number of learned commentators have noted. However, what we must observe is that this is only a partial, one-sided presentation of Marx's view *even in this early period*: his fast-growing, splendouring vision of the good society, his sublime ideal, is accompanied by his maturing, sobering, cooling insight, slower in growth and in taking effect but nevertheless there. Marx in fact displays a scientific attitude long before he advances his claim to being a scientist, his sense of reality and moderation antedate his historical and political realism as the latter manifests itself in the fully grown theory. Marx's insight, as we shall see later, opens up a *grand* theme in his understanding of communism, to be distinguished from the *sublime* theme which issues out of his vision. And since we have just alluded to the Judaeo-Christian origins of the Marxist vision, and noted likewise Marx's stand concerning the superiority of modern over ancient philosophy, it will be as well to repeat the point made earlier concerning the Hellenic character of Marx's insight: the 'grand' in Marx conjures up Hellas, as the 'sublime' in Marx conjures up heaven, the *earth* dominating the former and the *gods* the latter.

In the early period Marx's insight or his sense of reality comes to the fore in numerous and often unrelated ways, a few instances of which can be briefly noted here; the context does not demand a very strict adherence to chronology within the period in question. As early as his doctoral dissertation Marx makes it quite clear, in discussing Democritean and Epicurean atomic theory, that he is opposed to individualism in the customary modern sense and the notion of freedom connected thereto. 'Abstract individuality is freedom from being, not freedom in being. It cannot shine in the light of being.'[19] Marx does look upon the 'freedom of self-consciousness' as one of the most valuable principles of Epicurean philosophy (the early harbinger of 'Enlightenment'), but also believes that if 'self-consciousness which knows itself only in the form of abstract universality is raised to an absolute principle, then the door is opened wide to superstitious and unfree mysticism'.[20] In the text this is meant directly as a criticism of Stoic philosophy (again, calling to mind Hegel's similar stance on Stoicism in the *Phenomenology*), but it is also an indication of Marx's later scornful rejection of 'bourgeois' freedom and his insistence that the desired new society, and the freedom accruing to human beings therein, must be firmly rooted in 'being'. Marx also frequently shows his understanding and acceptance of the endemic, eternal, ineradicable uncertainty and openness attaching to radical changes, even though he insists that the human being is now 'enlightened', has rejected superstition, and is self-confident in his 'moral autonomy'. Marx rejects the notion of absolute perfection, just as he rejects absolute individuality. 'What undergoes development is imperfect. Development ends only with death.'[21] And: 'The human body is mortal by nature. Hence illnesses are inevitable . . . even the doctor is an evil. Under constant medical tutelage, life would be regarded as an evil . . . A perpetual physician would be an illness in which one would not even have the prospect of dying, but only of living. Let life die; death must not live.'[22] Further: 'The state cannot go against the nature of things, it cannot make the finite proof against the conditions of the finite, against accident . . . you will have learned that everything earthly is transitory . . .'[23] Then: 'A *true* state, a *true* marriage, a *true* friendship are indissoluble, but no state, no marriage, no friendship corresponds fully to its concept . . . No moral *existence* corresponds to its *essence* . . .'[24] The press, Marx thinks, 'like life itself', 'is always in a state of becoming, and never of maturity.'[25] And so on. In a curious way, we might say, Marx's sense of reality is somehow even more pronounced in these early years, gaining a clear though only intermittent expression placed alongside his more stridently visionary statements, than in the more mature period when the two themes are coalesced and Marx becomes more self-confident, not to say dogmatic, regarding his 'advanced' communist consciousness. Another point to mention here, but only in passing as the theme will be taken up again later in a different context, is Marx's suspicion and flexibility regarding *all* external, institutional forms, not merely what he then understands by the 'true state' and by 'communism'. He declares at one point, for example, referring to the radical newspaper he had himself edited a short while earlier, 'the *Rheinische Zeitung* has never given special preference to a *special form of state*. It was concerned for a *moral and rational commonweal*; it regarded the demands of such a commonweal as demands which would have to be realized and could be realized under *every* form of state.'[26] Of course from an avowedly *communist* standpoint (which was to become Marx's own dominant standpoint later), such statements would appear jejune, eclectic, and idealistic; but at the same time from the more detached position of the academic observer whose business is to make sense of Marx's concept of communism they will appear surely in a more favourable light, as early and subdued signs of the latent realism of Marx's thought.

We must proceed further, however. The period between Marx's radical journalism and his decisive move towards communism in 1843–44 is, theoretically speaking, an interlude or transition period in the sense that his earliest ideals in the formulations we have seen above disappear from view, while there is not yet a definite, explicit formulation of what becomes his permanent standpoint, i.e. communism. Such terms as the law of nature, law of reason, association of free moral beings, the true state and true liberalism, etc. are thrown overboard by Marx as so much unimportant, indeed intellectually detrimental, ballast. But although this in a sense is a 'negative' period, its significance for Marx is enormous, for it is now that he achieves the first of his decisive conceptual 'breakthroughs', and thus more or less sets the direction of the subsequent development of his thinking. The most important pointers are here, accordingly: his rejection of the state and politics altogether, his growing concentration and increasingly critical perspective on modern 'civil society', the formulation of his general standpoint as 'criticism' rather than positive conceptual construction, his insistence on the necessity to 'realize philosophy', and finally his discovery of the proletariat as the material weapon of philosophy. These steps lead straight forward and directly to the dominant themes of the *Manuscripts* and make Marx's position in this text more or less fully intelligible; we shall survey them in what appears to be a logical sequence.

Marx's repudiation of the state is one of the most fascinating turning-points in his thought, for here the change in his stance occurs visibly, gradually, to be observed at close range in his manuscript critique of some sections of Hegel's *Philosophy of Right*, to be shortly followed by his published article, *On the Jewish Question*. It is at first painful agony, struggle, perspiring labour, but then come the vital cries of the new-born infant who is of course at first nameless and shapeless and only later gets baptized as communism (and never entirely happy with it, as most human individuals are not, with their given names). The umbilical cord connecting Marx's original radical state ideal and his emerging stateless ideal (if we are allowed to continue just a little longer with the obstetric analogy, never very far from Marx's own thinking itself, to be sure) is represented by his notion of 'democracy' which he opposes to Hegel's constitutional monarchy and calls in the critique 'the solved *riddle* of all constitutions'. 'Here,' Marx proceeds, 'not merely *implicitly* and in essence but *existing* in reality, the constitution is constantly brought back to its actual basis, the *actual human being*, the *actual people*, and established as the people's *own* work. The constitution appears as what it is, a free product of man.'[27] In the same vein Marx argues, and notable here is his recourse to New Testament phrases in a conscious effort to paint in the contrast to the 'Old Testament' forms of state, like monarchy, that 'man does not exist for the law but the law for man – it is a human *manifestation*; whereas in the other forms of state man is a *legal manifestation*'. 'That', so Marx concludes, 'is the fundamental distinction of democracy.'[28] Now here Marx's point could I think be easily missed if one simply identified *his* notion of 'democracy' with what 'democracy' usually means in modern political parlance, including political radicalism. That is to say, democracy in the accustomed sense, as universal franchise, equality, popular control of government, etc. still presupposes a certain set of institutional arrangements and a body of rules, i.e. a kind of *state* (as in Rousseau, Paine and Jefferson, for example). But this is not Marx's meaning; the inner logic of his absolute justification of democracy as the 'free product of man' already pushes beyond 'democracy' as any possible political *form*, any definite set of rules and institutions which would still make man (inevitably) a 'legal manifestation'. Marx, we may remark here in passing, in the strictly limited context of democracy proves far more clear-sighted than the majority of radical democrats, in his time and later: 'government' and 'popular control' *are* contradictory, the state (in any form) *is* necessarily a barrier to any kind of abstract, speculative equality and freedom of 'man'. The crucial distinction Marx draws here is between 'democracy' and the 'republic': 'The *political* republic is democracy within the abstract state form. The abstract state form of democracy is therefore the republic; but here it ceases to be the *merely political* constitution.'[29] *Here* we see *travail* at its most intense and agonizing; here the cries of the mother (Marx's fading 'true liberalism' and his submerging Hellenism) are intermingled with the as yet feeble wailing of the infant, there are the same bloodstains on both bodies, slowly coming apart. The 'political' nature of democracy in the republican form pulls us back, its recognition by Marx that here it ceases to be a 'merely' political form pushes us forward. Marx sees democracy as a 'particular content of the people' and thus not *merely* a constitution which in all other state forms 'rules' only abstractly, nominally, 'without materially permeating the content of the remaining, non-political spheres'.[30] Of course, once there is 'material permeation' of form by content, the 'political' sphere in any recognizable shape and colouring is left behind altogether; there is no longer any state, true or otherwise.

Marx's extremely incisive article composed around the same time, *On the Jewish Question*, makes the conceptual breakthrough concerning the inadequacy of politics and the insubstantiality of the state entirely explicit, and here we also see the next, closely related, breakthrough represented by Marx's penetrating critique of modern civil society. In a dazzling theoretical synthesis, foreshadowing the character of his further syntheses soon to follow, Marx grasps the two separate and opposed phenomena, the modern political state (monarchical *or* republican) and non-political 'civil' or 'bourgeois' society, the sphere of private concerns and interests, as essentially united, as two sides of the same coin. The state is 'heaven' abstractly contrasted to the 'earth' of society, and the opposition, in Marx's view, is made necessary only by the 'earth' having here a contorted shape, being *itself* a bewitched, unreal kind of reality. We are only one step away from Marx's concept of alienated labour, and only two short steps removed from the 'capitalist mode of production', conceived by Marx, as we had occasion to see in the previous chapter, as an 'upside-down, topsy-turvy' world. Citizens of the state are, according to Marx, by definition 'religious' because they 'treat the political life of the state, an area beyond their real individuality, as if it were their true life.

They are religious in so far as religion here is the spirit of civil society, expressing the separation and remoteness of man from man.'[31] 'The so-called *rights of man*' here are 'the rights of egoistic man, of man separated from other men and from the community.' The right to liberty here, Marx goes on, 'is based not on the association of man with man', but on their severance.[32] The practical application of this right consists essentially in the 'right to *private property*'. 'It makes every man see in other men not the *realization* of his own freedom, but the *barrier* to it.' '*Security* is the highest social concept of civil society, the concept of *police* . . .'[33] Society here is not the real 'species-life' of individuals; the 'sole bond' holding people together 'is natural necessity, need and private interest, the preservation of their property and their egoistic selves'. The 'bourgeois' is 'considered to be the *essential* and *true* man'.[34] 'Man as a member of civil society, *unpolitical* man, inevitably appears . . . as the *natural* man.'[35] And thus Marx, driven on by the logical thrust of his arguments and by the further deepening of his vision of the good society, concludes here that 'political emancipation' is inadequate: 'Only when the real, individual man re-absorbs in himself the abstract citizen' and human capabilities are recognized and properly organized as 'social forces', and man 'no longer separates social power from himself in the shape of *political* power, only then will human emancipation have been accomplished.'[36] Thus the earlier form of the vision, 'free association of moral human beings', is now superseded by the notion of 'human emancipation'. The process of Marx's development here signifies a temporary loss or blurring of form altogether: 'emancipation' is an *act*, not a mode of being, though it is reasonable to assume that in Marx's thinking the human being 'emancipated' is no different from the human being fulfilling his 'true moral nature'.

But again, so as to be fair to Marx, we have to note the qualifications. Marx's radical, absolutist, visionary language is to some extent misleading, and it is not the case that he is drawing a sharp, absolute divide between the ideal and the existing, or a kind of true heaven contrasted to sordid earth. He seems conscious even now, though his critical armoury is not yet fully developed, of the need to avoid the mistake of opposing a 'shadowless ideal' of the real to the real itself. In a manner similar to his earlier rejection of 'abstract individuality', here, in the manuscript critique of Hegel's *Philosophy of Right*, he argues that 'universality is no essential, spiritual, actual quality of the individual'.[37] Human emancipation, whatever it may be (and this *is* and remains a big question, made ever more pressing by Marx's tendency to dismiss and blur forms), is not the realization of the 'illusory sovereignty' of members of the modern state, not the 'unreal universality' of abstract citizenship. Later, as we shall see in due course, Marx will experience some difficulty in reconciling his sublime vision of human 'universality' with his grand insight telling him that universality, in the direct, literal sense, is an impossible pipe-dream, a 'shadowless' fantasy projecting the *illusions* of the existing world. Here another relevant point is Marx's distinction between human 'will' and 'reason'. The former is associated by him with, at first, individual 'arbitrariness' and wanton egoistic self-interest, but not much later also with too impatient, too naive radicalism. Changes in the existing world cannot be a matter of arbitrary, voluntary fancy, and they cannot be wilfully, arbitrarily accelerated either. In the context of his arguments in favour of democracy, which we surveyed just a minute ago, Marx also argues that making constitutions 'is really a matter of knowledge and not of will. The will of a people can no more escape the laws of reason than the will of an individual.'[38] In an interesting way, Marx connects the recognition that 'will' is subordinate to 'reason' to his view concerning the inadequacy of politics and merely political emancipation. Politics pertains to the will, whereas reason takes us beyond politics and enables us to see the really determining factor of human life, society. Again, we are almost on the threshold of Marx's materialist conception of history. The failure of the Lyons workers' uprisings in the 1830s, Marx writes in 1844, was due to the proletariat having committed the error of thinking 'in the framework of politics', seeing 'the cause of all evils in the *will*, and all means of remedy in *violence* and in the *overthrow* of a *particular* form of state'. Thus here 'their *political understanding deceived* their *social instinct*'.[39]

Yet another point worthy of our brief attention is Marx's quite resolute and perfectly logical distancing of himself from the ancient Greek ideal; this runs parallel to his abandonment of the notion of the 'true state' and results in the classical ideal being more and more relegated in his thought to formlessness, to serve merely as a remote poetic inspiration. In a letter published in 1844 he writes still with his youthful classicism: 'The self-confidence of the human being, freedom, has first of all to be aroused again in the hearts of these people. Only this feeling, which vanished from the world with the Greeks, and under Christianity disappeared into the blue mist of the heavens, can again transform society into a community of human beings united for their highest aims into a democratic state.'[40] But only a few months later, in the same piece as contains his rueful judgment on the social immaturity of the Lyons proletariat, he resolutely condemns the ancient state together with the modern state, and on identical grounds. 'For this fragmentation, this baseness, this *slavery of civil society* is the natural foundation on which the *modern state* rests, just as the *civil society of slavery* was the natural foundation on which the *ancient* state rested. The existence of the state and the existence of slavery are inseparable.'[41] The bridges are thus burned, there are apparently no compromises possible with existing social and political *forms*; the emerging, ever more crystallized Marxist vision of free and moral human existence, of final human emancipation towards which 'political' emancipation (equivalent to 'democracy' in the customary sense) is an historically necessary but inadequate step, is travelling fast into formlessness, into becoming 'critique' pure and stark (though by no means simple), into negativity.

It is here that we have to take cognizance of Marx's declared aim, formulated in March 1843 (but published as a letter in 1844), to confine and concentrate his journalistic work as a radical to 'criticism'. Noting the 'general anarchy' that 'set in among the reformers', he believes that 'everyone will have to admit to himself that he has no exact idea what the future ought to be'. He proceeds: 'On the other hand, it is precisely the advantage of the new trend that we do not dogmatically anticipate the world, but only want to find the new world through criticism of the old one . . . if constructing the future and settling everything for all times are not our affair, it is all the more clear what we have to accomplish at present: I am referring to *ruthless criticism of all that exists*, ruthless both in the sense of not being afraid of the results it arrives at and in the sense of being just as little afraid of conflict with the powers that be.'[42] Further he adds: '. . . we do not confront the world in a doctrinaire way with a new principle: Here is the truth, kneel down before it! We develop new principles for the world out of the world's old principles.' Thus, he concludes, 'it will become evident that mankind is not beginning a *new* work, but is consciously carrying into effect its old work'.[43] Marx's grasping the essential nature of communism as the 'movement' of the existing world a few years later is of course but a more expressive, punchier formulation of this same negative and critical view. In neither instance, of course, is this

Full Vision

anything that ought to be or indeed could be taken entirely literally, fastening on the actual words themselves; Marx doesn't do this himself, to be sure. What he does, as we shall observe later, is ostensibly repudiate future 'ideals' and 'construction' only to give them a transformed expression and present them as the emerging critical-revolutionary consciousness *of* the present. This is by no means wrong or invalid as a style of argument, but we must try to be clear as to Marx's *real* position, what Marx logically *must* do in order to present a plausible view, and we should not be misled by his forceful yet often arcane mode of expression. It would not only be foolish but totally meaningless to criticize 'ruthlessly' if you didn't know *why* you were doing it, and you could not have a clear conception of your grounds or reasons, unless you also had *some* notion of that which your 'ruthless criticism' – perhaps indirectly – is intended to help come into being. Marx knows as well as any sane person that you cannot criticize *groundlessly* and that it is incoherent to talk about a 'movement' that doesn't go anywhere, has no intelligible destination, whose motion is comparable to that of a person stamping the ground desperately in front of an 'Engaged' lavatory door. It is partly his impatience and anger with more simple-minded radicals (matching almost his venom for apologists of the existing order) that makes Marx sometimes emphasize rather one-sidedly the *negative* stance of criticism; partly it is also an indication of his maturing insight, his deeply philosophical understanding of the nature of reality. This is why his own concept of communism is so difficult to comprehend. And this is why comprehending it is worth our effort.

In fact at this time, just before becoming a communist and an historical materialist, Marx does give us quite a few – oblique but unmistakable – indications as to the *grounds* of his intended ruthless criticism of the existing. One such ground is provided by his conception of human nature, frequently cited in the foregoing paragraphs, couched at first in terms of freedom and morality, then reformulated in terms of the Feuerbachian notion of 'species-being [*Gattungswesen*]', i.e. universal, species-wide consciousness and universal, free activity. The 1844 *Manuscripts*, which we shall look at in a minute, explains in some detail what Marx's notion of 'species-being' or universality is – this, again, changes in some important respects when Marx comes to work out his materialist theory of history. Another linkage, or positive ground for social criticism, is provided by Marx's conception of reason or rationality.

Insight and Vision

As we saw above, at first Marx appears to understand reason in the relevant sphere, i.e. human life and society, in terms of a 'law of reason' or 'natural law of freedom', in the manner of Rousseau, Kant and Fichte. It is, I think, mainly Hegelian influence which – for a short but crucial period – makes Marx concentrate on *philosophy* as the quintessence of reason, as, in a manner of speaking, the living embodiment of rationality. Very soon, of course, clearly under the influence of Feuerbach (which then makes him more receptive to non-German radical and communist ideas), he turns his back on philosophy altogether, in the *Manuscripts* crediting Feuerbach with the recognition that philosophy is but religion in a secular guise, both of course irrational and to be superseded, and in the *German Ideology* rather unkindly likening philosophy to masturbation.

However, with Marx nothing is simple. His rejection of philosophy is immediately preceded in the development of his thought by the intention, also to be voiced in the *Manuscripts* (somewhat incongruously, in view of the heavy Feuerbachianism of that text) but most forcefully expressed in 1843, to *realize* philosophy in practice. In the fiery, programmatic article composed at the close of 1843 and published the next year, 'Contribution to the Critique of Hegel's *Philosophy of Right*: Introduction', Marx advances the bold claim that although Germany is backward compared to France and England in respect of social development and political institutions, the Germans are nevertheless philosophically the equals of these most advanced nations, their thought constituting the distilled 'theoretical consciousness' of the modern epoch. The German philosophical understanding of the state and law is, unlike German history, '*al pari* with the *official* modern reality'.[44] This view smacks very strongly of Hegel, in that it basically accepts the distinctly Hegelian idea of philosophy transcending objective reality by comprehending it. Indeed, here Marx openly credits Hegel's view as being the 'most consistent, richest and final formulation' of German legal and political consciousness, its 'most universal expression', 'raised to the level of a *science*'. Thus the critique of Hegel is at the same time the critique of modern reality. However, for Marx this critique itself is also *Hegelian*, in the very crucial sense of accepting the fundamental reality, or validity, of that which is to be criticized. Hegel's philosophy is to be criticized not because it is wrong, but on the contrary because it is correct, perfect in its fundamental insights – except that its own correctness, perfection is *unconscious*, hence its mode of expression mystical, self-contradictory. And likewise with social reality: *it* doesn't lie, it is there, solid, to be recognized and accepted as it fundamentally *is* – except that the truth of it lies deeply beneath the surface, to be uncovered by criticism. Hence Marx's seemingly paradoxical statement in this article that in order to realize philosophy you must supersede it and in order to supersede it you must realize it. 'In a word – *you cannot supersede philosophy without making it a reality.*'[45] It is obvious that there would be no point in wanting to realize philosophy unless philosophy was basically right in its comprehension of the world, unless it was reason, rationality distilled and summarily formulated. This point is important to bear in mind, for Marx's more mature theory, as it were, *sinks* reason and philosophy *into* reality, into communism as the 'movement' of reality. But this is no significant alteration of the innermost substance of Marx's view: it is the vital core of his insight being fused with his vision.

In this same article the further and final linkage to the *Manuscripts* is provided by Marx's asking the crucial question of *how* philosophy is to be realized, how the rational is to be made actual. Philosophy by itself cannot effect secular changes, its movement or revolution is ultimately impotent. 'Theory can be realized in a people only in so far as it is the realization of the needs of that people.' Revolutions 'require a *passive* element, a *material* basis'.[46] This is provided 'in the formation of a class with *radical chains*, a class of civil society which is not a class of civil society . . . which can no longer invoke an *historical* but only a *human* title . . . which, in a word, is the *complete loss* of man [*völlige Verlust des Menschen*] and hence the complete *rewinning of man*. This dissolution of society as a particular estate is the proletariat.'[47] And Marx concludes with resounding, pithy rhetoric: 'The *emancipation of the German* is the *emancipation of the human being*. The *head* of this emancipation is *philosophy*, its *heart* is the *proletariat*. Philosophy cannot be made a reality without the abolition of the proletariat, the proletariat cannot be abolished without philosophy being made a reality.'[48] Soon Marx will be talking in a very different language, adopting the *grand* manner of his historical and economic science, ridiculing and dismissing philosophy, and coming to look upon the proletariat or 'working class' (the latter term itself having a decidedly different flavour and connotation) in more positive terms, not as the 'passive element' in the revolution and the most 'suffering' class, but as the sole creator of value, the leading force in production, and hence the class which, historically speaking, *embodies* reason and progress. But the grand style should not make us oblivious of the *sublime*, visionary origin of Marx's view, its very heavy and unmistakable Judaeo-Christian content. The 'free association of moral human beings' as well as 'human emancipation' as well as the 'realization of philosophy' are as ideas (or ideals) quite unintelligible if not understood as stemming from that tradition which begins by declaring that the 'Word is made flesh and came to dwell among us'. Hegel's philosophy is an attempt to reconcile this out-and-out spiritualism with Hellenic substantiality, in his calling on us to comprehend 'substance as subject'. We need not go into the problems raised by his attempt here – to be sure, they are considerable. But we must grasp Marx's communism as being, fundamentally, the same *sort* of attempt and we ought to be able to pinpoint the problems *it* raises and contends with. The visionary in Marx urges the leap ahead, towards the *certainty* of human emancipation, guaranteed as God guarantees salvation. The grand in Marx, or his insight, urges caution and circumspection, intimating the dilatoriness, the graduality, the heterogeneity, the uncertainty of this emancipation; Marx bows to the weight of 'substance', of the world, nature, history, retarding the power of the Word.

Before we move on to the 1844 *Manuscripts*, one of the most crucial texts in Marx's entire literary output, another important aspect of Marx's early thought needs to be commented upon. I have already alluded to this, the point concerning Marx's suspicion of the doctrine of 'communism' in the forms he found it abroad. The suspicion and scepticism are carried on into the *Manuscripts* (alongside Marx's seemingly unreserved and enthusiastic adoption of communist views), and indeed they can be detected even later. The point is, at first Marx looks upon communism as merely a particular *doctrine*, very far removed from the philosophical comprehension of human emancipation, and one that has merely an external, institutional reference, i.e. communism as would be defined in a dictionary, as 'common ownership'. Nothing necessarily follows from this external form that would be determinant of a certain content, which is one reason for Marx's scepticism. Another is the theoretical poverty, frequently combined with religious fanaticism, of the communist sects and groups Marx came to know at first. In an article as editor of the *Rheinische Zeitung* Marx asserts that his paper 'does not admit that communist ideas in their present form possess even *theoretical reality*, and therefore can still less desire their *practical realization*, or even consider it possible . . .'[49] One ought certainly not to read too much into this, or similar statements; while we could not be entirely sure of how exactly to interpret Marx's attitude to communism here, it seems reasonable to infer his relative ignorance. However, Marx is both more explicit and shows himself more knowledgeable in a letter to Arnold Ruge (composed in 1842), where, referring to a German radical group whose adherents bombarded him with articles for publication, he condemns these 'heaps of scribblings, pregnant with revolutionizing the world and empty of ideas, written in a slovenly style and seasoned with a little atheism and communism (which these gentlemen have never studied)'.[50] He goes on: 'I stated that I regard it as inappropriate, indeed even immoral, to smuggle communist and socialist doctrines, hence a new world outlook, into incidental theatrical criticism, etc., and that I demand a quite different and more thorough discussion of communism, if it should be discussed at all.'[51] Here then Marx displays a detached, scholarly attitude, neither hostile nor favourable, enjoining the study of communism, though evidently he does not regard this study as being very important. In 1843 he writes, again in a letter printed in the *Deutsch-Französische Jahrbucher*, about communism as a 'dogmatic abstraction', meaning thereby not 'some imaginary and possible communism [*eingebildeten und möglichen Kommunismus*] but actually existing communism as taught by Cabet, Dezamy, Weitling, etc. This communism is itself only a special expression of the humanistic principle, an expression which is still infected by its antithesis – the private system. Hence the abolition of private property and communism are by no means identical . . .' Marx goes on here to say that communism is 'itself only a special, one-sided realization of the socialist principle', and further that 'the whole socialist principle in its turn is only one aspect that concerns the *reality* of the true human being'.[52] There is a great deal that puzzles the reader here, and what I think is especially important for us to note is Marx's paradoxical conjunction of communism as 'still infected by its antithesis' and as something that is not 'identical' with the abolition of private property. It seems that Marx here is talking about *two* separate things, not one, viz. communism as it is, 'infected' and hence wrong, inadequate; and 'imaginary and possible' communism, something that would transcend altogether the private property system. This duality is worked out by Marx in greater detail in the *Manuscripts*; his overall endeavour is to lift up existing communism and endow it with the spirit of this fuller, transcendent, ideal communism; he soon (in 1845) comes to regard the former as itself *almost* the real thing, communism as transcendent, yet he never entirely loses his sceptical approach to it.

The 1844 *Manuscripts*, also called *Economic-Philosophic Manuscripts*, is dominated by Marx's concept of 'alienation [*Entäusserung*]' or 'estrangement [*Entfremdung*]' which constitutes the most important bridge between his earlier, so-called 'philosophical' views and his matured (and so-called) 'scientific' views. Alienation is a bridging or integrating or mediating concept in Marx's thought, and it defies any intended interpretative categorization as belonging exclusively to the young or to the mature Marx. In the *Manuscripts* Marx talks in literally the same breath, in a logically inseparable manner, about general 'human alienation', the 'estrangement of man from himself', and about the 'alienation of labour' in capitalism. Already in the *Holy Family* (composed in fact almost at the same time as the *Manuscripts*) there is ridicule poured upon 'human estrangement', while the notion is dealt an explicit death-blow in the *German Ideology* (written in 1845–46). However, the concept 'alienated labour' not only remains with Marx – and *all* his theoretical writings, including *Capital* and *Theories of Surplus-Value*, are very liberally sprinkled with the term – but constitutes the very basic, central *principle* of literally everything he says about capitalism, his 'critique of political economy', his secular predictions, his 'immanent laws', his notion of surplus-value, the lot. More about this later. The point to note here is Marx's original derivation of the notion of alienated labour, on the one hand from his earlier philosophical views, his visionary notion of an essentially 'moral' and 'free' human nature, his looking towards 'human emancipation', his belief in the coming practical realization (and superseding) of philosophy (all these ultimately stemming from the Christian tradition), and on the other from his relatively new acquaintance with the science of political economy. It is the latter that suggests to him, indeed defines for him, the concept of 'labour' as the basis and central agency in the creation of social wealth, the historical mainstay of human society. While on the one hand Marx takes his concept of essential human nature, in part derived from Hegel's Spirit and in part from Feuerbach's 'species-being', to the study of political economy, endowing now the 'worker' with the spiritual, self-transcendent qualities of 'man', on the other hand in the *Manuscripts* he reads 'labour', and through that the basic principles of political economy, back into Hegel. From this point on Marx's development becomes more unitary (though obviously there are important changes still to come) and from the *Manuscripts* on it becomes increasingly difficult to identify various 'influences' on Marx. Now *Marxism* proper, a distinct message and a distinct style of thought, comes to the fore. This essential 'Marxism' – already communist but not yet scientific or historical materialist – is centred on the synthesis of philosophy and political economy, this being a more inspired, more informed and more commanding expression of 'the gods in the centre of the earth'. Man is now sunk into the worker, essential human nature is redefined in terms of labour, materially creative activity. Hence here also the equation of human self-estrangement and the alienation of labour; Marx can later safely afford to jettison the former term, since his seemingly new understanding of human nature – man whose 'species-activity' is labour and who progressively changes his own nature in the historical development of production-creation – already contains in itself, in a terminologically novel shape, the original visionary notion.

Of course, estrangement or alienation, as applied predominantly to 'labour' and the 'worker', do not just emerge out of the void. They are prefigured in Marx's calling the proletariat the 'complete loss of humanity', preceding any explicit documentary evidence we have of his studying political economy, and even earlier in his referring to the 'natural right' of the poor to gather fallen wood. In the *Manuscripts* all these various strands and gropings are definitively *conceptualized* in 'alienated labour'. Here then we find, operating from this firm conceptual base, Marx describing in extremely vivid language the various aspects, dimensions and effects of alienation, describing the worker's alienation from nature, from his labouring activity, the product of his labour, his fellows and human society in general, his divided and alienated consciousness of himself, and the alienation of the 'non-worker'. The nature and institutions defining capitalism are explicitly derived by Marx from alienated labour. 'Through *estranged, alienated labour*, then, the worker produces the relationship to this labour of a man alien to labour and standing outside it. The relationship of the worker to labour creates the relation to it of the capitalist . . . *Private property* is thus the product, the result, the necessary consequence, of *alienated labour*, of the external relation of the worker to nature and to himself.'[53] This general state of alienation, significantly and in a way again reminiscent of his earlier views, is described by Marx as a veritable *animal* kingdom where 'man (the worker) only feels himself freely active in his animal functions – eating, drinking, procreating, or at most in his dwelling and in dressing-up, etc.; and in his human functions he no longer feels himself to be anything but an animal. What is animal becomes human and what is human becomes animal.'[54] The worker in alienation, his present existence being the direct result of the alienation of his *own* human essence, his species-activity as production, is 'unhappy', and he 'does not develop freely his physical and mental energy but mortifies his body and ruins his mind'. He 'therefore only feels himself outside his work, and in his work feels outside himself . . . His labour is therefore not voluntary, but coerced; it is *forced labour*. It is therefore not the satisfaction of a need; it is merely a *means* to satisfy needs external to it.'[55]

Of particular importance in the present context is for us to note the explicit, totally unromantic way in which Marx depicts here the *actual* nature of the worker, spelling out the meaning of the proletariat as the 'loss of humanity'. The worker is 'man', morally autonomous, free, rational, divinely creative even, but only in visionary terms, in the depth of his essence and *in potentia* as the 'material weapon' of philosophy. Alienated production, however, 'produces him in keeping with this role as a *mentally* and physically *dehumanized* being [*entmenschtes Wesen*]. Immorality, deformity, and dulling of the workers and the capitalists.'[56] While for the masters, the owners of the means of production, estrangement manifests itself in 'the sophistication of needs', it also produces 'a bestial barbarization, a complete, crude, abstract simplicity of need . . .'[57] This unromantic, matter-of-fact, indeed almost contemptuous, view of the actual worker, it may be noted in passing, is also to be found in Engels' *Condition of the Working Class in England*; unlike Marx, Engels had by then (1844) extensive personal experience with factory workers and at least some of the statements Marx makes in the *Manuscripts* are based on information he directly gained from him.[58] This point is important, since Marx continues to make numerous similar observations later, clearly noting the less than fully ideal features of human nature as manifested in actual workers,[59] and so this very lack of romanticism, of wishful, pious attribution of ideal characteristics, presents one abiding problem for Marx's communism, or shall we say it remains one of the enduring, central aspects of the problem of communism in Marx. To

Full Vision

pose the question squarely, anticipating our further discussion of this topic in subsequent chapters: how can you expect 'humanity to shine forth' from its actual base of complete 'dehumanization'? Why should one expect workers, who at present we are told are immoral, bestial, dull and deformed, to be the chief agents of human emancipation and inaugurate the 'human' society of the future? Marx certainly seems aware of this as a problem and it also seems reasonable to assume that it is this theoretical unease that leads him sometimes towards quasi-miraculous solutions, asserting the *unintelligibility* of communism (as we noted in the previous chapter) or calling for the 'revolutionizing' of practice and consciousness. Bernard Shaw may have exaggerated a little, calling this attitude to the working class 'perverse stupidity',[60] but it is certainly not easy to fashion into a coherent, intelligible view. We do indeed find in Marx's writings, starting with the *Manuscripts*, a running *dual* definition of the proletariat, a 'low view' of actual workers running *side by side* with a 'high view' denoting the same actual workers. In the *Manuscripts*, for example, Marx mentions in glowing terms French socialist workers for whom 'association' is an end in itself: 'the brotherhood of man is no mere phrase with them, but a fact of life, and the nobility of man shines upon us from their work-hardened bodies'.[61] These two views certainly *appear* to be in glaring contradiction with each other, and as far as I can see neither a sober and timid empirical approach, i.e. that some workers are deformed and some are noble, etc. (which Marx tends to avoid anyway), nor an historical approach, which Marx takes up later, i.e. that workers in the mass are now deformed, but they are becoming ennobled, etc., is entirely satisfactory in offering up a convincing theoretical solution.

And thus we come to Marx's first full-length and most intriguing discussion of communism, found in the *Manuscripts*, which in its stark duality parallels the Marxist view of the proletariat. Already here, foreshadowing his theory of history proper and indeed suggesting the direction in which this theory will soon develop, Marx is emphatic that the transcendence of estrangement, which is what communism is, basically, will take a gradual, protracted course. However, I shall endeavour to argue here and in Chapter 5 where I shall analyse Marx's 'lower' and 'higher' phases of communism that what Marx ostensibly presents as successive *stages* are also capable of being interpreted as distinct, alternative and conflicting *types* of communism. At any rate, in the *Manuscripts* Marx argues that the 'first form' of communism is only a 'generalization and consummation' of private property relations. Here 'the dominion of *material* property bulks so large that it wants to destroy *everything* which is not capable of being possessed by all as *private property*'. Here talent is disregarded in an arbitrary manner, and the sole purpose of life is 'direct, physical *possession*. The category of the *worker* is not done away with, but extended to all men.' Private property persists as the relationship of the community itself to material things. This opposition of 'universal private property' to capitalist private property finds 'expression in the brutish form' of opposition to marriage, instituting instead the community of women, 'in which a woman becomes a piece of *communal* and *common* property'. Thereby the 'secret' of this 'completely crude and thoughtless communism [*rohen und gedankenlosen Kommunismus*]'[62] is given away. 'Prostitution' here characterizes both human relations and the relation to wealth. 'This type of communism', Marx goes on and we need not read anything significant into his (probably chance) use of the word 'type', 'is but the logical expression of private property, which is this negation'. Now the community is the 'universal capitalist'. The dominant qualities are greed and envy, and the intention is a general levelling-down. This is the communism then, in Marx's view, that befits bestialized, deformed, dull and immoral workers, proving itself to be 'the abstract negation of the entire world of culture and civilization, the regression [*Rückkehr*] to the *unnatural* simplicity of the *poor* and crude man who has few needs and who has not only failed to go beyond private property, but has not yet even reached it'.[63] Not much gloss is needed here. Marx the 'communist' in this section of the *Manuscripts* pours forth a contemptuous and uncompromising denunciation of communism that is hardly equalled, and certainly not surpassed, in the most intransigent and unreasoning kind of conservative literature. Note that Marx clearly looks upon this crude communism as being, from the *immediate* human and moral point of view (whether or not it is 'historically' justified), lower, more objectionable than estrangement in capitalism: it represents 'regression' and it denies culture and civilization which, by implication, are acknowledged to be present in the capitalist world.

In brief and somewhat enigmatic terms, Marx then proceeds to postulate a second, intermediary type or stage of communism, one which is 'still political in nature – democratic or despotic'. Interestingly he defines this stage as one that has already achieved the

Full Vision

'abolition of the state', yet it is 'still incomplete' and 'affected by private property, i.e. by the estrangement of man'. 'In both forms,' Marx goes on, 'communism is already aware of being reintegration or return of man to himself', but it is still captive to the 'human nature of greed', not yet having 'grasped the positive essence of private property', although it has already grasped its 'concept'.[64] This rather difficult distinction, I think, signifies Marx's adaptation of Hegelian logical categories, and in the context it seems to refer to a consciousness that already understands fully *what* it has to oppose and transcend, i.e. its own 'human nature of greed', but as yet does not see *how* this transcendence can be effected and has no clear conception of the full quality of this transcendence either. Crude communism, by contrast, would then be characterized as a type of consciousness that has not even grasped the 'concept' of private property as estrangement, i.e. one that is fully satisfied, happy with its 'unnatural' qualities of greed and envy. Note here that in Marx's terms, not granting full understanding of what communism is really, truly about even to this intermediary stage, let alone to crude communism, how *futile* must be the effort to comprehend it, standing this side of the shore, sunk in self-estrangement, bewitched by the world of capitalism all around us and within us. What lies beyond can only be poetically divined, yearned after, conceived in ecstasy.

The paragraph immediately following here in the *Manuscripts* bears out this seemingly far-fetched interpretation, containing as it does the most audaciously extravagant philosophical claims ever advanced on behalf of what at first glance appears an historical mode of being, a form of society. Marx's definition of communism in its full plenitude is probably unparalleled in modern radical thought, in its metaphysical depth, in its boldness, in its absolutism. This communism is *more* than religious eschatology in that it seeks to present divine perfection without a transcendental divinity. And this communism is *more* than utopia, for unlike the utopian vision which conjures up a perfect way of life and perfect happiness to suit human beings *as they exist*, it envisages perfection on both counts: in society as well as in individuals who must be radically, dimensionally *changed* in their nature and outlook to be able to comprehend it and live in it. The passage where Marx thus defines the third stage of communism as the 'positive transcendence of private property as human self-estrangement' must be quoted in full, so as not to lose its force and aesthetic appeal: 'This communism, as fully developed naturalism, equals humanism, and as fully developed humanism equals naturalism; it is the *genuine* resolution [*wahrhafte Auflösung*] of the conflict between man and nature and between man and man – the true resolution of the strife between existence and essence, between objectification and self-confirmation, between freedom and necessity, between the individual and the species. Communism is the riddle of history solved and it knows itself to be this solution.'[65]

In ensuing passages where Marx goes into considerable detail as to how he envisages this state of 'genuine resolution' the tone is lowered somewhat, but the picture presented is still impressive in its boldness and visionary inspiration. The key notions are unity and a concrete, 'direct' relationship of human beings to one another and to nature. At one point Marx resorts to the sex-relationship of 'man and woman' as being the essential prefiguration of human relationships in communism, for as he sees it this 'is the *most natural* relation of human being to human being'. 'This relationship also reveals the extent to which man's *need* has become a *human* need . . . the extent to which he in his individual existence is at the same time a social being.'[66] Humanity and nature are here thus concretely united and also personalized. Sexuality in human terms unites *persons* who 'need' each other, and not abstract units who go about indiscriminately to satisfy their 'natural' sexual appetites. This latter Marx clearly regards as 'animal' existence, befitting estrangement only, and his denunciation of the general 'prostitution' of crude communism, a special manifestation of 'abstract' human relationships, is as we have seen uncompromising. Further, Marx makes the emphatic point that in full communism there is no such thing as 'society' as 'an abstraction *vis-à-vis* the individual'. Individuals here are 'social beings' whose 'particularity' does not set them apart and in conflict with their 'species-character'.[67] Then again, man's relation to external nature is depicted here in terms of 'comprehensiveness' where the different senses experience nature in their genuine, concrete human manner. Private property, Marx says, made us 'so stupid and one-sided' that we can relate to nature only through the sense of 'having' (here referring to Moses Hess, a German radical contemporary, who according to some sources was chiefly responsible for Marx's 'conversion' to communism). In communism, by contrast, 'the eye has become a *human* eye, just as its *object* has become a social, *human* object . . . The *senses* have therefore become directly in their practice *theoreticians*.'[68] Further-

Full Vision

more, Marx argues here that in communism the solution of 'theoretical antitheses' becomes possible in a 'practical way', seeing 'how the history of *industry* and the established *objective* existence of industry are the *open* book of *man's essential powers* . . .'[69] 'The *rich* human being is simultaneously the human being *in need of* a totality of human manifestations of life – the man in whom his own realization exists as an inner necessity, as need.'[70] Finally, Marx's vision encompasses the future unification of knowledge, of science. 'The *social* reality of nature, and *human* natural science, or the *natural science of man*, are identical terms.'[71] And so on. There is a wealth of fascinating detail compressed in a few paragraphs in the *Manuscripts*, which we have not the space here to subject to a minute analysis, but the above should cover all the outstanding points. Obviously there is a great deal that is sensible in Marx's evocations, and equally obviously a lot of it is quite hair-raising. The essential point, surely, is Marx's equating of communism as 'genuine resolution' with human social unity and harmony, the eradication of social conflict and estrangement, and as far as the later dominant *visionary* presentation of communism in his thought is concerned, this essential point is never explicitly repudiated as such. As we shall see later, it is communism as 'genuine resolution' that lends credence and coherence to Marx's later emphases on communism as 'free development' and the 'satisfaction of needs'.

For now it will be more to the point to concentrate on the meaning of this key passage in Marx's characterization of full communism, where, as quoted above, he calls it 'genuine resolution' and the 'riddle of history solved'. What is crucial to note here is that in spite of immediate appearances, and perhaps to some extent contrary to Marx's own immediate consciousness and intentions in composing these sentences, it is by no means obvious that by full communism he means an actual state of society, an historical mode of being, projected on to the future. Ostensibly this is so, but even the language used by Marx suggests that there may be a more important, as it were esoteric, meaning attached to his views. It can, in the first place, be taken for granted, and needs no elaborate argumentation, that 'genuine resolution', etc. cannot *literally* apply to a form of society as its definition in empirical, institutional terms. It can only serve as a definition of the substantial *quality* of a kind of life or a kind of society, and of course once we recognize this we immediately become aware of the logical *gap* (narrow but nevertheless there, and significant) between this quality and any given particular institutional 'form'. There is a difference between 'communism' and 'communism', between its visible, external form and its inner, invisible content. The two are brought together by Marx only by way of a dialectical synthesis, but their integral relationship has no absolutely waterproof, logically compelling demonstration – and of course this would be impossible to accomplish anyway. That Marx is aware of this difficulty, and that it concerns him, can I think be shown by reference at least to two things. Firstly, in the *Manuscripts* itself his usage of the term 'communism' is quite clearly inconsistent – as far as I am aware, this is the only place in the entire corpus of Marx's writings where such an obvious discrepancy can be shown to exist (which says a great deal about Marx's staggering intellectual qualities, remembering that we are here talking about rough notes jotted down, not intended for publication). In the passage quoted above 'communism' is defined as a kind of substance, a quality, and *not* an external form; it is equated, identified, defined in terms of, 'humanism'. However, in another section of the *Manuscripts* (where, admittedly, the actual text is fragmentary and thus one can never entirely divine Marx's actual meaning)[72] Marx falls back on his earlier (as seen above) understanding of 'communism' as external form *only*, as simply a means to an end lying beyond itself. Here communism is presented as merely 'the negation of the negation', as the *'actual* phase necessary for the next stage of historical development'. *'Communism* is the necessary form and the dynamic principle of the immediate future, but communism as such is not the goal of human development, the form of human society.'[73] And again, he sees communism as merely a kind of 'mediation', the 'advent' only of 'practical humanism', a 'necessary premise'.[74] This 'necessity' is, of course, only asserted, but not demonstrated; or, more tolerantly, we might go as far as conceding that while communism (as external form) is shown by Marx to be a necessary condition of 'genuine resolution', it is not shown to be its *sufficient condition*. Secondly, and connected to this discrepancy in the *Manuscripts*, we find Marx later, and increasingly, becoming prone to define communism as the mere 'possibility' of human development, freedom, happiness, etc. In fact, Marx constantly hovers between communism as form and communism as substance, which is but one aspect displaying the diverging paths of his vision and his insight, and we shall have to consider as we go on whether either of these is intelligible by itself, and whether or not they can be either fully united or separated in analysis.

Full Vision

Communism as substance then, as 'genuine resolution', to come back to the *Manuscripts*, is not to be seen as referring directly to any particular form of social organization. Its direct and essential reference is to a *quality*. But in fact we can go a step further even. The point to note is that there are clear indications in the *Manuscripts* that Marx might not be thinking about 'genuine resolution' in historical terms *at all*. That is to say, what we have already recognized as a disembodied inner *quality*, on further probing undergoes another – subtle but all-important – conceptual transformation and becomes a *standpoint*. Full communism is not, literally, a kind of society, and it is not even the quality of a kind of society; it is the consciousness, the comprehension, the theoretical vantage-point, of given but categorially different, qualities and social forms. Full communism has perhaps nothing directly to do with history; it has all to do with, or rather it *is*, in Marx's understanding, philosophy. Already, I think, the sentences quoted above, where Marx talks about the resolution of essence and existence, and of freedom and necessity, and the 'riddle of history' of which communism *knows itself* to be the solution, suggest the way in which his 'vision' could also be read. It is, undoubtedly, a vision in the proper sense of the term, including substantive and representational elements, but it is also a cognitive act, an expression of philosophical comprehension, and as such an important step towards the articulation of Marx's insight, in that it postulates, however subtly and by implication, the existence of a *gap* between actual, empirical, historical reality on the one hand, and our understanding of it on the other. Full communism refers to the latter but not to the former; historical reality is, indeed, amenable to change but not to visionary transfiguration. The direct relationship of this passage, again, to Hegel's *Phenomenology of Spirit* is unmistakable, once we have reflected on it a while; Marx's full communism, his 'positive transcendence' and his 'genuine resolution', are in this sense but transliterations of the Hegelian climactic category of 'absolute knowledge'.[75] Consider the following sentence, for example, which comes immediately after communism has been called the self-conscious solution of the riddle of history: 'The entire movement of history, just as [communism's] *actual* act of genesis – the birth act of its empirical existence – is, therefore, also for its thinking consciousness the *comprehended* and *known* process of its *becoming*.'[76] This time, I would argue, it is not a chance accident that Marx should put all the heavy emphasis on knowing, on comprehension, on thinking consciousness; this full communism, which unlike the 'immature' variety seeks no 'historical proof' of its own being, is the conscious solver of history because it stands above and outside history: it is simply the *way* in which history is to be understood or the way in which history understands *itself*. And here we must note and stress a point which is so glaringly obvious that it might easily escape our attention: whereas crude communism and immature communism *are* historical existents, full communism is not. It is Spirit seeking its incarnation in the world, and finding the task rather difficult indeed. Marx certainly understands the difference between 'knowing', from the vantage-point of full communism, the 'positive transcendence' of private property, and the 'actual', 'practical' accomplishment of the same. 'History', as he puts it somewhat hopefully, 'will lead to it; and this movement which in *theory* we already know to be a self-transcending movement, will constitute in actual fact a very rough and protracted process.'[77] A clear understatement.

And so to conclude this chapter, having taken the story down to Marx's first communist 'manifesto' in the *Manuscripts*. Marx's concept of communism here, 'genuine resolution', is full of tension and its interpretation stretches in two opposed directions. In the visionary idiom it appears as the basic defining quality of the good society as Marx understands it, the full statement of his communist vision. In the insightful idiom, however, it presents itself to us as a superior standpoint which indeed *has to do* with history, with the world, but is not itself directly translatable or realizable in the world. As insight or as philosophical vantage-point, 'genuine resolution' suggests the manner in which Marx begins now to look at the world, close range. This world, as he understands it clearly, displays various – and mostly objectionable – features which he interprets from his vantage-point of communism in terms of 'estrangement', and in terms of 'crude' and 'thoughtless' movements seemingly opposed to estrangement but in truth merely representing a generalized version of it. It is a dark, unregenerate world which can gain illumination from above only, which makes sense only from the communist point of view and which then *may* be improved upon if human action is informed by this point of view. But how? The abyss separating present existence, including crude communism, and the 'genuine resolution' of essence and existence, and of freedom and necessity, is infinitely great, almost unbridgeable. As Marx begins to realize still in his young age, it is not enough for thought to move towards reality: reality also has to move towards thought. The subsequent development of his thinking in general, and his formulation of its central concept, communism, in particular, will take precisely this course: to chart this movement of reality out of darkness and towards the light of Spirit, to effect a philosophical synthesis between the two, to conceive and present them as one and united.

After the *Manuscripts*, both the notion of crude communism *as such* and communism *qua* 'genuine resolution' *as such* disappear entirely from view in Marx's writings. They are already, as we have seen in this chapter, the outcome of a succession of imposing conceptual breakthroughs in Marx's thought, representing his endeavour to define a substantive ideal in such a way as to render it also credible, leavening it with his sense of reality. In 1844 there is still a clearly visible dualism in his thinking: the gods (communism as 'genuine resolution') are not yet properly speaking in the centre of the earth, except in the philosophical sense, as the communist standpoint, or alternatively in the futuristic, visionary sense, as the defining quality of the expected good society. The world is inhabited by people estranged from themselves and some even 'regressing' to barbarity, unnatural simplicity, crudeness. Marx now embarks on a course which promises to bring the gods and the earth really together; his developing concept of communism is to be seen as an endeavour to resolve the duality by dialectical synthesis or fusion, in other words to continue with his conceptual breakthroughs.

3 Strengthening Insight

With the formulation of 'genuine resolution' Marx reaches, figuratively speaking, the full extent and height and magnificence of his vision of communism, the infinite horizon which cannot be stretched any further or superseded in thought and understanding. The only possible way to progress from this point, to continue with the metaphor, is to take one's eyes away from the dizzying distance and look down at things lying in the immediate vicinity of the observer. In that, as we suggested in the previous chapter, 'genuine resolution' in the *Manuscripts* is open to interpretation as philosophical *standpoint* as well as the basic defining *quality* of the good society, it already represents a change in the direction of Marx's thinking; as highest vantage-point, it so to speak compels one to 'look down' at things here and now, to concentrate on reality. Marx's thought then in 1844–45 begins to assume more resolutely the character of the downward gaze: his vision of communism becomes paler, less pronounced, and instead there is now a continually sharpening focus, a constant strengthening, intensification and clarity of his insight. Marx embarks now on the task of re-locating and redefining the object of his vision in terms of his strengthening insight; in some ways it could be seen as an attempt at *re-cognition* in the literal sense of the term, since the seemingly quite drastic terminological changes in Marx's writings and his apparent redefinition of communism in 1845 do not substantially alter the visionary essence of this concept; these changes, as we shall see later, alter things for Marx mainly in the sense of accentuating his problems or bringing the underlying problem of communism in his thought, the problem of harmonizing, uniting his vision and his insight, into sharper relief.

The period we shall be mainly concerned with in this chapter is Marx's 'revolutionary' period proper, the years stretching roughly from 1845 to the early 1850s, the period which provides the connecting link between Marx's early 'humanism' and his scientific doctrine of political economy, the latter to some extent chronologically overlapping with this middle, revolutionary period but analytically quite distinct from it. In other words, diverging from the usual run of interpretations, in this study I shall endeavour on the one hand to stress the underlying continuity between Marx's humanist, philosophical communism and his revolutionary, proletarian communism, and on the other to highlight the (interesting and analytically relevant, though often unnoticed) discontinuity between his revolutionary communism and his science of capital; the reasons for taking this line will become more intelligible as we go on. This middle period of Marx's intellectual development, at any rate, is one full of drama and excitement in the European political arena, some of it obviously reflected in Marx's change of focus (though it would be rather useless to attempt a vulgar Marxist reading of Marx; there is always a great deal more to individual thinkers than their conscious expression of either their 'social being' or the 'spirit of the times'). However, what is unmistakable here and of some significance is Marx's being visibly drawn towards the *spirit* of revolution which reached its climacteric in 1848–49. Marx becomes now more and more caught up with the actuality of revolution, with the rapid succession of secular events, bringing with them fervent hopes of imminent and far-reaching radical changes. It is this gradually brightening (and quite slowly fading, in the early 1850s) solar focus that seems to explain as well perhaps as any other factor usually resorted to in interpretations, Marx's optimism, impatience and intransigence as countenanced in his enthusiastic espousal of the proletarian movement and his contemptuous rejection of humanism and the 'German ideology' in general. The spirit of revolutionary confidence and optimism lends a distinct tone to Marx's 'materialist conception of history', first articulated in 1845, and it perceptibly infuses the concomitantly altered Marxist understanding of communism, the emphasis shifting in a more 'worldly' direction, away from substance towards form, away from 'genuine resolution' to 'free development' and the 'satisfaction of need', and reaching the climax in Marx's virtual identification of communism with revolution. Movement is in the air. The Marxist stance is now best epitomized in the renowned statement of the *German Ideology*: 'Communism is for us not a *state of affairs* which is to be established, an *ideal* to which reality will have to adjust itself. We call communism the *real* movement [*wirkliche Bewegung*] which abolishes the present state of things.'[1] Resounding and resolute, but to what extent and in what sense is this stance *really* different from 'ideals', from the 'positive transcendence of estrangement', and indeed from the 'free association of moral human beings'? We shall try to deal with this question in the course of our rudimentary survey in the present chapter of some prominent aspects of Marx's development in the period, and we shall conclude, in the main, negatively: in spite of the unquestionable strengthening of the Marxist insight, the notion of the proletariat, the worldly understanding of communism, historical materialism, and the notion of revolution itself, only succeed in determining the nature of 'real movement' *abstractly*, separate from and in opposition to what Marx himself accepts as *reality*. The gap is still there, dividing the gods and the earth; insight and vision are not (as yet) properly fused.

Let us begin then by surveying the Marxist adoption of the proletarian standpoint, given a resolute shape at first in the *Holy Family* where Marx and Engels, in this first joint publication, declare war on the 'spirit', i.e. the idealistic humanism of the two authors' erstwhile Left Hegelian associates. Opposed to the 'spirit', for Marx and Engels signifying radicalism still in tutelage to idealist philosophy and through that to religion, is the 'mass', representing the real existing world, actual society in turmoil, the proletariat rising in revolutionary consciousness. '*Real humanism* has no more dangerous enemy in Germany than *spiritualism* or *speculative idealism*, which substitutes "*self-consciousness*" or the "*spirit*" for the *real individual man* . . .'[2] The 'hidden meaning' of the opposition of 'spirit' to the 'mass' is revealed as 'the *speculative* expression of the *Christian-Germanic* dogma of the antithesis between *Spirit* and *Matter*, between *God* and the *world*'.[3] Communist and socialist writers, Marx and Engels assert, have however realized that '*all progress of the Spirit* had so far been *progress against the mass of mankind*, driving it into an ever more *dehumanized* situation'. Hence communist 'criticism' of existing society, paralleling 'the movement of the *great mass*'. And so we must realize 'the moral energy and the unceasing urge for development of the French and English workers to be able to form an idea of the *human* nobility [*von dem menschlichen Adel*] of this movement'.[4] This theme, the nobility of the proletarian movement, which we have already noted in the *Manuscripts*, carries an increasing weight in Marx's writings in the later 1840s, but it still continues to be counterbalanced by far less effusive statements concerning the actual state of the 'mass'. In the *Holy Family*, for example, the authors insist that it would be wrong to regard workers as 'gods'. Marx and Engels go on: 'Rather the contrary. Since in the fully-formed proletariat the abstraction of all humanity, even of the *semblance* of humanity, is practically complete ... since man has lost himself in the proletariat', the proletariat must now become conscious of its 'absolutely imperative need [*absolut gebieterische Not*]' to revolt against the 'inhumanity' of its life and living conditions, and so 'it follows that the proletariat can and must emancipate itself'.[5]

In the very same paragraph, however, we find what may be seen as the revealed 'secret' (if we may adapt Marx's polemical style for the moment) of this dualistic stand taken on the proletariat. A sharp distinction is drawn by Marx and Engels here between the proletariat as actual individuals, living now, and the essential being of the proletariat *qua* 'man lost to himself'. 'It is not a question of what this or that proletarian, or even the whole proletariat, at the moment *regards* as its aim. It is a question of *what the* proletariat is, and what, in accordance with this *being*, it will historically be compelled to do [*geschichtlich zu tun gezwungen*].' Again, hopefully it is added that 'a large part of the English and French proletariat' is already conscious of its 'historic task' of emancipation.[6] Now these two things, what the proletariat actually wants and what its true 'being' will compel it to do, are brought by Marx and Engels as closely together as possible, yet it is not difficult to note the *logical* gap still separating them. That is to say, it is not argued by Marx, let alone established, that the historical validity (and ethical desirability) of this essential, true being of the proletariat is logically *dependent* on what any proletarian, or 'even the whole proletariat' may think or desire now. The texts clearly suggest that the present aims of the proletariat are important and relevant to the Marxist argument concerning the validity of communism only to the extent that they provide additional corroborative evidence, but no more, in spite perhaps of appearances. That many proletarians are now becoming 'communists' (whether that is true or not, empirically) is not the chief *reason* for arguing that communism is valid; on the contrary, Marx and Engels *approve* of the communism of the proletariat because of their pre-established conviction regarding the validity of communism as the true 'being' of the proletariat. Communism, as it were, historically comes alive in the 'being' of the proletariat, but it does not directly proceed from the actual proletariat; on the contrary, this true historical being of the proletariat is opposed to the actual, present being of workers, to what 'this or that proletarian' may think at the moment. The vital connecting link or synthesis of actual and ideal is projected by Marx on to the future realm only, i.e. to something that is itself still ideal, existing only in the mind, in imagination; although this future realm is presented as *almost* here, as imminent, as being a matter of historical 'compulsion', the gap still persists. In other words, in spite of their apparent *volte face* and derisive denunciation of the Left Hegelian 'spirit', Marx and Engels have not wholeheartedly gone over to the side of the 'mass' either.

The mass or the proletariat is as it were spiritualized by Marx, endowed with qualities that are not, or not yet, present in their actuality but must be attributed to them in their hidden essential form if the movement *qua* communism is to make any sense. The earlier and *obviously* visionary terms, like the 'transcendence' of human 'self-estrangement', are now jettisoned as so much disturbing ballast, but they all make their transformed reappearance in the visionary shape of the proletariat. The spirit is simply read as the revolutionary communist proletarian movement.[7] Or rather, there is a simultaneous, parallel reading of the proletariat as self-redeeming humanity *and* another reading which takes cognizance of what is actually going on in the world: the proletariat for Marx is both a visionary object and a part of actual reality as revealed to his insight. *Some* of what is going on is certainly taken as corroboration of the spiritual presence in the human struggles of the proletariat, but as I have argued above this spiritual presence is not validated by its putative empirical occurrence. It cannot be, for the simple reason that there are (as Marx and Engels do not fail to note) *many* empirical occurrences going on, and one has to make a prior choice of what is to be approved and what is not, what is the 'human nobility' of the movement, and what are effects of estrangement or false consciousness or immaturity, etc. Thus it is that Marx's seemingly hard, non-philosophical, non-visionary 'proletarian communism' at this stage is revealed on analysis to be not much more than a reformulation of his earlier views, discussed in the previous chapter. Thus it is still the continuity of Marx's thought that lends it meaning and significance. The proletarian communist movement is god or spirit incarnate in history, it is the movement to establish a 'free association of moral human beings', it is the re-gaining or creating human 'species-being', it expresses 'essential human nature' in its unfolding at present, it is 'genuine resolution' in the process of becoming.

The proletariat in Marx's thought is and remains a disturbingly ambiguous concept. The working class is, in a manner of speaking, both here and there, both the creature, integral part, maintaining support of the existing system, and its actual, conscious denial or 'negation'. The most succinct and conspicuous form in which this duality is expressed in the Marxist texts is the simultaneous assertion that the proletariat constitutes a 'class' in capitalist society, but that it is *not* a class in the obvious, ordinary sense. Marx's writings abound with references to this duality, and while there is of course absolutely no novelty in simply observing this point, it is of great importance in the present context to note the full implications of it and to be clear concerning *both* sides of the duality. I shall cite here only a few representative statements from the texts. It says in the *German Ideology*, for instance, that the coming 'communist revolution', aimed at abolishing the present mode of production, also 'abolishes the rule of all classes with the classes themselves, because it is carried through by the class which no longer counts as a class in society, which is not recognized as a class, and is in itself the expression of the dissolution of all classes . . .'[8] Marx and Engels continue: 'the revolution is necessary, therefore, not only because the *ruling* class cannot be overthrown in any other way, but also because the class *overthrowing* it can only in a revolution succeed in ridding itself of all the muck [*Dreck*] of ages and become fitted to found society anew'.[9] Later in the same work it is repeated that in capitalist society 'there develops the universal character and the energy of the proletariat, which are required to accomplish the appropriation, and the proletariat moreover rids itself of everything that still clings to it from its previous position in society'.[10] And in the concluding section of the *Poverty of Philosophy* Marx poses the rhetorical question of whether the successful proletarian communist revolution will mean 'that after the fall of the old society there will be a new class domination culminating in a new political power?' He answers resolutely: 'No. The condition for the emancipation of the working class is the abolition of all classes, just as the condition for the emancipation of the third estate, of the bourgeois order, was the abolition of all estates and all orders.'[11]

What interests us here especially is the present actual *class* character of the proletariat, in its positive significance, as the *part* of bourgeois society, as that aspect which is theoretically *contrasted* to the putative 'historic mission' of the proletariat to abolish itself and thus create or redeem full humanity. Now the positive, *actual* class character of the proletariat is undoubtedly recognized by Marx and it is also logically demanded by the terms of his own theoretical construction. To put the point simply: if the proletariat did not at present exist as a class, why should it aspire to 'abolish' itself in the communist revolution in the first place? And why is the success and the genuinely communist character of the proletarian revolution considered by Marx to be dependent on the self-abolition of the proletariat as a class? From one angle, of course, we have already suggested a possible (and I think valid) answer to this question, viz. that since the proletariat for Marx bears the spiritual mantle of humanity (i.e. the proletariat *qua* communist movement), it necessarily and quite logically follows that the proletariat will have to shed its partial, deformed, class character: the establishment of true moral humanity is incompatible with the continuation of class divisions and conflict, and class-based consciousness. However, illumination is required also from the opposite angle. That is to say, we must take seriously Marx's somewhat underemphasized (understandably) but nonetheless clear recognition that the proletariat has 'muck' attaching to it in and from the present. In so far as it *is* a class, a proper object of insight, an aggregate of actual people, the proletariat is an integral part of capitalist society, and it has *being* and *intelligibility* in the context of this society only. As spirit pure and simple, communism has no *reality*, as Marx notes in 1845. Hence the recourse to the proletarian movement which is deemed communist and spiritual by implication. But on the other side the *reality* of the proletariat as an actual social formation, as a class, as an aggregate of existing human beings, now very clearly confronts its own ideal shape. Furthermore the proletariat as an actual class and workers as actual human beings can have nothing to do directly with 'dehumanization' and consequently with 'human' emancipation; these sublime ideals and aspirations pertain to the working class only in its visionary aspect of negativity, i.e. *unreality*. The positive, existing, real proletariat, either individually or as an aggregate, have sundry aims, wants, demands, all proceeding directly from their present life and consciousness, from their reality and not from their unreality. The 'worker' in so far as he *is*, by definition, is a part of capitalist society. It is only in so far as he is *not* that he figures as the negation of this society.[12] And here the point is *not* that workers, as actual human beings in capitalist society, may choose not to become communists or need not be communists. The point, once the true and full meaning of the Marxist stand is properly grasped, is that workers *as such* cannot become communists at all, they are divided from communism by the barrier of their own present *being*. Communism is open to the worker only if the worker ceases to be what he is, and becomes – what? A 'moral human being'? Or 'nothing', a completely 'dehumanized' object? But how can a worker become 'human' through his non-being, nothingness? Why should he want to? Who in his right mind would want to 'abolish' himself? Who wants 'human' emancipation instead of the satisfaction of his/her *own* concrete wants, understood in present terms? Who *really* wants to go to heaven, instead of having more of this world?

The contrast needs to be painted in thus vividly in order for us to understand the significance of Marx's ever-present impatience and anger with his radical and socialist competitors. It is not just that he found most of them intellectually inferior, a nuisance and an irritation, and rivals in organizational and power-political terms. It is rather that he knew that others could get closer to the working class, approaching it through its being, and not through its nothingness. Marx realized that there was a very real possibility of the proletariat not becoming 'communist' in his sense *en masse* and speedily enough. They could be retarded or diverted from the path leading to human emancipation. Now why this should be such a serious threat becomes intelligible once we grasp the significance of the *reality* (and not just mistaken fancy) of the dual character of the working class. Really, and not just in imagination, the proletariat occupies two worlds; this is why they can be pulled two ways; their imputed 'nothingness' might draw them towards communism, but their existence and actual consciousness would tend to keep them firmly here, not indeed making them supporters directly of the bourgeois order as it is, but turning them towards seeking improvements for their class *within* this wider world.[13] Here it may be possible to go a step further than usual in our interpretation of the well-known Marxist view concerning the 'bourgeois' or 'petty bourgeois' outlook of the working-class or 'false consciousness'. What I am suggesting here is that it would be misleading to regard the so-called bourgeois outlook of workers as 'false', except in vulgar or propagandistic terms. This outlook is 'false' only if we assume that the proletariat as a class has a unitary character. But if we recognize that the proletariat sports a dual character, then both outlooks are 'true', proper and fitting, and one could even argue that the bourgeois outlook is the 'truer', in that it pertains to the actual reality of the workers. Capitalism as mode of production and bourgeois society with its culture dominate, nay essentially constitute and define, the existing world; capitalism is reality, with the working class being just as much a part of this reality as the other classes. Communism in the shape of the proletarian movement confronts this world still abstractly as 'nothing', thus the working class is opposed by, or contrasted to, its own negation. The reality of the proletariat is capitalism, its mode of production and its consciousness. Hence when Marx comes to draw his distinction between the 'antagonistic' classes of bourgeois society, *objectively* (empirically) he might well be talking about different groups of people, but *subjectively* (pertaining to aims, wants, etc. – consciousness in one word) the opposition is between the real, existing wants and aims of *anybody*, irrespective of objective class position, and the projected, negative, non-existing consciousness of communism.

In this connection it is important to note that in both the *Holy Family* and the *German Ideology* the ostensive contrast between the 'spirit' and the 'mass', and between pseudo-radical 'ideology' and the 'proletarian movement' (Marx and Engels espousing the latter), is paralleled by a less conspicuous contrast between the existing bourgeois world and the projected human ideal of communism. That is to say, while ostensibly the 'ideal' is repudiated by Marx and the 'real' extolled, at the same time the Marxist position also involves a repudiation of the real world in favour of the ideal world of communism. In modern civil society, as Marx and Engels see it, a man is 'linked with other men only by the ties of private interest and *unconscious* natural necessity, the *slave* of labour for gain and of his own as well as other men's *selfish* need'.[14] Free industry and free trade 'produce the universal struggle of man against man, individual against individual'.[15] The point here is, of course, that this judgment describes the *whole* of bourgeois society, not just the bourgeois class. 'Competition separates individuals from one another, not only the bourgeois but still more the workers, in spite of the fact that it brings them together.'[16] Clearly, this separation would be inconceivable if workers did not share the dominant form of consciousness. The *existing* worker is regarded by Marx as the 'crippled' individual and thus all attempts to liberate *this* individual appear to him as being the greatest sin and betrayal. This is why Marx shows so much scorn towards Max Stirner and Proudhon, and others, accusing them of advancing 'petty bourgeois' perspectives; of course, the petty bourgeois outlook does befit the working class, too, in its actually existing form. Stirner, for example, is denounced for regarding communist aims to achieve 'all-round development' (which we shall discuss later) as something 'holy', while Stirner allegedly 'seeks to free them [i.e. workers] from this by defending the individual who has been crippled [*zerstümmelt*] by the division of labour at the expense of his abilities . . .'[17] Well, it might be said that the communist view that 'the vocation, designation, task of every person is to achieve all-round development of all his abilities' would *necessarily* appear 'holy' from the point of view of the existing world, *including* actual workers. Marx and Engels also argue here that 'it could only occur to a discontented school-master to base his arguments about revolution and rebellion on satisfaction and dissatisfaction, moods that belong wholly to the petty bourgeois circle from which' Stirner is said to derive 'his inspiration'.[18] The contrast is instructive: on the one hand, 'dissatisfaction' as a mere 'mood' stemming from the existing world, on the other 'revolution' from the human point of view which has nothing to do with the demands of 'crippled' individuals. Stirner's individualism is a 'perfectly consistent postulate that coincides with the sentimental desire of the petty bourgeois for a world of hucksters [*Welt des Schachers*], in which everyone gets his advantage'.[19] Bray too, the 'equalitarian' socialist, is dismissed for having a 'corrective ideal', which is 'nothing but the reflection of the actual world'.[20] The 'philanthropic school' of socialism, again, 'denies the necessity of antagonism; it wants to turn all men into bourgeois'. They 'want to retain the categories which express bourgeois relations, without the antagonism which constitutes them and is inseparable from them'.[21] Obviously, the Marxist argument here is that this 'antagonism' is necessarily hidden from the present, 'bourgeois' viewpoint which only sees 'struggle' and 'competition' between *individuals*; but again, this viewpoint *must* include the workers. Some years later, in 1850, Marx and Engels say in a review: 'But of course bourgeois socialism always presupposes that *society is exclusively composed of capitalists*, so as to be able then to resolve the issue between capital and wage labour according to this point of view.'[22] But for Marx, too, the capitalist world must contain, if not exclusively, then certainly predominantly, 'capitalists' *in spirit*, 'hucksters', people who have 'selfish needs', etc. Very interestingly, Marx defines the petty bourgeois class as being in a 'self-contradictory' position; in the true terms of his argument, however, this serves as a proper definition of the *whole* of bourgeois society and applies to the working class *par excellence*.

With the formulation of Marx's 'materialist conception of history', paralleling his view of communism as the 'real movement' of the present, there is undeniably an emerging understanding of communism by Marx which is altogether more attractive, more libertarian, more moderate and 'secular' in spirit than the heavily moralistic and visionary earlier view.[23] This is the emerging communism of Marx's insight, defined in terms of the satisfaction of individual 'needs' and the 'all-round development' of individuals. The communism pertaining to Marx's materialist conception of history appears at first sight to be truly 'negative' and a 'movement', an anthropologically and cosmically *indifferent* communism, and there is absolutely no reason to doubt that Marx's concern with the wants and aspirations of ordinary individuals is genuine. I would argue, however, that there is more of an unbroken continuity between Marx's earlier view and this one than might be apparent on the surface, and furthermore that the notion of an 'indifferent' communism is logically incoherent. Before we come to this, however, a problem concerning the *standpoint* which Marx now calls 'materialist' will have to be briefly noted. There is a duality concealed in this standpoint and its defining 'materialism' is questionable. The duality, which closely parallels Marx's essentially ambiguous concept of the proletariat, is so deeply embedded in the very definition of historical materialism, offered by Marx in several of his texts in the period under discussion, that it takes close analysis to extricate and present it. Ostensibly, the terms of the Marxist definition are 'hard', compact, unitary. To see a few of the most renowned instances: 'The premises from which we begin are not arbitrary ones, not dogmas, but real premises from which abstraction can only be made in the imagination. They are the real individuals, their activity and the material conditions of their life . . . These premises can thus be verified in a purely empirical way.'[24] 'The fact is, therefore, that definite individuals who are productively active in a definite way enter into [*gehen . . . ein*] these definite social and political relations.'[25] 'Men are the producers of their conceptions, ideas, etc., that is, real, active men, as they are conditioned by a definite development of their productive forces and of the intercourse corresponding to these . . .'[26] 'It is not consciousness that determines life, but life that determines consciousness.'[27] Again, 'we must begin by stating the first premise of all human existence and, therefore, of all history, the premise, namely, that men must be in a position to live in order to be able to "make history". But life involves before everything else eating and drinking, housing, clothing and various other things.'[28] These statements are all taken from the *German Ideology*, but the viewpoint expressed in them is reproduced without important alterations in numerous other texts, notably the *Poverty of Philosophy, Communist Manifesto, Eighteenth Brumaire* and Marx's famous 1859 'Preface'.[29]

Surely now the crucial point is to be able to determine with some degree of accuracy the nature of Marx's standpoint, which is here equivalent to the question of *what* or *who* Marx is talking about. Ostensibly the position is that human beings are shaped, conditioned, influenced (not strictly 'determined' in a fatalistic manner – Marx never actually says that) by their social powers of production and intercourse, from which they continually learn and improve their productive capacity and their lives, and this goes on. This is what history is about: as the human relationship to nature is beset by ignorance gradually overcome, so the relation of human beings to one another is beset by the conflict between classes, overcome in stages by revolutions. Thus history, if not entirely 'subjectless' and 'anti-humanist' (as presented in Althusser's Marxism), is nevertheless autonomous, and its subject is certainly not the human being as such, not thinking human beings, not 'mind' or 'spirit' or any other trans-historical entity. History is immanent, self-propelled change, acted by human beings who, however, do not figure directly as 'masters' of their destiny. There is no such thing as 'human nature' apart from history. The 'essence of man', Marx states in his *Theses on Feuerbach*, 'is no abstraction inherent in each single individual. In its reality it is the ensemble of social relations.'[30] And later: 'M. Proudhon does not know that all history is nothing but a continuous transformation of human nature.'[31] This is all very well, but some reflection will show that this position would be untenable in the strict, literal sense: changes, transformations must happen *to* something, otherwise they would have no intelligible meaning; social 'relations' do not relate themselves indiscriminately; they relate units which are not and cannot be *entirely* refashioned in every single 'ensemble'. Obviously this is not what Marx means either. The standpoint from which the process of human history becomes intelligible and understood as *one*, connected and continuous, process, must be conceived as being in a sense higher than the process itself, not necessarily occupying a position external to it, but representing its own highest point. With

Marx this highest point is the present in movement, or communism, i.e. 'genuine resolution' understood in its philosophical sense (as we defined it in the previous chapter). The point to be made here, however, is that this higher communist vantage-point is one that is now *read back* into history proper through the way Marx formulates his 'materialist conception'.[32] Thus in history there is a dual subject: one deriving from Marx's strengthening insight, the other still representing his vision. On the one hand, and ostensibly, there are 'men' continually changed through changes in production, etc. But on the other hand these units are *already* defined as 'men', and *then* presented as 'entering into definite social relations'. There is a sense in which human beings who are ostensibly the 'products' of their own history, are at the same time *ready-made* units, enacting and producing their own history, assumed as existing and recognizable *before* their various activities and relationships.

I do not wish to argue that this is strictly a 'contradiction' in Marx, but it *is* a very definite duality within the inner core of his maturing thought, and it is centrally relevant to an understanding of his communism. There are two, overlapping but nonetheless analytically distinct, subjects in Marx's historical materialism: one is the human being as the 'author and actor' of his own drama, essentially the same all through historical progression; the other is the human being who is continually under the influence of changes in his productive activity and relations and whose nature undergoes continual transformation. The two can be conjoined only with difficulty and their attempted integration in Marxist doctrine is rent with tension. The quintessence of Marx's realism, the synthesis of his insight and his vision, is arguably captured in his famous statement in the *Eighteenth Brumaire* that 'men make their history but not in any way they please'. However, reflective focus on communism reveals that these two subjects cannot be perfectly united, that their logic is different, that they indicate two diverging avenues towards communism or perhaps two communisms. Our foregoing analysis of the proletariat has already shown this: on the one hand there is 'spirit', stripped of its halo but still active in the world, the human being potentially divine and the 'master' of his relations and circumstances, morally omnicompetent and perfectly knowing, at present 'dehumanized' but at last recognizing the 'secret'[33] of his alienation, and progressing towards the 'abolition' of his present being and the realization of his essential humanity. On the other hand, there are 'definite individuals' with the 'muck of ages' on them, profane in outlook and in their life-conditions, with their various needs, wants, aims, aspirations, not 'humanity' but the *actual* proletariat, people who do not and cannot look beyond their present predicament and whose 'movement' is essentially negative, aimed at destroying the existing order.

This second picture is an *emerging* one in Marx's thought, subordinate to the first one and never, as far as one can see, wholeheartedly accepted by him, his later anti-philosophical scientific and unmoralistic terminology notwithstanding. The first visionary, or sublime, stance on communism presents communism as 'genuine resolution' in the *historical* sense, i.e. it suggests anthropological as well as ethical *finality*, it has almost cosmic significance. The second seems to indicate a communism that has no such finality, no such imported eschatology; it is *indifferent* in the larger context of the human historical 'drama'; it is communism that has *merely* to do with the present and the immediate future, being the necessary outcome (as Marx will later emphasize) of the prevailing form of society itself. And here an interesting point might be noted, just in passing. It is often argued by a number of interpreters of Marx that the introduction of historical materialism into Marx's thought signifies a turn towards 'determinism'. Marx's critical humanism, it is said, is predicated on freedom and voluntarism, whereas his scientific history (and political economy) postulate determination by objective factors. But in fact the opposite is the case, and the true terms of the opposition within Marx's thought become clear once we consider it from the perspective of communism. Critical humanism only *looks* like being libertarian and voluntaristic, since it shows itself (relatively) oblivious of history and the 'weight' of existing reality, but in truth it operates with a concealed categorical imperative, with a strict, absolute principle of *moral* determination.[34] And scientific Marxism only *looks* like being deterministic, since it postulates an essential continuity of past, present and future, but at the same time it is *relevantly* libertarian, precisely by virtue of its taking seriously the *mundane* desires, needs, aims and aspirations of people living in the present, promising their satisfaction.

What then presents itself to us at first glance as a kind of cosmically and anthropologically 'indifferent' communism is a seemingly *open-ended* conception, dominating Marx's definitional utterances on communism from 1845 onwards. In a sense this conception grows out of Marx's earlier view, commented upon in the previous chapter, of communism as merely a *form* of social organization, with no clearly defined substantive content. Communism is essentially 'possibility' or just 'liberation' from existing conditions. As the famous passage in the *German Ideology* has it, 'in communist society, where nobody has one exclusive sphere of activity but each can become accomplished in any branch he wishes, society regulates the general production and thus makes it possible [*möglich*] for me to do one thing today and another tomorrow, to hunt in the morning, fish in the afternoon, rear cattle in the evening, criticize after dinner, just as I have a mind, without ever becoming hunter, fisherman, shepherd or critic.'[35] Note that here it is not at all suggested that every individual *ought* to diversify himself in these ways, only that in communism they *could* do so, if they wished. Communism equals the absence of the present crippling division of labour, it means nothing else. What they do with their freedom is up to the people themselves. Of course, this open-endedness and almost infinite possibility for human freedom and diversity must imply, on the other side, the 'control and conscious mastery' of the forces and relations of production. As it is said: 'The reality which communism creates is precisely the true basis for rendering it impossible that anything should exist independently of individuals, in so far as reality is nevertheless only a product of the preceding intercourse of individuals.'[36] However, often Marx and Engels seem aware, nay quite emphatic, that the freedom and possibility communism offers does not mean that individuals will become holy or loving, completely transcending their present selves and aspirations. 'The communists have no intention of abolishing the fixedness of their desires and needs, an intention which Stirner, immersed in his world of fancy, ascribes to them and to all other men; they only strive to achieve an organization of production and intercourse which will make possible the normal satisfaction of all needs, i.e. a satisfaction which is limited only by the needs themselves [*normale, d.h.nur durch die Bedürfnisse beschrankte, Befriedigung* . . .]'[37] The renowned stance of the *Communist Manifesto*, likewise, has ostensible reference only to this indifferent kind of communism, baffling though in some respects the precise meaning of its relevant sentences might be. Contrary to bourgeois society, it is said there, 'in communist society the present dominates the past'.[38] Here again the dominant emphasis is on freedom, individual self-determination, without any connotation of transcendent goodness. And: 'In place of the old bourgeois society, with its classes and class antagonisms, we shall have an association, in which the free development of each [*die freie Entwicklung eines jeden*] is the condition for the free development of all.'[39] This, it seems to me, is the same in intent and meaning as the earlier, 'utopian'[40] passage in the *German Ideology*; it connotes simply the absence of the present division of labour, the abolition of class domination and class identity, the *possibility* of individuals – all of them – to develop their potential and satisfy their various human needs.

Alas, however, this is not the whole picture, attractive and stimulating though this open-ended, worldly, libertarian communism might appear. Communism as sheer human possibility and human liberation, the satisfaction of needs and the all-round development of capacities, would make just as little sense as would pure negative 'criticism' (as shown in the previous chapter) and literally understood historical materialism. That is to say, it makes no sense *without* certain presuppositions, and of course it will not take us too long to find these presuppositions in Marx's maturing thought. But first let us make an endeavour to see what is involved clearly; what we are asked to believe is that it is adequate to define communism as mere external social *organization* (of production and intercourse) and that it is enough to refer to the substantive values which this organization is intended to foster merely in terms of 'satisfaction of needs' and 'free development'. By themselves, these terms have no meaning at all, or rather (which is the same thing) they have *several* and *opposed* meanings. Nothing, in the first place, follows at all from any particular kind of social organization as to the *quality* of human relationships and life in general that it can necessarily be said to engender and/or maintain. Within the stricter terms of historical materialism (of which this 'indifferent' communism is a conceptual offshoot, or its *alter ego*), Marx can have no conception, no idea, no inkling, no 'vision' *whatsoever* as to the essential defining quality of this future and desired form of organization. It will be *different* from the present, all right, it may be something very exciting, very thrilling, really and truly 'movement', society dominated by the present and not the past, 'liberation' squarely and indeed *exclusively* from the outlook of existing bourgeois society where individuals are 'crippled' by the division of labour and where the proletariat is oppressed and exploited by the bourgeoisie. But Marx could never cogently argue that this communist society ('organization' only!) will be *better* in any definite sense – ethical, existential, eudaimonic – than capitalist society. It may or may not be; the terms of the argument leave this entirely open. (It could be said, though this is not Marx's position, or not his dominant position at any rate, that it is this very *uncertainty*, volatility and excitement, that makes the communist revolution *worth* embarking upon.) From the judgment that capitalism is 'crippling', whether sensible or not, one cannot logically (without some hidden, underlying premise) move on to the judgment that another kind of society, not existing but only wished-for and projected, will not be crippling, or if not crippling, will not have some other, equally or even more objectionable, basic defining quality. We simply don't know. 'Form' is always only *mere* form.

Communism as the satisfaction of needs and the free development of individual capacities fares no better than communism *qua* organization when it comes to an attempt to determine its precise meaning. Needs and development, of course, do seem to refer to *substantive* aspects of communist society, and not to its organizational form. However, it is easy to see that (in the absence of *really* substantive assumptions) they do not reach the core, do not reveal anything unitary or unambiguously essential about the quality of life and human relations in this projected form of society; they, too, are ultimately revealed as *formal* aspects only and hence meaningless, i.e. multi-directional in signification. What are human 'needs' or 'human' needs? The mind boggles. The point is of course not just to offer here a lengthy description of recognizable human needs, 'basic' or more refined, physical, emotional, social, intellectual or what have you. Variety and multiplicity in themselves have no consequence, for communism or anything else. The point is that human needs *as we know them* necessarily involve conflict and some 'crippling' in their process of satisfaction. How about, for instance, the need for individual self-assertion, for triumph over others, for rivalry and competition, for the exclusive possession of others, etc., etc.? *Of course* we are arguing here from the 'present point of view'. And why shouldn't we be arguing from the present point of view? After all, communism is here, not in the clouds of 'German ideology' and an affair of the 'spirit', it is supposed to be the 'real movement' of the present. And who can tell us with certainty, or moral authority, which needs are genuinely human, to be upheld, and which are not, to be eradicated – from the outlook of the present (where they *all* exist) only?[41] And in addition to this, as it were, qualitative heterogeneity of needs, there is also the problem of quantitative satisfaction. Not only: *what* are human needs? – but:

when can needs be said to be satisfied? What is the satisfaction of hunger or the quenching of thirst? How do you ever satisfy your creative urge? Do you dance all night long? Do you need to recognize all Beethoven's symphonies? Where do we ever stop? How can it ever be proven that needs are really self-regulating?

The same goes of course for the catchy but in truth quite vacuous phrase concerning the 'free development of each'. This can also mean literally *anything*, under, within and over the sun. It is obvious that no individual can develop simultaneously in all directions – this would defy all possible logic and common sense. So you have to choose, but when can you ever know that you have chosen 'freely' and truly in accordance with your own 'potential'? Choice itself logically entails some 'crippling', some restriction: is it really *better* for you to fish in the afternoon and criticize after dinner, or to forego one of these and become a truly, fully 'developed' critic or fisherman? You may never know, or if you do come to know, it is long after the event of your 'free choice' and you can scarcely go back. And what if my 'potential' is for destruction, for violence, for all-consuming self-regard, for idleness, for bloody-mindedness, for arrogance and superiority, for wanton indifference, for fickleness? Why shouldn't I 'develop' these; who can convince me that I am not 'free' then and not fully 'human'? Why is your humanity better than mine? There is undoubtedly a certain amount of exaggeration in the way in which these problems of understanding communism are presented here, and I am also fully aware of their figuring in wholesale denunciations of Marx's thought, which is certainly not my purpose in this study. My intention here is not to criticize Marxism *per se*; it is only to show that this open-ended, libertarian communism is in the strict sense an incoherent notion. Yes, communism may possibly allow for the free development of *some* capacities of *all* individuals or perhaps all capacities of *some* individuals; but literally the 'free development of each' cannot be the 'condition' of the free development of all. This indifferent communism is sheer *chaos*. It cannot as such be entertained in thought, it is inconceivable in practice.

So we must conclude that, in spite of appearances, Marx's more mature understanding of communism, reflecting the development of his thought after 1844, must have more to it than an organization of production making possible the satisfaction of needs and the free development of individual capacities. In fact, the most telling way in which to come to terms with Marx's *real* position in this period will be to proceed from the notion of 'indifferent communism' itself, which the foregoing remarks suggested is an incoherent notion. For it, for communism in general, to become intelligible, its openness and 'indifference' must be *resolved* and decided in one of two ways. One way, and this is without much doubt Marx's intended and *coherent* meaning, is to make explicit Marx's assumptions concerning genuine humanity, the defining quality of being human which he approves and sees as being the very *rationale* as well as the historical guarantee of the future success of the proletarian communist movement. We do not have to go very far to find these, they are stated in the *Manuscripts* under 'genuine resolution' and openly expressed in scattered remarks as well as by implication in later texts also. Without therefore this continuity on the level of substantive values, of beliefs as to what it means to be 'human' and what is hence desirable (and not merely abstractly 'possible') in terms of human development, communism in Marx's thought simply melts into indifference, inconsequentiality, meaninglessness. Communism then *must* still mean, and it cannot mean anything less than, the genuine resolution of the 'conflict between men and men, and between men and nature'. The latter aspect seems the only assumption justifying and explaining Marx's emphatic and continuing belief in human 'mastery' over the forces and relations of production. And the former aspect, suggesting as it does mutual harmony of interests, complementarity of needs and wants, the pure historicity and artificiality of destructive, violent and anti-social tendencies, can *alone* justify the Marxist expectation of communism as the 'free development of all'. There is then no problem: once it is maintained that to be 'human' means to be basically good, to have fellow-feeling and naturally to desire to help others, and to be rational, then it *does* follow that 'needs' can be universally satisfied and individual talents and inclinations pursued to the full, without conflict and disturbance. Then the diversity of desires creates no antagonism. Then needs are transparently self-regulating and abilities are complementary.

In one expression: *morality* must be read into human nature for communism to make any sense at all. It must be maintained by Marx that human beings, though on the surface 'dehumanized' in bourgeois society, are essentially moral and, given the 'conditions' provided by the communist organization of the future, will soon learn to pursue goals that lead them to happiness without the undue 'crippling' of any particular group or individual. The 'freedom' defining communist society is predicated on goodness and rationality. It, freedom, pertains to human beings only in their essential 'species-character'; it does not, properly speaking, befit them as long as they are dominated by 'selfish needs' in existing society and have a crippled consciousness. So communism as the free development of all is the same thing as communism *qua* 'genuine resolution', and the latter is the same thing as the 'free association of moral human beings' and the 'true liberalism'. While Marx's adoption of a 'materialist' conception of history does signify some important changes in his thought (and fresh problems, too), it makes on the whole no decisive difference to his original *moral* stand and his visionary humanism. In the *Holy Family* we learn from Marx and Engels that 'materialism' of the correct variety 'leads directly to *socialism* and *communism*'. 'There is no need for any great penetration to see from the teaching of materialism on the original goodness and equal intellectual endowment of men, the omnipotence of experience, habit and education, and the influence of environment on man, the great significance of industry, the justification of enjoyment, etc., how necessarily materialism is connected with communism and socialism.'[42] All this is expressed somewhat naively, of course, and one would have to note that Marxist historical 'materialism' differs in some important respects from eighteenth-century 'French' materialism, extolled here. Nevertheless, this postulate of 'original goodness' remains incorporated in Marx's theory. Marx and Engels add the following, quite significant, sentence to the above eulogy of materialism: 'If correctly understood interest [*wohlverstandne Interesse*] is the principle of all morality, man's private interest must be made to coincide with the interest of humanity.'[43] The notion, 'correctly understood interest', would self-evidently be a *petitio principii*, were it not for the prior substantive assumption of essential, true, genuine humanity. Morality *is* human interest, and conversely, human interest is morality. In the *German Ideology* it is argued, in a somewhat moralizing language, that the present epoch sets a 'very definite task' to existing individuals. 'It has set them the task of replacing the domination of circumstances and of chance over individuals by the domination of individuals over chance and circumstances.' Further: 'This task [*Aufgabe*], dictated by present-day relations, coincides with the task of organizing society in a communist way.'[44] That this is described as a 'task' suggests that the moral authority for it does not directly or exclusively proceed from *existing* aspirations (a point which we discussed earlier), but from substantive humanity. And here, incidentally, we find it pretty clearly stated by Marx and Engels that the communist 'organization' of society is inadequate by itself; it is only 'coincidental' with the 'task' of human beings' acquiring mastery over their lives.

This is then one alternative: if libertarian, indifferent, formal, materialist and proletarian communism is to make sense, it is to be read in line with Marx's earlier notion of 'genuine resolution' which in turn connects us up with the notion of human morality. But there is another alternative also. Indifferent communism can – indeed, must – resolve either into something *good* or into something *bad*. And here I want to suggest that its 'bad' resolution should be read in line with Marx's denunciation of 'crude communism' in 1844, paralleling his formulation of 'genuine resolution'. A couple of explanatory remarks first. Concerning 'indifferent' communism: I hope I have succeeded above in showing that communism (and any other notion referring to a way of life and a kind of society) is meaningless if understood merely in *formal* terms, be they 'organization', 'satisfaction of needs', 'free development' or the like. For Marx these formal terms acquire meaning solely by virtue of the substantive assumptions read into them. It is because communism is expressive of true humanity that it is meaningful, good, desirable. But if we don't resolve the chaos and tension of indifferent communism into this *good* communism, then we have to resolve it into its moral and conceptual opposite: it cannot remain in this amorphous state of uncertainty and multi-directional signification (i.e. self-contradiction).

Concerning now 'crude communism': there is of course a very evident, and in Marxist terms perfectly legitimate, reason for Marx's ostensive abandonment of the use of this category: the proletarian movement, in his eyes, had already grown beyond the crude and immature stages in the mid-1840s. Interestingly, and anticipating our discussion in the last two chapters, Marx continues to refer to the *objective* features of crude communism in his later texts also (notably in *Critique of the Gotha Program*), but this time endowing these features with a *subjective*, moral significance which is the direct opposite of what we have found in the *Manuscripts*. However, the point to make now is that the various terms of criticism and denunciation directed by Marx at 'bourgeois socialism' and the 'petty bourgeois' standpoint – surveyed and analysed at some length earlier in this chapter – are readily *recognizable* as erstwhile putative features of 'crude communism'. That is, we can quite easily establish the continuity of Marx's thought on *both* sides, in positive as well as negative terms, concerning what Marx upholds and finds desirable, and what he rejects as undesirable. Egoism, the selfish need, 'huckstering', 'false consciousness', 'dissatisfaction' as a 'mood', searching for 'shadowless ideals', regarding the whole society as consisting of 'capitalists', endeavouring to keep bourgeois relations without class antagonisms, what any proletarian 'may want', etc. – all these undesirable manifestations of *seemingly* radical and socialist sentiment can be seen as essentially belonging to the consciousness, the culture of bourgeois society. It is these very same features which in the earlier terminology are described as effects of estrangement, or its 'generalization'. They only *look* like the real thing, viz. the movement towards communism, but in truth all they do is affirm the existing world. Thus, in summary, indifferent communism is *either* the complete transcendence of capitalism (i.e. Marx's vision) *or* just the continuation of capitalism (Marx's insight); it cannot as yet be seen as these two things united, and it cannot refer to any third alternative.

These two things – capitalism and communism – *will* of course be dialectically united in Marx's thought, yielding us his completed, 'fused' concept of communism, but before we turn to a presentation of this climax (in the following chapter), another advance in Marx's thought, representing the further strengthening of his insight after the formulation of 'indifferent' communism, will have to be sketched in here. As was remarked at the beginning of the present chapter, towards the later 1840s Marx and Engels became increasingly caught up in the atmosphere of revolution, which led to significant theoretical results, going even beyond the optimism expressed in the first formulation of the materialist conception of history. It was not merely that Marx came to endow the proletarian movement with an advanced communist consciousness and, more or less, equated communism with what he looked upon as the proper aims of this movement. In this equation, as we argued earlier, one can detect an endeavour towards uniting two erstwhile opposites: the proletariat, with its crudeness and simplicity, is lifted up as it were into the 'spirit', into the philosophical consciousness of 'genuine resolution'; together they make up communism as 'real movement'. But the further important point to grasp here is that Marx now came to see the communist revolution as *imminent*: it was in the air, it was advancing rapidly, it gathered momentum with every year and every month, it was expressive of a climactic concentration of social antagonisms and the bursting forth of the new world. Marx never believed, either in his youth or in his mature years, that the proletarian communist revolution will *at once* change the quality of life and human relations, that light will immediately follow darkness; this he always rejected as idle dreaming and utopianism. But he did, in this period, come to conceive of the revolution as a true cataclysm, as an event, or cluster of events, which will in itself encapsulate the death of the old and the birth of the new, the phenomenon in which the 'movement' of the present is accelerated so rapidly as to appear *also* as a new quality, like a disc that revolves so fast as to appear perfectly clear and stationary. The important point for him therefore was not to look beyond the revolution; in his terms this was impossible, since the revolution itself was not confined to (though it included) external political events, like raising the red flag and mounting barricades, but also signified the 'revolutionization of practice' and consciousness. The message was, as we have seen earlier, to await and work towards the creation of a new 'content' which as yet has no name; this stance is sharply opposed by Marx to the utopian-petty bourgeois endeavour to postulate a 'shadowless ideal' and contrast it to the existing. But if you don't thus oppose something different, something outside, something that is beyond the existing, what are you left with? You must contrast the existing to itself, which means recognizing and fastening on its own negative, its movement. This movement itself is the ground as well as expression of radical aims, it itself expresses the 'ideal' if you like *of* the existing world. But this movement is the *revolution*. Thus present antagonism and present struggle, the plight of the proletariat, its dehumanization and its radical needs, the agony, the misery, the self-contradiction, the fullness and hence temporality of the existing world *as well as* the final, irrevocable termination of all these and the concomitant inauguration of the new, with the possibility of genuine human life and relationships are all there, condensed in the concept of the revolution. To be a communist means to be a revolutionary in this total sense; it means intending to destroy and thereby to create. The two processes cannot be separated, either conceptually or historically, as a succession of events. Destruction means creation. Communism is nothing less and nothing more than the revolution.

This new breakthrough in Marx's thought, a further and hitherto the most decisive move to make the 'gods become the centre of the earth', is accompanied by a hardening and impatience of his attitude towards the static, *positive* character of the existing world. The tone in which Marx denounces 'the cowardly, hypocritical presentation of communism not as "destruction" but as "fulfilment" of existing evils and of the illusions which the bourgeoisie have about them'[45] gets visibly angrier, more intolerant. Communism is not to be confused with 'communion', it is not the 'old fantasy of religion'. 'Faith in the holy spirit of the community' is 'the last thing required for the achievement of communism.'[46] Communists do not want to 'improve the human race'. 'We are too modest and too few to want to compete with the reverend fathers in that humanitarian industry.'[47] Not benevolence but struggle is the watchword; indeed, struggle is presented now as one of the basic principles of the materialist conception of history. 'No antagonism, no progress. This is the law that civilization has followed up to our days.'[48] In the present, the proletariat is inevitably locked in the antagonistic encounter between itself and the bourgeoisie. 'In this struggle – a veritable civil war – all the elements necessary for a coming battle unite and develop.'[49] 'Indeed, is it at all surprising that a society founded on the *opposition* of classes should culminate in brutal *contradiction*, the shock of body against body, as its final denouement?'[50] Further: 'The social principles of Christianity preach cowardice, self-contempt, abasement, submissiveness and humbleness, in short, all the qualities of the rabble, and the proletariat, which will not permit itself to be treated as rabble, needs its courage, its self-confidence, its pride and its sense of independence even more than its bread.'[51]

For Marx the proletarian revolution becomes so much the condensed expression of communism, the realization of humanity and the fulfilment of morality, that he is led to the dismissal and ridiculing of ordinary moral rules and moral scruples. Communism alone embodies true morality, hence communism *qua* revolution contains in itself all valid moral principles; there is no room for a separate morality which is, or fancies itself to be, above the struggle waged at the present. The revolution legitimizes everything that, from the point of view of the existing in its static and positive character, would appear objectionable. The revolution cannot be waged in an 'amicable fashion'. The bourgeois are becoming aware that 'in revolutions the *rabble* gets insolent and lays hands on things'.[52] It is motivated not by the 'religious heart', but by 'the heart made bitter by real need'.[53] As Marx very openly puts it in a letter, talking about the new era of 'communist propaganda': 'Our means will be increased, the antithesis between bourgeoisie and proletariat will be sharpened. In a party one must support everything which helps towards progress, and have no truck with any tedious moral scruples [*langweiligen moralischen Skrupel*].'[54] Repudiating 'weak, cowardly minds' in June 1848, in the *Neue Rheinische Zeitung*, Marx insists that 'the best form of state is that in which the social contradictions are not blurred, not arbitrarily . . . kept down. The best form of state is that in which these contradictions reach a stage of open struggle in the course of which they are resolved.'[55] And as he repeats the point in 1853: 'In a state of society founded upon the antagonism of classes, if we want to prevent Slavery in fact as well as in name, we must accept war.'[56] The June revolution of the Paris proletariat in Marx's eyes was 'the ugly revolution, the nasty revolution'.[57] The historical example of the Roman slave war is adduced by Marx to justify this present battle between two classes as a battle between 'respectable people and rogues'.[58] In the context this is ostensibly meant as a sarcastic rejoinder to an anti-revolutionary article in another German newspaper, but Marx's overall attitude is not in doubt: the revolutionary proletariat *must* fight as 'criminals', 'cannibals', 'murderers' and 'plunderers'. After all, it is bourgeois society that made them such, that caused them to lose completely their 'humanity' in the first place. Then again, also in the revolutionary *Neue Rheinische Zeitung*: *'We have no compassion and we ask no compassion from you. When our turn comes, we shall not make excuses for the terror.'*[59] In 1850, in his 'Address of the Central Authority' of the Communist League, Marx urges the workers (i.e. communists) to 'compel the democrats to carry out their present terrorist phrases'. 'Revolutionary excitement' must be kept alive as long as possible. 'Far from opposing so-called excesses, instances of popular revenge against hated individuals or public buildings that are associated only with hateful recollections, such instances must not only be tolerated but the lead in them must be taken.'[60] Again, as Marx says later, in 1853 in an article in the *New York Daily Tribune*, 'I am far from defending the aimless acts of violence committed by the Wigan colliers'; but, he goes on, there is a great difficulty especially for the 'inferior elements of the working classes' to be peaceful and orderly 'when they are driven to acts of frenzy by utter destitution and by the cool insolence of their masters'.[61] And so on.

The revolution, then, is not merely a secular course of events, but it is in the deepest sense humanization, the visible birth of the communist quality of mankind, the culmination and resolution of history in a conscious manner. However, as with need satisfaction and individual development, revolution as the reality of communism cannot be conceived in an 'indifferent' form, as *just* struggle, just change, just the overthrow of one particular set of social institutions and their replacement with another set. Acts of external violence, rising passion, frenzy, are all transvalued and justified in the name of this immanent, integral *end*, as labour pains acquire meaning only by reference to the act of birth. And just as the 'means', revolutionary actions, have no meaning in separation from the end, communism, so communism is no outlying, transcendent culmination but this very process of *becoming*, the dizzying, accelerating movement itself. You cannot, need not and ought not look beyond the revolution; it is already, essentially, communism the *quality*, the present no longer shackled by the past but 'dominating' itself.

Interestingly, and in a curious way endorsing the materialist conception of history, the final *conceptual* culmination in Marx's thought bringing together communism and the revolution takes place after the *historical* climax, viz. the events of 1848–49. The 'revolution', of course, failed, there was no doubt about that, after a year or so of fervent hopes and anticipations the world settled down again in essentially its old shape, irrespective and in spite of superficial achievements, like liberal constitutions. For Marx these signified only the entrenchment of bourgeois rule and by implication the failure of the proletariat to become humanity and to inaugurate communist society. Hence Marx's increasing recognition in the 1850s of the need for patience and a war of attrition, and his increasing – and fascinating, in point of theory – preoccupation with the nature of the existing, i.e. his 'science' of political economy, not born of but certainly nourished by frustration. There is a corresponding, subtle but very significant, shift of emphasis in his understanding of communism also, which will be the subject matter of our next chapter. However, the point here is that the clearest identification of the revolution with communism occurs in Marx's thought after the close of the secular events externally constituting the revolution, but still within the live embers of revolutionary fervour. The spirit of revolution not only lingered on after the demise of its body, but it acquired its highest excellence and inspiration only at this time. As though, if we are permitted another

Insight and Vision

frivolous analogy, the intoxication of the last glass of wine obscured the fact that the bottle was empty and that soon the painful process of sobering up must be entered into. When the revolution had already run its course and finally fizzled out, Marx crystallized the notion of 'permanent revolution' which was to play such a controversial role in the subsequent history of Marxism. In his 'Address', already referred to, Marx insists that 'it is our interest and our task to make the revolution permanent, until all more or less possessing classes have been forced out of their position of dominance, the proletariat has conquered state power, and the association of proletarians, not only in one country but in all the dominant countries of the world, has advanced so far that competition among the proletarians in these countries has ceased and that at least the decisive productive forces are concentrated in the hands of the proletarians.'[62] The 'battle cry must be', he concludes the 'Address': 'The Revolution in Permanence'.[63] It seems reasonable to suggest that what Marx is formulating here is not merely a strategic plan or a timetable of desired secular events; the strategy of revolution is only the external translation of the essential nature of the revolution into political terms and would be meaningless without it; the struggle can be continued indefinitely only on the assumption of an essentially volatile, dynamic world, on the view of the present as 'movement'. Thus the concept of the permanent revolution signifies not merely, or not so much, a projected chronological list of events, but the lifting up of the revolution from the temporal plane altogether. The revolution is *nothing* in time (since it has already ended), hence it becomes *everything*; it is not taking place at all in the external world, but in truth it is there always, it is 'permanent'. The movement, revolution, communism thus express the most important truth, the very meaning, of the existing world.

Let us then close this chapter by briefly recapitulating the prominent aspects of Marx's thinking concerning communism in this middle, and theoretically most fertile, period; and at the same time we shall attempt to put these aspects into the perspective of our overall interpretation of Marx's communism in this study. Communism is the essence of Marx's thought, it is the innermost core of his understanding of the world, it is his way of achieving the reconciliation and unity of reality and the idea, thinking and existence, vision and insight. In the youthful period, as we saw in the previous chapter, Marx looks upon communism itself in a dualistic manner, as rent, divided, bifurcated into the two opposites of communism of the idea, 'genuine resolution', and the crude, heterogeneous communism of the world, the generalization of estrangement. From 1845 onwards Marx engages in the gigantic task of synthesizing these opposites, at first the synthesis being formulated in his materialist conception of history, together with its implied ideal, the 'indifferent communism' of free individual development. Communism now seems to shed its pure ideal, philosophical character, and appears as the 'real movement' of the world, expressing the 'radical need' of the proletariat. The proletarian movement, with its predominantly negative, mundane, destructive, oppositional attitude towards existing society, comes then to be identified with communism: you don't look beyond the movement. However, as I tried to argue in the foregoing pages, this is no complete *volte face* in Marx's position, since, in the first place, the erstwhile visionary ideal is read into the proletarian movement, and in the second place, the erstwhile opposition of the idea and the world is carried on, this time the antagonist being presented as 'petty bourgeois' attitudes to which the proletariat is prone. Communism as the satisfaction of human needs and as the free development of individuals only *seems* an open-ended, libertarian position; its coherence requires the continuing presence of assumptions concerning the true nature of humanity. Further, it has been shown that Marx's elevation of the proletarian movement as the visible, worldly manifestation of communism is inextricably tied up with his belief in the imminence of revolution. The 'movement' is communism because it is radical transformation, it leads directly, immediately to changes which inaugurate communist society. In the final synthesis, then, communism is revealed as the revolution itself, movement *as such*, ideal and real at the same time.

At once, then, we also come to see Marx's dilemma, or the gnawing *problem* of communism in his thought, and this dilemma goes a long way indeed towards explaining the direction of Marx's *further* development, from the emphasis on history to the emphasis on political economy. The question we have to pose here is this: has Marx up to this point succeeded in demonstrating the *reality* of communism? Is 'revolution' an adequate way of arguing that communism is *here*, that it is imminent, the real movement of society, a quality of life and human relationships that is reasonable to expect as coming into being? Does 'revolution' succeed in convincing us that communism is not merely a figment of the radical imagination, a 'shadowless ideal' of the existing, impotent utopian construction, pure vision, gods in the ether and far away from the inhabited world? The answer seems obvious and it is, inevitably, a *negative* answer. Marx himself saw no successful communist revolution and the desired transformation of society. Revolution in his thought, together with the worldly, libertarian aspects of communism, remained as such mere ideals, visionary objects, still sharply opposed to the existing world. There was still something outside for Marx's insight to penetrate, something yet insufficiently explained and integrated; communism *qua* proletarian movement still confronted the world as an Hegelian 'bad infinity', intending to but still incapable of penetrating and conquering the world outside. Hence Marx, who as a thinker really had a gigantic stature and would not stop at obstacles that might render his thought sublime but impotent, was forced to go further. The next advance in his thinking on communism, to be judged in my view the highest point of development his thought ever achieved, was to take him much closer to the existing world than his understanding of communism as 'revolution'. This crowning achievement will be the subject matter of our next chapter.

4 Fusion

Marx achieves his highest stature as a thinker in his scientific critique of political economy or, which is the same thing, his study of capital. It is, and informed opinion appears almost unanimous on this point (by no means confined to Marxists), as a theorist of capitalism that Marx achieves his distinct elevation from the ranks of modern radical and socialist writers, whereas (as general opinion would have it) *qua* revolutionary and *qua* 'communist' Marx is merely an ordinary, though particularly forceful and respected, member of that confraternity. However, it is my central argument in this study that Marx's 'communism' and his critical-scientific theory of capitalism cannot be separated. First of all, and from one side, it is established that Marx's critique of capitalism presupposes the standpoint of communism and gains its meaning only if understood from this standpoint. This was argued in our first chapter. Now it is our task to attempt to illuminate the same connection from the other side and show that Marx's communist standpoint itself assumes the being, and very distinct character in terms of the succession of historical formations, of capitalism. Communism and capitalism are closely, dialectically united: this is the complete fusion of Marx's vision and Marx's insight. One useful and initial way in which this conceptual fusion, the very climax of Marx's intellectual achievement, can be grasped is by our comprehending capitalism as 'movement'. This will provide a link with the subject matter of our previous chapter where it was argued that Marx's understanding of communism in the middle period (1845–51 approximately) comes to be concentrated on the notion of 'real movement', associated then with the rising revolutionary consciousness of the proletariat and the expected revolution.

However, we have already intimated at various points that the notion of 'movement' in Marx's thought should not simply be interpreted as a political and social phenomenon, i.e. certain people 'moving', joining radical organizations, engaging in strike action, demonstrating, fighting, manning the barricades, etc., though all these of course are *parts* of Marx's meaning. But we would entirely miss the point of Marx's communist theory if we confined the meaning of 'movement' to these important, but nonetheless derived and, in terms of the materialist conception of history, 'superstructural', events and processes. The 'contradictions' of capitalist society, as Marx says in his 1859 'Preface', are merely 'fought out' on the conscious, political level; but these contradictions lie deeper in the objective being of capitalism. 'Movement', too, must ultimately be understood in this deeper, objective, one might say *ontological*, sense. Communism is the 'real movement' of the revolutionary working class, but the point is that this revolutionary class 'moves' towards communism, or comes to embody communism in this very movement, *by virtue of* being a part of capitalism. Through the proletariat it is capitalism *itself* that moves towards communism and – though this might sound somewhat far-fetched at first – actually reveals itself as communism in its innermost and dynamic essence. The proletariat is at first presented by Marx as the 'negation' of capitalism, as the class excluded from capitalist society and from 'humanity' altogether, but as the later unfolding of Marx's thought shows, this negative character of the proletariat itself presupposes its very positive involvement with capitalism: the working class, or 'labour' as the chief value-creating agency, constitutes the basis of capitalist society, and thus it is the *basis* of capitalism that is at the same time its Achilles' heel, its weakest point and the agency of its demolition. Capitalism is overthrown not by any kind of transcendental intervention, but from within itself: '. . . the new forces of production and relations of production do not develop out of *nothing*, nor drop from the sky, nor from the womb of the self-positing Idea; but from within and in antithesis to the existing development of production and the inherited, traditional relations of property.'[1] The overthrow of capitalism, or the proletarian revolution, is communism; hence communism is the affair, the business, as it were, of capitalism itself.

To look at this from another angle: Marx's distinction from 'utopian' and similar kinds of socialists and communists, as seen by himself, is his ability to show that the overthrow of capitalism and the (conceptually equivalent, though chronologically spread out) inauguration of communism is an historically, scientifically 'necessary' event; communism is not a wished-for, empty, pious dream, a shadowless ideal, the cry of the impotent imagination, something which is merely, and moralistically, *desirable*; it is the actual movement *of* existing society. It is, however, to some extent misleading to read Marx's remarks *literally* that his aim is 'to reveal the economic law of motion of modern society',[2] or his famous conclusion in

Fusion

Capital that 'capitalist production begets, with the inexorability of a natural process [*mit der Notwendigkeit eines Naturprozesses*] its own negation'.[3] In part, Marx was perhaps too impressed by contemporary advances in natural science (especially by Darwin) and in part his Germanic use of the term 'science' connotes a much broader category than the customary Anglo-Saxon usage anyway, and by 'natural' here he obviously does not refer to a mechanical, autonomous, and from the human point of view fatalistic, process. It is evident that for Marx the science of capital, political economy, is not mechanistic but *dialectical*; indeed, the very last term in the statement above, referring to capitalism begetting its 'own negation', shows this clearly. (Whether or not Marx, like Engels, conceives of *natural* science itself in dialectical terms is a question wholly irrelevant in our present context.) In his 'Postface' to the second edition of *Capital* itself, Marx very openly and unequivocally professes to his adaptation of a 'dialectical method', differing in its materialism from Hegel's, but nevertheless drawing on the 'rational kernel' found in Hegel's system.[4] At this time Marx certainly appears to 'take the dead dog Hegel seriously',[5] more so, in fact, than in the earlier writings. The main and relevant point of Marx's 'rational' dialectic, which, as he biblically expresses it, 'is a scandal and an abomination to the bourgeoisie', is its inclusion 'in its positive understanding of what exists a simultaneous recognition [*zugleich auch das Verständnis*] of its negation, its inevitable destruction'.[6] We have to emphasize here the very crucial point of dialectical understanding being the *simultaneous* recognition of the 'positive' and the 'negative'; it won't do, it won't lead to a proper appreciation of Marx's thought, to place all the emphasis in jejune, vulgar, idealistic 'Marxist' fashion on the 'negative', on destruction, and letting the 'positive' aspect go by default, relegating it to oblivion. There *is* no negative without positive, no destruction without construction, no communism without capitalism.

In what sense then should we understand Marx's dictum that the future demise of capitalism and the thereby connected establishment of communism constitute a 'necessary' process? As we have indicated above, Marx's understanding of history and human society is not mechanical or positivist or empiricist or non-humanly, fatalistically 'materialist'. The relationship of communism to capitalism is not one of merely external, temporal succession, or abstract juxtaposition. *This* kind of projection, besides being patently absurd on commonsensical reflection itself, would also be alien to Marx's thinking: Marx, as we have seen earlier, strenuously denies the rational possibility of divining, conjecturing, foretelling a 'future' which is wholly *different* from the present and has at the same time *definite* features and contours. In this Marx's approach is genuinely Hegelian – and it is a different question, not to be entered into now, whether or not he could consistently *keep* to this Hegelianism in everything that he said about communism coming to replace capitalism, and indeed whether or not this Hegelian position is itself coherent, tenable. The point then is that while on the one hand the move from capitalism to communism cannot be pronounced (by Marx or anybody else) to be an event that is absolutely, empirically necessary (e.g. there might be natural disasters, etc.), on the other hand it is not quite enough for Marx to suggest, in the manner of a natural scientific 'hypothesis', that capitalism just might be altered or destroyed in the future. This would make Marx's theory merely, and anti-climactically, probabilistic, and Marx never says anything anywhere, or even intimates indirectly, that the coming overthrow of capitalism and the arrival of communism are just uncertain projections, inconsequential 'scenarios', matters of idle 'futurological' speculation. This kind of academic pusillanimity would not only have minimized the political significance of Marx's thought, but would have rendered it devoid of its very core meaning, its innermost theoretical substance and its intelligibility. Communism *is* necessary, Marx's thought stands or falls with this assertion.[7] But then, if communism cannot be seen as absolutely necessary in empirical terms (because the future is unknowable and because we cannot surmise a wholly different future), its necessity must lie in its present existence, its actual reality. Communism is the necessary outcome of capitalism, because communism is *already here*. And conversely the overthrow of capitalism is necessary because, in a manner of speaking which in fact reveals the very *essence* of Marx's meaning, capitalism is *no longer here*, it merely lingers on on the surface of things, it is already an anachronism, a malevolent ghost, the 'undead' which haunts us from the grave dug by itself. Capitalism, as we recognize it on the surface, is the merely temporary turbulence of waters deep and calm, the mist ever so imperfectly obscuring the clear horizon in front of us, the tatty, torn, dirty decoration hiding the exquisite mahogany from our view, our own very *being* falsified by our own retarded consciousness. Capitalism is the living 'contradiction' with its own *reality* which is communism. The necessity of the overthrow of capitalism is also the

Fusion

impossibility of capitalism, its ephemeral, transitory, untenable and in the last resort merely illusory existence.

We must qualify this point somewhat, and thereby we shall come face to face once again with the underlying *problem* of communism in Marx's thought. While it is true, and will be argued at some length in the ensuing part of this chapter, that Marx comes at the highest point of his intellectual development to recognize and to assert the dialectical unity of capitalism and communism, and with this to argue the point of the 'necessity' of the demise of capitalism in a cogent, dialectical manner, it is also true that Marx's thought does not remain firmly occupying this dizzying theoretical position. Eventually, as we shall endeavour to show in the next chapter, his thinking finally comes to rest again in a dualistic stance, accepting that communism as idea or vision on the one hand, and the reality of the world on the other, are two separate things, disunited and incapable of being synthesized. And more relevantly here, the point to note is that even this highest trajectory in Marx's understanding of communism is always accompanied by the lingering doubt and rueful recognition, as witness his numerous and (understandably) bitter denunciations of 'petty bourgeois' tendencies and the venality of the actual working class, that capitalism in its 'contradictory' form of existence might in fact linger on much longer than expected, might just survive (for all revolutionary intents and purposes) indefinitely. Marx's thought, while strictly necessitarian in a dialectical manner, yet by implication allows for two, and only two, alternatives concerning the future. Dominantly it is asserted, as has been indicated above, that since the underlying reality of capitalism is communism, capitalism must also and imminently change to communism in its *visible* aspects. The contradiction expressing the existence of capitalism *as* capitalism must be resolved, and it can only be resolved in communism (which, in the pregnant phrase of the *Manuscripts*, is 'genuine resolution'). However, this resolution of capitalism into communism *can* be temporarily suspended, held back, retarded, resisted – if I am forgiven yet another frivolous analogy, the triumphant climax of communism can be spoiled by the involuntary *coitus interruptus* of capitalism indefinitely salvaging itself, and lingering on and on, irrationally and ever more anachronistically. There are and can be only two alternatives, given the present 'contradictory' existence of capitalist society: *either*, what is rationally to be expected and to be 'fought for' on the conscious, political level, the rule of capital is wholly destroyed, and this equals communism; *or* the rule of capital is perpetuated, carried on, under various and perhaps unsuspected *disguises*. This is a point of utmost significance and must be clearly grasped if we are to comprehend Marx: petty bourgeois 'social democracy', utopian construction, the 'equalitarian' socialism of the radical disciples of Ricardo, 'academic' socialism, the anarchism of Proudhon, the co-operative socialism of Louis Blanc and Lassalle, etc. are all in Marx's view merely 'solutions' in appearance, on the surface, but in reality they represent the continuing domination of *capital*, i.e. the lingering contradiction of capitalism with its *own* reality. And of course behind these sundry and lamentable deviations from the true path of communism as 'genuine resolution' we see the awful, ghost-like, equally lingering presence of *crude communism*, gone underground in Marx's writings, but still *the* ultimate threat to the validity and credibility of his dominant message. Either capital destroyed or capital surviving; either estrangement annulled or estrangement 'generalized'. The rule of capital is contradictory, irrational, and its overthrow is dialectically 'necessary'; yet capital can still carry its shrivelled carcase on a while longer, can still go on oppressing us and sucking human blood, it ought to be dead, but it is in truth the *undead*. Will then capital *ever* be destroyed? Or is it the case that what we can rationally, 'dialectically' read out of the dynamic character of capitalism, its very existence as 'movement', amounts merely to its *generalization*? This is the gnawing question at the very heart, and actual completion, of Marx's thought considered from the point of view of its essential core, the concept of communism. We shall have more to say on this point later.

For now, let us concentrate on the subject matter of this chapter, the dialectical unity of capitalism and communism. This unity is given its clearest expression in Marx's mature work on political economy. But it would be wrong to be too schematic about this and assume that Marx's thought is thus subject to a lifeless academic periodization. I think it could be cogently argued that the basic principles of Marx's critique of political economy are already to be found, more or less completed, in the *Manuscripts*; there, in the concepts of alienated labour and of communism as 'genuine resolution', is to be found already the thesis which, in its full development, becomes the dialectical unity of communism and capitalism. That is, in 1844 Marx already conceives of that which dehumanizes, oppresses and exploits the worker as 'labour in alienation', i.e. we have here the embryonic notion of the fundamental *identity* of

Fusion

labour and capital, on which notion the whole of Marx's science of political economy rests. However, it is to be noted that it takes a certain length of time for Marx to work this conception out fully, and that, in spite of definite foreshadowings present in sundry writings before the 1850s, this crowning achievement of Marx's lifework does not appear in its full splendour before the *Grundrisse* and *Capital*. In truth, therefore, it is not absolutely necessary to resort to extraneous explanations to account for Marx's development; in a valid sense, it *is* just the result of intense intellectual application, Marx's ability to follow out his arguments with relentless logical rigour.

Yet on a different level it is also helpful to explain Marx's truly amazing concentration on, almost obsession with, the reality of 'capital' by reference to political events, notably the failure of the 1848–49 European revolutions. We have, of course, already alluded to this at the end of the foregoing chapter, and it is a form of explanation frequently resorted to in commentaries. It certainly does make sense: the dramatic events of these years showed to Marx (and other revolutionary leaders and writers involved) that the existing system possessed a much greater degree of resilience, strength in terms of military potential, political sway and ideological appeal, than had been believed. The communist and allied revolutionary groups, and the working class in particular, proved too weak in confrontation with the concealed might of bourgeois society; some sections were physically liquidated (as in June, 1849 in Paris), others cowed, yet others, the great 'mass', came to acquiesce in the situation and sought accommodation with petty bourgeois values and bourgeois culture in general. Particularly galling to Marx was the accession of Louis Bonaparte, causing him partially to modify his political theory (willy-nilly allowing more importance to the 'state') and to denounce in extremely vituperative terms the peasants and the urban 'lumpenproletariat' who, according to radical expectations, could well have been caught up in the revolutionary movement (though the *Manifesto* already brands this 'scum' [*Lumpenproletariat*] as the likely 'tool of reactionary intrigue').[8] Marx's strictures in the *Eighteenth Brumaire* concerning the 'petty bourgeois' peasants and the 'reactionary' lumpenproletariat again bear a certain, and in our context quite significant, resemblance to both the tone and terms of his earlier rejection of crude communism. It might be said, therefore, that it was natural, nay imperative, for Marx to turn his full attention after the debacle (and in spite of intermittent flashes of revolutionary optimism, e.g. in 1857) to the existing, and entrenched, bourgeois system; he had to find out *why* it was so unexpectedly, irritatingly and 'irrationally' enduring, and why the attributed 'communist' consciousness of the working class was taking so long to materialize. Hence his emphasis, in years to come, on the need for patience, for education and for organization (culminating in his work with the International in the 1860s and 1870s). And hence also his fully worked-out science of political economy, designed to uncover the 'laws of motion' of capitalism. The existing system is thereby elevated, promoted, distinguished: it becomes an object *worth* serious study. The point to note is, however, that this modification in Marx's orientation need not be interpreted as a kind of conscious 'pessimism' setting in: Marx does not in any political sense cease to be a revolutionary, communist, and implacable enemy of the capitalist system which he obviously would not be if he were to believe that capitalism was *that* durable. The gnawing doubts and uncertainties, and the basic ambiguity and dualism characterizing Marx's *thought* on the reasonableness of communism, are there all the time and not specific to this period. What happens now, as we have already indicated in this chapter, is that the notions of movement, revolution and communism itself are shifted, ever so subtly but ever so significantly, so as to embrace the whole capitalist system: there is now a unity of perspective, an integration of large and small things, the whole and its parts, the distant gaze and short-range concentration.

The point should on no account be missed – and it only *seems* paradoxical – that it is when Marx's thought becomes most pronouncedly scientific that it also becomes most determinedly dialectical, when it is most 'materialist' it is at the same time the most 'Hegelian', not in the mistaken, one-sided sense of 'Hegelian Marxism' read into Marx's early writings (which, in truth, display the imprint of *Left* Hegelianism and the anti-Hegelianism and 'humanism' of Feuerbach), but in the sense of the *immanentist*, substance-oriented core of the fully-grown Hegelian philosophical enterprise.[9] It is Hegel's dictum concerning the rationality of the real that is adapted by Marx in his argument concerning the dialectical unity of communism and capitalism. There is, of course, no novelty in making this observation. It was the 'materialist' Lenin who noted the intrinsic, substantial connection between *Capital* and Hegel's *Science of Logic*. And it was the structuralist, anti-idealist Althusser who noted, if not quite unequivocally and consistently

Fusion

perhaps, the identity of approach to history connecting Marx and Hegel. Accordingly here, in our present endeavour to advance an interpretation of Marx's thought from the point of view of communism, we shall concentrate on the philosophical foundations of Marx's theory of political economy, the *rationale* of his principles guiding his empirical observations, and not on what is often *taken* to be important, i.e. Marx's mathematical equations, the wealth of historical detail woven into his theory, his description of working-class life in capitalism, and so on. To fasten on Marx's theory of political economy as a purportedly 'exact' and quantifiable science assumes, to my mind, either arguing from an already committed, communist standpoint, or the mistaken attempt to prove Marx 'wrong' on a level which is wholly inconsequential. Here, of course, we are not arguing from a communist standpoint but trying to determine what that standpoint is. And we are of the view, voiced sufficiently often in these pages, that the validity of Marx's theory does *not* depend on such secondary, derivative conclusions as the falling rate of profit or the extraction of relative surplus-value. All these make initial *sense* only on the assumption of the reality of communism. And, in turn, the reality or which is the same thing 'necessity' of communism only acquires its highest, clearest sense if recognized as forming a dialectical unity with capitalism. Thus the emphasis must be on Marx's dialectic.

Particular attention is to be focused on the *Grundrisse* which, from our point of view, is undoubtedly the most significant Marxist text. Here, in these lengthy and at times bewilderingly difficult and turgid notebooks composed by Marx in the 1850s, we have the most pregnant concentration of everything that is crucial to an understanding and appreciation of Marx's thought, the 'early' philosophical concern and the 'mature' scientific interest brought together. It is by studying the *Grundrisse* that we can gain not only the clearest glimpse of Marx's conception of the dialectical unity of capitalism and communism, but also, from this highest vantage-point, a more adequate comprehension of Marx's earlier, predominantly visionary and abstract conception of values to be promoted in communist society, such as the realization of the universal 'social individual', the satisfaction of human need, and 'free development'. All these, and many other things, are now put into their proper perspective, and as a result no longer appear in a one-sided, idealistic light (on account of which we criticized these Marxist notions in the previous chapter), once seen in the powerful prismatic illumination provided by the *Grundrisse* theme. In its philosophical wealth, the *Grundrisse* provides an extension, and definitive conclusion, of the central argument of the *Manuscripts*. And in the way in which these philosophical premises are visibly integrated with Marx's more technical-sounding, scientific and seemingly mundane pronouncements in the language of political economy, the *Grundrisse* supplies us with the proper background, or context, for an informed understanding of *Capital*. The latter work, unrivalled in Marxist literature in its sheer aesthetic appeal on account of the fullness, enclosedness, detailed as well as systematic presentation of the Marxist theory of political economy, also reveals, I believe, Marx's conception of the dialectical unity of capitalism and communism. However, the value of *Capital* is lessened for us precisely by virtue of its character as a complete, polished, definitive work. Its very clarity, neatness, argumentative certainty as well as its confident, didactic tone and style all but reduce it to a 'text-book', however substantial and sophisticated; its presentation is cut-and-dried, committed, unspeculative, almost pedestrian, suitable reading perhaps for communists already semi-consciously committed and for academic, unimaginative Marx-baiters alike. And its *dominant* message, as I shall argue in the next chapter, represents a clear descent from the height of the *Grundrisse*, in that here Marx comes once again to acquiesce in a dualistic reading of communism and the real world. But the *Grundrisse*, no doubt on account of its being a collection of unpublished notes and jottings, shows us the *whole* Marx, Marx's thought in its live, dynamic, titanic struggle with itself, with all its parturitive perspiration and subterranean rumblings. The *Grundrisse*, together with the *Manuscripts*, provides the best key to a comprehension of the essential core of Marx's thought. And while the *Manuscripts* is by far the more readable and more immediately striking of these two seminal texts, the relevant value and excellence of the *Grundrisse* lies in its very messy, very complicated, agonizingly repetitive and often forbiddingly technical, but nonetheless unmistakably concentrated attention on Marx's chief argument and achievement as a thinker, and what is only speculatively, half-implicitly stated in the *Manuscripts*: the dialectical unity of the 'real' and the 'rational', of capitalism and communism. Here only Marx's science is fully revealed as what it truly is, the *phenomenology* of capital in the genuine Hegelian sense, the thinking *development* of capital to the point where it itself is truly revealed as what it is, the communist essence of mankind.

Fusion

What, then, do we mean by the 'dialectical unity' of capitalism and communism? Perhaps it will be in order, and not too condescending to the reader, to make the obvious but essential point that 'dialectical' unity does *not* mean abstract, empirical identity or even resemblance or similarity open to simple, unaided perception. This resemblance is there, and we shall come to it in a minute, but its significance can only be appreciated if we are first able to grasp the concept. Not wishing to overburden the discussion, I shall not resort here to any kind of technical elaboration involving Hegelian terminology. We shall in any case be able, as we go on, to learn the nature of this concept through observing Marx's own, for the most part Hegelian-derived, formulations. For now, just a couple of crude, simplistic, commonsensical illustrations. Communism and capitalism are 'united' not in that they represent two identical eggs, or one egg in two forms. They are, respectively, the chicken and the egg. Eggs only come from chickens; this is what we *mean* by an 'egg'. And out of chickens only eggs can come, not tadpoles or maggots or human babies. This is what we *mean* by a chicken: a bird that reproduces by the laying of eggs. Or, a bit less frivolously: a musical score is composed in order for it to become 'music', to be performed. There is no 'performance' and no 'rendering' which is not that *of* a 'composition' (not excluding 'ad-libbing' as in jazz, which is merely the *immediate* rendering of a composition in the musician's mind). And a score, only written on paper or in the mind, is not yet fully music, but *becomes* so only in its performance, translation, execution. Marx's renowned contrasting example of human action and animal behaviour in *Capital* is also illustrative of this point: human 'action', properly conceived, is the accomplished unity of two things, design in the mind and execution in external reality. The two things, like chickens and eggs and score and music, are inseparable. Of course, it will have been noted, and the point does not lose its significance by being obvious and well-attested in exegetical literature, that this way of thinking about things and about the interconnections of things is characteristic of Aristotelian philosophy, and that in so far as Marx's way of connecting capitalism and communism is at all seen to correspond to this pattern, Marx is revealed to us as an Aristotelian thinker. And indeed, this is precisely the case: Marx's connecting capitalism and communism is really not much more than a peculiar and striking adaptation of the Aristotelian categories of potentiality and actuality, and it is certainly not an accident that Marx's later theoretical writings (the

Insight and Vision

Grundrisse as well as *Capital*) are replete with references to Aristotle, in revealing contrast to the earlier texts. Of course, Marx's immanentist 'Hegelianism' and his increasing reliance on and preoccupation with Aristotle are not in any sort of contradiction; Hegel himself does not need a great deal of analysis for *his* Aristotelianism to be discovered; it's there, unmistakably, in his intense concentration on the 'real', his concern with 'substance' being recognized as 'subject'. But again, neither Hegel nor Marx is a simple *interpreter* of Aristotle. Marx's project, and in this he more or less carries further and perhaps culminates the Hegelian philosophical enterprise, is an attempt at a gigantic synthesis of classical and modern thought; it will be recalled that we noted this tendency in the young Marx's thinking in Chapter 2 above. This time, however, the synthesis is brought forward in much weightier, more compelling terms. The classical element in Marx's conception of the relationship between capitalism and communism lies, as we noted above, in the way in which *substance*, the heavy, perceptible, intelligible, existing world is seen *by itself* to give rise, create, generate, 'necessarily' move towards a new, and ideal, world. The modern element lies, in the first instance, in Marx's subjectivist humanism, his belief in the (near) omnipotence of human reason to recognize consciously, and actively assist and accelerate this substantial movement (this being epitomized in the communist *standpoint*), and in the second instance in his adaptive subsumption of classical Aristotelianism in a unilinear conception of history. Capitalism is not just any, recurrent or accidentally hit upon, 'potentiality' which has its 'actuality' in communism. Capitalism is a *unique* development in human history and its full actualization in communism is the *end* of history as we know it; in Marx's renowned phrase, it marks the end of the 'pre-history' of mankind and the beginning of its real, proper 'human' history. The point to grasp here though (to repeat) is that the full meaning of this unique, cataclysmic event is in the *connection*, dialectical unity, of capitalism and communism, the two seemingly discrete and antithetical entities must be *thought* together.

First, then, let us survey some of the more obvious, *visible* characteristics of capitalist society, noted by Marx, which reveal its essence as the potentiality or prefiguration of communism. Broadly, these fall into three categories: the victorious struggle waged by humanity under capitalism against the might of external nature; the generation of free, universal human individuality in capitalism; and the secular, progressive requirements of the capitalist organization of production, which point beyond this organization itself (only this third, incidentally, gains full recognition in committed exegetical accounts of Marx's 'science'). On the first count, already in the *Communist Manifesto*, composed at the height of revolutionary excitement, Marx and Engels go out of their way to extol the 'wonders' of bourgeois society, thereby demonstrating yet again the decisive difference of their communism from the one-sidedly negative, utopian variety. The bourgeoisie as a ruling class 'has been the first to show what man's activity can bring about. It has accomplished wonders far surpassing Egyptian pyramids, Roman aqueducts, and Gothic cathedrals; it has conducted expeditions that put in the shade all former Exoduses of nations and crusades.'[10] And even more emphatically: 'The bourgeoisie, during its rule of scarce one hundred years, has created more massive and more colossal productive forces than have all preceding generations together. Subjection of Nature's forces to man, machinery, application of chemistry to industry and agriculture, steam-navigation, railways, electric telegraphs, clearing of whole continents for cultivation, canalization of rivers, whole populations conjured out of the ground – what earlier century had even a presentiment that such productive forces slumbered in the lap of social labour?'[11]

In a letter published in an English newspaper in 1854 Marx writes: 'The labouring classes have conquered nature; they have now to conquer man.'[12] This conquest has obviously taken place within capitalism. In the *Grundrisse*, enlarging on this theme, Marx refers to the 'exploration of the earth in all directions', the discovery of 'new things of use as well as new useful qualities of the old', and the thereby connected general result of the development of 'the natural sciences to their highest point', as being all conditions of 'production founded on capital'. He goes on: 'Thus capital creates the bourgeois society, and the universal appropriation [*universelle Aneignung*] of nature as well as of the social bond itself by the members of society. Hence the great civilizing influence of capital; its production of a stage of society in comparison to which all earlier ones appear as mere *local developments* of humanity and as *nature-idolatry*. For the first time, nature becomes purely an object for humankind, purely a matter of utility; ceases to be recognized as a power for itself; and the theoretical discovery of its autonomous laws appears merely as a ruse so as to subjugate it under human needs . . . capital drives beyond national barriers and prejudices as much as beyond nature worship, as well as all traditional, confined, complacent, encrusted satisfactions of present needs, and reproductions of old ways of life. It is destructive towards all of this, and constantly revolutionizes it . . .'[13]

Marx here emphasizes the superiority of the modern age, i.e. bourgeois civilization, to ages past, a superiority which is not always apparent if one merely looks at the surface. The prevailing 'objective connection' among individuals, although defined in terms of estrangement, is still 'preferable to the lack of any connection, or to a merely local connection resting on blood ties, or on primeval, natural or master-servant relations'.[14] In a very revealing comparison with the values and reality of classical antiquity, Marx argues that 'the old view, in which the human being appears as the aim of production, regardless of his limited national, religious, political character, seems to be very lofty when contrasted to the modern world, where production appears as the aim of mankind and wealth as the aim of production. In fact, however, when the limited bourgeois form is stripped away, what is wealth other than the universality of individual needs, capacities, pleasures, productive forces, etc., created through universal exchange? The full development of human mastery over the forces of nature, those of so-called nature as well as humanity's own nature?' The 'childish world of antiquity' appears 'loftier' only because as yet the modern world gives no satisfaction or only satisfaction that is 'vulgar'; antiquity is really 'loftier in all matters where closed shapes, forms and given limits are sought for'.[15] But of course antiquity is essentially *static*, whereas the principle of the modern world, of capitalism turning into communism, is *movement*. In a different but relevant connection Marx makes the interesting point that the primitive 'indifference' towards various kinds of labour and modern 'universality' of skills and capacities are two essentially different things, and his contrasting examples also have present-day political poignancy: 'One could say that this indifference towards particular kinds of labour, which is a historic product in the United States, appears e.g. among the Russians as a spontaneous inclination. But there is a devil of a difference between barbarians who are fit by nature to be used for anything, and civilized people who apply themselves to everything.'[16] Communism is an affair and the consequence of 'civilization'; it has nothing to do with the return to childishness or barbarity.

This leads us to the second point which concerns the generation of free, universal individuality in capitalism. It is not merely the case that, as we saw above, capitalism *externally* leads to, and indeed actually realizes, communism; adding just a little bit of interpretative gloss to Marx's statements quoted above, we might well say that in the larger context of the relationship of mankind as such to nature capitalism is *already* essentially communism; in this sphere the communist 'transformation of society' adds nothing concrete and nothing qualitatively different to the 'subjugation of nature to human needs', which is the historic achievement of bourgeois civilization. But *internally* also capitalism prefigures communism, in that its mode of production and productive relations necessarily create free and universal individuals, though again, this essential feature of capitalism is not always easily recognized for its progressive, communist significance. 'Universally developed individuals', Marx says, 'whose social relations, as their own communal relations, are hence also subordinated to their own communal control, are no product of nature, but of history. The degree and the universality of the development of wealth where *this* individuality becomes possible supposes production on the basis of exchange values as a prior condition, whose universality produces not only the alienation of the individual from himself and from others, but also the universality and the comprehensiveness of his relations and capacities.'[17] Alienation and universality are hence not two different and *merely*, on the surface, antithetical things: they are two integrated aspects of the very same process. Again, in Marx's graphic expression: 'Universal prostitution appears as a necessary phase in the development of the social character of personal talents, capacities, abilities, activities.'[18] In Marx's view the development of 'surplus labour' under the rule of capital, and 'the severe discipline [*die strenge Disziplin*] of capital, acting on succeeding generations, [which] has developed general industriousness as the general property of the new species', allied with various other progressive elements in bourgeois society, are acting together so as to create 'the material elements for the development of the rich individuality [*reichen Individualität*] which is as all-sided in its production as in its consumption, and whose labour also therefore appears as no longer labour, but as the full development of activity itself . . .'[19] And 'the cultivation of all the qualities of the social human being, production of the same in a form as rich as possible in needs, because rich in qualities and relations – production of this being as the most total and universal possible social product, for, in order to take gratification in a many-sided way, he must be capable of many pleasures, hence cultured to a high degree – is likewise a condition of production founded on capital'.[20] Marx thus puts special emphasis on the 'universalizing tendency of capital' which is the 'presupposition [*Voraussetzung*]' of a new mode of production, the latter having as *its* 'presupposition' the 'free, unobstructed, progressive and universal development of the forces of production'.[21] Either then 'presupposition' is used by Marx in two very different senses (almost in the same breath!), or, which is the likelier interpretation, capitalism *itself* is approximated to this 'new mode'. The latter certainly seems to be born out by Marx's reference, a couple of pages later, to the 'tendentially and potentially general development of the forces of production' in capitalism based on the 'universality of intercourse' and the 'world market'.[22]

It is to be noted here that in the full terms of Marx's dialectical understanding the very expressly, from the communist point of view, objectionable and negative features of capitalism – e.g. the seemingly passive, hedonistic, consumer-oriented ethos of bourgeois society, and even the relationship of 'exchange' – also possess a directly progressive, communist significance. These negative features are still rather one-sidedly subsumed under the general category of 'estrangement' in the *Manuscripts*, but in the *Grundrisse* they come to be presented in their full nature, as simultaneously both static and retrogressive, and projective, forward-looking phenomena in the existing world. 'Out of the act of exchange itself', as Marx puts it, 'the individual, each one of them, is reflected in himself as its exclusive and dominant (determinant) subject. With that, then, the complete freedom of the individual is posited . . .'[23] And, 'when the economic form, exchange, posits the all-sided equality of its subjects, then the content, the individual as well as the objective material which drives towards the exchange, is *freedom*'.[24] Further, Marx notes the rather obvious fact that in capitalist production owners of capital wishing to sell in the market are related to workers as consumers. But from this he draws the conclusion, somewhat surprisingly perhaps, that it is as consumers also that human beings, and workers in particular, are being transformed into universal 'social individuals'. 'It is', in Marx's expression, 'precisely this side of the relation of capital and labour which is an essential civilizing moment, and on which the historic justification, but also the contemporary power of capital rests.'[25] A little later Marx adds the relevant point that although the absolute 'devaluation' of the worker is a presupposition of capitalist production and the reverse

Fusion

side of so-called 'free labour', nevertheless the capitalist feature of 'free labour' is not to be regarded as 'a step backwards'. It is not to be forgotten, he argues, 'that the worker is thereby formally posited as a person who is something for himself *apart from his* labour, and who alienates his life-expression only as a means towards his own life'.[26]

From these and similar statements then it seems reasonable to conclude that for Marx the 'subjective' character of individual consciousness in capitalism, workers as well as capitalists seeing and accepting themselves as self-seeking, need-possessing individuals, people actively engaged in exchange-relationships and consuming as well as producing wealth, and understanding all this as being essential to human *freedom*, is not anything that need be, will be, or ought to be, totally 'overcome' or 'transcended' in communism. Quite the contrary: the freedom, the many-sidedness, the sociality, the universality, the 'rich need' of communism are all already here, contained in the deepest reality of capitalism, and gain their credibility, intelligibility as well as ideal desirability from thus being so indubitably *real*. Here at last then Marx is descending to the real, existing world, or now he truly succeeds in locating the 'gods' in the 'centre of the earth'; his gaze becomes all-encompassing and intensely concentrated at the same time. In the light of this progression of Marx's thought, culminating in the recognition of the dialectical unity of capitalism and communism, we have of course to modify to some (considerable) extent the critical judgment passed on the communist ideals of 'free individual development' and 'satisfaction of needs' in the previous chapter. In a dualistic and dominantly visionary framework these notions *do*, indeed, evoke scepticism and deserve dismissal as being, literally, *groundless* and thus, in the proper sense, 'utopian' notions: if free individuality and need-satisfaction refer merely to *thoughts*, abstract ideals, futuristic projections, then there is no good reason to accept their credibility, and they can only be understood in terms of purely visionary assumptions concerning 'true' (but non-existent) human nature. If, however, as I am arguing is the case, there is a real progression in Marx's thought towards the overcoming of this dualistic standpoint, the fusion of vision and insight, and the near-achievement of a dialectical stance, then these notions will appear now credible, sensible, realistic: free individual development and the satisfaction of human need are veritable ideals because (and only because) they are *already present*, necessary to the very being, the dynamic

Insight and Vision

character, of the existing capitalist system. There is still, for Marx, true or moral human nature, but it is located already in the modern bourgeois 'ensemble'.

It won't be necessary to dwell too long on the third feature of capitalism revealing its necessary movement to culminate in communism as mentioned above, viz. the organizational requirements of capitalist production, since on the one hand this has received the lion's share of attention in exegetical literature (Marxist as well as anti-Marxist), and on the other hand this feature is not as clear-cut a pointer as the other two, already discussed, to the hidden but intelligible communist *quality* of capitalism as existing. The facts that capitalism has achieved victory over nature and that it generates and realizes free, universal individuality through capitalist discipline, exchange and consumption, show up bourgeois society as being already, essentially communist. The Marxist arguments concerning how and why capitalist organization must eventually shed its own retrograde 'capitalist' character or form are of course important in their own right, on the appropriate level of analysis. But they hardly touch on what is here taken to be the core of Marx's position, i.e. the reality and necessity of communism. The famous scientific theses concerning the growing concentration of capital, increasing misery, the falling rate of profit, the changing 'organic composition' of capital, and the prevalence of relative surplus-value over absolute surplus-value, etc., could only show, by themselves, that capitalism is *changing* – abstractly, hypothetically, open-endedly, and thus, in the last resort, inconsequentially. They do not show that it is *communism* which is 'tendentially and potentially' involved in capitalist development. For this, Marx must somehow indicate that communism is inherent and implied in capitalism, and this necessitates a mode of argument that reaches beyond empirical 'science', certainly in the analytical and positivist sense.

Nevertheless, it is relevant to observe here that for Marx the dynamic, forward-pressing quality of capitalism is also manifest in the way capitalist institutions themselves are changing. It is the 'ceaseless striving towards the general form of wealth', characterizing capital, that 'drives labour beyond the limits of its natural poverty'[27] and makes for the expansion of production and productive units, for diversification and sophistication of exploitative techniques, the tendency to monopolization, and thus also for the inevitable *socialization* of capital. Capitalist production, predicated on the maximization of profit (which is, of course, nothing but the appropriation of 'alien' labour), in this very process creates conditions which make the continuing extraction of surplus-value problematic for the individual capitalist (i.e. the falling rate of profit), and from the dynamic point of view of production as a whole – and this is where, on the profoundest level, the capitalist viewpoint *shades into* the viewpoint of communism – individual capitalist profit becomes irrelevant, irrational and self-defeating. This process is, as it were, prematurely reflected in the manner in which purely capitalist institutions become socialized institutions. An interesting illustration of this partial, arrested development of capitalism into communism is found in the posthumously published third volume of *Capital* where Marx describes joint-stock companies as being the 'social form of capital', asserting that 'this is the abolition of capital as private property within the confines of the capitalist mode of production itself'.[28] Moreover, according to him, 'this result of capitalist production in its highest development is a necessary point of transition [*notwendiger Durchgangspunkt*] towards the transformation of capital back into the property of the producers, though no longer as the private property of individual producers, but rather as their property as associated producers, as directly social property'.[29] The joint-stock company is 'private production unchecked by private ownership', and it is hence a 'self-abolishing contradiction [*sich selbst aufhebender Widerspruch*]'.[30] The 'company' then, it might be said, is already an infantile manifestation of communism as 'association' in its essential *content*, in that it embodies, necessitates 'rational' production processes, i.e. planning, co-operation and some genuine 'sharing' of the proceeds; however, it is capitalist in its *form*, in that it is still based on 'alien' wage-labour, directed to the accumulation of profit, and functioning in a pluralistic, competitive framework. Needless to say, Marx would never intimate, and even less would he assert, that capitalism in its most highly developed stage is *positively*, immediately communistic, and *smoothly* transforms itself to the *form* of communism; what I think he does argue here, however, is that this advanced form of capitalism is *negatively*, mediately communistic, and that the future coming 'form' of communism is the appropriate form of *this* same content. There is another side to this, to be discussed in our next chapter, concerning the way in which, for Marx, the 'form' of communism itself is to some extent approximated to the 'content' as existing in capitalism: but this belongs to another story, to the final story of Marx's de-fusing his insight and his vision.

At any rate, to continue with our present theme, it seems to me that it is not so much Marx's discussion of the sundry and visible features of capitalism displaying communistic tendencies that is chiefly indicative of his, at this stage, dialectical understanding of communism; rather, the most important pointers are to be found in his use of language in describing and analysing capital, the wealth and varied nature of his images and metaphors. There is an even better, more convincing way in which to glean the dialectical unity of capitalism and communism in Marx's thought than by reference to the triumph over external nature, the generation of free, social individuality, and the secular tendencies of capitalist productive organization. None of this would obtain, or would not have the required significance, were it not for Marx's fundamental conception of capitalism as *movement*, and it could I think be argued that on this fundamental level, in terms of its one basic defining quality, capitalism becomes almost indistinguishable from communism. We have already noted the telling remarks in the *Communist Manifesto* concerning the 'wonders' of bourgeois society. In the same text we find also pointed references to the 'revolutionary' character of the bourgeois epoch: the bourgeoisie, as Marx and Engels say here, 'cannot exist without constantly revolutionizing the instruments of production, and thereby the relations of production, and with them the whole relations of society'. Now 'all that is solid melts into air, all that is holy is profaned, and man is at last compelled to face with sober senses, his real conditions of life, and his relations with his kind'.[31] Let us reflect a bit on these statements.[32] There is, of course, a seemingly obvious, unproblematic meaning to them, but it is by no means certain that the attribution of this simplistic meaning would show up the earlier Marxist vision of communism in a credible light. That is, if we *confine* this 'revolutionary' character to capitalism only, if we say that it is only here and now, in bourgeois society, that productive forces are 'constantly revolutionized', and that it is in this epoch only that we are facing 'with sober senses' the 'real conditions' of our lives, then to what *can* communism refer, in contradistinction? Is it not the case that for Marx (as we have frequently observed in the foregoing pages) it is *communism* that signifies constant change, dynamism, revolutionization of human relations, as well as perfect knowledge and mastery of productive forces? Thus, if we were to say that it is *only* capitalism that is to be conceived in these *profound* and *total* terms of movement, then communism can only be understood as a kind of *rest* coming after the turmoil, a *static* form of existence. But this would very definitely turn Marx's communism back into a *utopia*, an inconsequential and impotent dream, a childish way of conjuring up 'shadowless' illusions, and of course this is exactly the approach that Marx himself came to dismiss so unceremoniously in the later 1840s.

So while on the surface, on the level of institutions and consciousness, capitalism and communism do appear glaringly different and totally opposed, they converge deep below in their essential characteristics, as movement and revolution. Communism cannot be anything else but this movement and revolution being *conscious* of themselves as essential humanity; it cannot be anything else but our drawing clear conclusions from what we already understand with 'sober senses' as the 'real conditions' of our lives, and acting on these conclusions. Nothing is more fundamentally real for human beings than movement and revolution, and these not only must go on in communism but become more intensified and total. As Marx says in the *Poverty of Philosophy*, citing the poet Lucretius, 'there is a continual movement of growth in productive forces, of destruction in social relations, of formation in ideas; the only immutable thing is the abstraction of movement – *mors immortalis*'.[33] If movement itself is 'immutable', it cannot grind to a halt in communism either, but on the contrary communism must signify the unrestrained growth of productive forces and continual revolutionization (construction through destruction) of productive relations and ideas. We recall here Marx's striking definition of communist society also in the *Manifesto* that, in contradistinction to bourgeois society, here 'the present dominates the past'. Past and present can meaningfully be contrasted only in terms of the static, stagnation, petrification on the one hand and liberated, continuous, self-propelling movement on the other. The present *means* dynamism, mobility, turbulence, it is 'content' freely developing in all directions, and it can only be opposed to and by the deadweight of fossilized structures, forms. But the opposition of domination by the past and by the present is inadequately grasped if seen merely in terms of the opposition between bourgeois society and communist society. That 'solution' of the opposition, communism, would not *be*, would appear as something wholly unintelligible, if it did not itself *partake* of the opposition played out in front of our eyes, in the existing world. Marx never in fact says or argues that capitalism is opposed or 'contradicted' by communism; what he does say, repeatedly, is that capitalism contradicts *itself*, and this can only be interpreted as a contradiction of capitalism and communism *within* capitalism, which must mean that communism is not only contained in capitalism, but that it is the very essence of capitalism, its own dialectical truth, its own 'negative' moving principle. The self-contradiction of capitalism *is* communism, nothing more need or indeed can be added.

The self-contradiction of capitalism lies in its inability to become truly itself, to bear out its ideal principle also in ostensive visible structures and relations. 'But from the fact', as Marx writes in the *Grundrisse*, 'that capital posits every such limit as a barrier and hence gets *ideally* beyond it, it does not by any means follow that it has *really* overcome it, and, since every such barrier contradicts its character, its production moves in contradictions which are constantly overcome but just as constantly posited.'[34] Note that it is the 'character' of capitalist production itself which is thus constantly contradicted. And again: 'By its nature, therefore, [capital] posits a *barrier* to labour and value-creation, in contradiction to its tendency to expand them boundlessly. And in as much as it both posits a barrier *specific* to itself, and on the other side equally drives over and beyond *every* barrier, it is the living contradiction [*lebendige Widerspruch*].'[35] Here then the opposition is defined as occurring between the 'nature' and the 'tendency' of capitalism, and it seems to parallel the contrast between 'past' and 'present', stagnation and movement, continual repetition and liberated, progressive movement. It also very closely resembles the Hegelian contrast between bad infinity and true infinity as well as the Aristotelian categories of potential and actual. Capitalism, which Marx defines in the *Grundrisse* as the 'most extreme form of alienation', 'is a necessary point of transition – and therefore already contains in *itself*, in a still only inverted form, turned on its head, the dissolution of all *limited presuppositions of production*, and moreover creates and produces the unconditional presuppositions of production, and therewith the full material conditions for the total, universal development of the productive forces of the individual'.[36]

It is, furthermore, stated by Marx quite clearly that 'alienation' is simply an appearance, the hidden meaning and principle of which is liberation, universality. 'The barrier to *capital* is that this entire development proceeds in a contradictory way, and that the working-out of the productive forces, of general wealth, etc., knowledge, etc., appears in such a way that the working individual *alienates* himself ... But this antithetical form is itself fleeting [*verschwindend*]...'[37] Then: 'The last form of servitude assumed by human activity, that of wage-labour on one side, capital on the other, is thereby cast off like a skin, and this casting-off itself is the result of the mode of production corresponding to capital...'[38] It's all *there*, in capitalism; Marx's images unmistakably suggest that we are dealing with the existing world and nothing else: what *appears* as capitalism, alienation, etc., is just 'inverted form', the world 'turned on its head', the real body that comes to light once its 'skin' is discarded. Of course, capitalism is not merely a matter of definition or something that exists merely in the imagination; it is a real existent and cannot be spirited away by redefining our terms; while, as Marx argues in *Theories of Surplus Value*, in the real productive process capital is 'a mere *name for, and rechristening of,* labour itself', it does not follow that capital is 'the power dominating and engendering labour'.[39] However, this very distinct reality of capital is itself forward-pointing and demands and *needs* to be completed in communism. And conversely, communism is not a matter of simply desiring and willing a better, perfect world, a figment of the imagination, either; its own reality, in turn, is backward-pointing and must be understood as the completion *of* capitalism. As Marx puts it, 'this twisting and inversion is a *real* [phenomenon], not a merely *supposed one* existing merely in the imagination of the workers and the capitalists. But obviously this process of inversion is a merely *historical* necessity, a necessity for the development of the forces of production solely from a specific historic point of departure, or basis, but in no way an *absolute* necessity of production; rather, a vanishing one, and the result and the inherent purpose [*Zweck (immanente)*] of this process is to suspend this basis itself, together with this form of the process.'[40] Capital is not an 'absolute necessity' of production, it is the 'skin' that will be cast off in the progressive interest of production – here Marx obviously adopts the pure standpoint of the future, for which capital is merely a 'specific historic point of departure'. However, in the same breath he asserts, in a clearly recognizable Aristotelian idiom, that capital *is* a 'historical necessity' and moreover one whose inherent or immanent 'purpose' is to suspend itself, i.e. to become communism. Here, in other words, the communist standpoint becomes more fully presented, in a manner of speaking, as something which is thus *impure*, vision as mediated by insight, and which by the same token assumes greater credibility.

We have at this point to ask the most intriguing and crucial question, for communism and for Marx's thought in general: what is 'capital' really? Why should it be seen by Marx as essentially 'self-contradictory'? Why is it to be expected that it will progress to the point of suspending itself? Understanding the notion of 'capital' in Marx means understanding Marx's communism and thus the innermost essence and moving principle of his thought. Mistaking the meaning of capital for Marx means missing the entire point of his thought and thus getting hopelessly confused and abstract about the meaning of communism, too. It is not really the case, or rather it is only the immediately apparent part of the story, that capital is, as it were, the arch-villain or arch-enemy in Marx's thought, the foe to be exterminated, the demon to be exorcised, the vampire that sucks the human blood of workers, the 'hideous pagan idol' or 'dead labour' which enslaves and oppresses living labour, human essence in alienation. Capital is all this, to be sure, but the extent as well as intensity of Marx's preoccupation with something the importance of which is, after all, only *negative*, still raises some puzzling questions. It could be said without undue exaggeration that as a scientist and philosopher Marx was interested in capital *only*, nothing else, the rest of his concerns being either preparatory sketches or attemps at circumvention. In the earlier period he is searching for an adequate way of conceptualizing capital (first formulated in terms of 'alienated labour'), then in the *Grundrisse* embarking on an ambitious and staggering phenomenology of capital, and in the book *Capital* finally writing the 'science of logic' of capital. His progression is not only superficially similar to Hegel's, but it is essentially the same kind of progression; the end result of Hegel's search is the notion of 'Spirit', that of Marx is the notion of capital, and *both* are substantive, and not merely negative, concepts (negative, that is, in the ethical sense). Here, inevitably, we have to raise again the simplistic-sounding but most pertinent question: why did Marx write so much about capitalism and (relatively) so little about communism? Enough, I hope, has been said in these pages to dispute the validity of such commonly found and temptingly obvious, but in truth pointless and evasive, answers as that Marx was not 'interested' in communism in a constructive way or that he did not think that the future could be defined or that he thought 'critique' or 'science' was his main task, not utopian blueprints, etc., etc. All these are of course true, but they merely restate the problem in different terms. *Why* was Marx not interested constructively in communism, *why* did he believe that communism was essentially undefinable, and *why* in spite of all this did he profess to be a critic and enemy of capital and a revolutionary fighter for communism? We have to persist relentlessly in asking these questions, until a satisfactory answer is found. Marx's almost exclusive concentration on capital in his theoretical writings, and as long as capital is interpreted in merely *negative* terms, would appear equivalent to Plato writing only about democracy and not about the 'republic', Augustine only about the terrestrial city and not about the 'city of God', Hobbes only about the state of nature and not about the commonwealth, Rousseau only about civilization but not the social contract, Burke about the French Revolution but not about the British Constitution, Hegel only about nature but not about Spirit, etc. We would be puzzled as to what these writers *mean*, what they are *after*. So why has there been, relatively speaking, such a lack of scholarly interest concerning Marx's meaning?

The argument of this study is, of course, that a finally satisfactory answer to the problem can be found only through grasping the dialectical unity of capitalism and communism as the highest achievement of Marx's thought. This means recognizing capital also in ethically *positive* terms. Capital, that is, is not merely the *alienated* essence of mankind, it is the alienated *essence* of mankind. The first thing to note here is the elusive, 'spiritual' nature of capital in Marx's understanding, the second its ubiquity in bourgeois society, the third its close, inseparable links to living labour. Marx never ceases to emphasize (especially in the *Grundrisse* and in *Theories of Surplus-Value*) the spiritual, ethereal, intangible character of capital, and he regards it as the greatest mistake of socialist economists to see in capital a 'thing'. Referring to the views of the so-called Ricardian Socialists in England, for example, he dismisses the belief that in socialism 'we need capital, but not the capitalist'. If capital is regarded in this way, 'then capital appears as a pure thing, not as a relation of production which, reflected in itself, is precisely the capitalist'. 'The *capitalist*, as capitalist, is simply the personification of capital, that creation of labour endowed with its own will and personality which stands in opposition to labour.'[41] And against the apologists of the existing capitalist system he argues that capital is not a necessary condition of production. 'The catch', as he puts it, 'is that if all capital is objectified labour which serves as means for new production, it is not the case that all objectified labour which serves as means for new production is capital. *Capital is conceived as a thing [Sache], not as a relation [Verhältnis]*.'[42] In other and simpler words, it is not the case that industrial plants as such, machinery and tools as such, or raw material or finished products or various goods in storage, or shops and marketplaces, or even money as such, is capital. You cannot see anything, or point to anything, and call it capital. Plants and other things, especially institutions like banks or the stock exchange, are only visible expressions of capital, but not capital itself. The capitalist is an expression of capital, but not capital itself, and neither are his shares, his legal certificates, his storehouses, workshops, offices capital as such, only its empirical representations. Capital is in them, it animates them, and it makes them what they are in bourgeois society, but capital itself is not confined to any of these, and it is not 'essentially' represented in one institution rather than another.

Capital, in Marx's rather puzzling expression, is not a thing but a 'relation', and not even a 'simple relation' but a 'process'. Relations cannot be seen or observed, they can only be understood: relations are ideas, concepts. Bourgeois society or the capitalist mode of production as a *totality* is defined in terms of capital, capital is in everything that is contained in this society, it is a vast, penetrating network of invisible relations, transforming human actions and 'bewitching' human minds, it is like a dense cloud or fog or some particularly powerful drift of *dampness* that gets into the marrow. Marx likens bourgeois society to an 'organic system' in which 'every economic relation presupposes every other in its bourgeois economic form and everything posited is thus also a presupposition...'[43] Capital is 'the communal substance [*gemeinschaftliche Substanz*] of all commodities',[44] it is there embodied in exchange-values and exchange acts, in trading and producing, in keeping accounts and paying out wages and dividends, and beyond these it is also there in non-productive institutions, in courts of law, in the police and military, in politics, in culture, in the newspapers, in homes and schools and hospitals, in sport and recreation, in the marriage-bed. Primarily, of course, capital is manifested in fundamental relations of *power* defined here as private ownership, and the capitalist owner of plants and employer of workers is undoubtedly the typical, *concentrated* representation of capital, but where could one in truth draw the line? Drawing the wage is expressive of the same *relation* as paying out the wage, purchasing commodities in shops is the same thing (only looked at from another angle) as the shopkeeper's accumulation of profit, receiving poor law relief is the reverse side of capital's control of the cost of labour, the constable who checks

Fusion

factory-gates at night, the housewife who queues for a loaf of bread, the minister of religion who preaches ways to the salvation of the soul, the teacher who teaches history, the worker who orders his pint of ale, the charitable lady who dishes out hot soup for the destitute, the ascetic who turns away from the world in disgust, etc. are all *aspects* of capital, they are capital itself in their mutual *relations*. Capitalism is a *system* of production where everything hangs together (capital, as it were, 'hanging' in the air); bourgeois society is a *society* which embraces all its members.

Of course, Marx does draw a line, very emphatically so, but it is not difficult to see that the intended line of division is just as much a line of unification. Capital is confronted by 'living labour'. As Marx says, 'the only thing distinct from *objectified* labour is *non-objectified* labour, labour which is still objectifying itself, *labour* as subjectivity'.[45] Now the interesting point to note here is not just that in bourgeois society, according to Marx, capital and labour are intrinsically related, united in deadly conflict, mutually defining each other's character and limits, existing by virtue of their antagonistic interpenetration. What is to be noted is that Marx's distinction here is not, essentially, an empirical one, and it couldn't be an empirical distinction either, if we recognize the *all-pervading* nature of capital. Capital is the *whole* of bourgeois society, it *is* the existing world. There cannot be anything *in the world*, in actual reality, that is *not* capital. (As the point was made in an earlier chapter and in a different context: workers *as workers* are just as much an integral part of the capitalist system as capitalist employers.) Thus the opposition of capital to 'living labour' is not and cannot be an opposition between two natural objects or 'things' (even though Marx might use the term 'thing' sometimes unguardedly); if capital is not a thing but a 'relation', then labour cannot be a thing but also a relation, and moreover the *same* relation.

Capital, as we have seen above, has for Marx an almost spiritual quality, it is intangible and inarrestible in its essence, it is *in* things and in *all* things, but not a visible, perceptible, natural object itself. However, capital has actual *reality*, precisely because it is manifested, expressed, represented, demonstrated in the things, institutions, people of bourgeois society; capital is not just spirit but spirit *incarnate*. By contrast, and this is a most significant contrast, 'living labour' is spirit *only*, it has no embodiment apart from capital, it has no *independent* manifestation in actual reality, it is much more elusive, much more ethereal, much more spiritual, much more to be conceived in other-worldly terms, and its being much more to be *inferred*, rather than directly understood, than capital. Capital is *being*, labour is *nothing*. In Marx's imaginative expressions, 'labour is the living, form-giving fire; it is the transitoriness of things, their temporality, as their formation by living time'.[46] Or, 'the product of labour, objectified labour, has been endowed by living labour with a soul of its own, and establishes itself opposite living labour as an *alien power*'.[47] 'Living labour', as Marx says later on, now 'appears as a mere means to realize objectified, dead labour, to penetrate it with an animating soul while losing its own soul to it . . .'[48] Even more pointedly, Marx refers to capital in some passages as the 'animating unity' of the production process, appearing as 'alien will' and 'alien intelligence', and as the 'animated monster' [*beseeltes Ungeheuer*] which 'objectifies the scientific idea'.[49] Again, 'The development of fixed capital indicates to what degree general social knowledge has become a *direct force of production*' and 'social life itself' has come under 'the control of the general intellect . . .'[50] And finally Marx also argues that 'in bourgeois society, the worker e.g. stands there purely without objectivity, subjectively; but the thing which *stands opposite* him has now become the *true community* [*das wahre Gemeinwesen*], which he tries to make a meal of, and which makes a meal of him'.[51]

Thus, as we can see, it is not even the case that labour is opposed to capital by Marx as the 'soul' of production contrasted to its corporeal body, or subjectivity contrasted to objectivity, or indeed 'living' labour to 'dead' labour, in a simple way of understanding 'living' and 'dead'. The point is that capital is *also* 'living', it too has not only a 'soul' but a substantial, credible soul, it, and not labour, is the 'animating unity' of production, it, rather than labour, is 'intelligence' and the 'scientific idea' objectified; capital is now the 'true community'. The curious and perhaps at first glance extravagant conclusion to which one is led by this examination of Marx's statements is that the *real* meaning of Marx's revolutionary and critical science of political economy is in diametrical, sharp, striking opposition to its *ostensible* meaning. Marx puts all the emphasis on labour, he derives everything and especially capital from labour, he fights for and identifies with labour, he almost apotheosizes labour and equates it with true 'human' nature, etc. Yet in the very unfolding of his arguments, and perhaps in spite of his conscious intention (which we could not incontrovertibly and accurately determine anyway), labour *vanishes*. In the full scheme of Marx's thought, labour in contrast to capital is not much more than a *deus ex machina*, a nebulous hypothesis or supposition, something which (Marx seems to believe sometimes) *must* be assumed in order to be able to explain and comprehend the world. Labour and capital are related in Marx in a similar way to the theological relationship between 'creation' and the 'universe'. God *must* be assumed, otherwise the natural universe has no meaning. Labour *must* be conceived as 'form-giving fire', otherwise the world of capital is incomprehensible.

However, Marx in his science of political economy is not only a theologian, and indeed not primarily a theologian but a profound thinker, an Hegelian philosopher. For Hegel God has no meaning apart from the world, He *is* the world, rightly comprehended, the world understood in its spiritual essence, 'substance as subject'. Similarly in Marx there is at least a strong intimation (let us not put it higher than that) that it is capital, and not labour, that has true subjectivity as well as substantiality; capital, that is, understood in its spiritual significance, as substance becoming subject. Capital is not merely the incarnation of labour or the completion of labour, but it represents the *highest* aspects of human 'species-activity', it is the will, the design, the intelligence, the rationality of human production and creation as well as the intelligible content of the human 'community'. Capital is not a thing, it is nothing 'natural', but a *human* aspect, and in so far as humanity is endowed by Marx with transcendent, quasi-divine qualities, these qualities are and must be consummated in capital. There is nothing else! 'Labour' is vanishing 'transitoriness', a 'hypothesis' which (as Laplace told the theologians, referring to the divine creator) is not really *needed* by Marx. Everything, the future, communism, proceeds from capital, all that is *human* is already contained in the relationships, accumulated knowledge, culture, productive capacities and processes, of bourgeois society. Capital, indeed, can truthfully be interpreted as the human species, the unity of human beings, their distinctive 'humanity'. Labour on its own is only human beings viewed in their *natural* and *animal* capacity, individuals severally and disunited, their sheer and unconscious energy, just the undistinguished, grey mass.

And if our foregoing interpretive remarks point in the right direction for an understanding of Marx's thought, viewed at its highest peak of intellectual development, with Marx's vision of the ideal and his insight into the real perfectly fused, then there is a further, and fascinating, conclusion following, which concerns the nature of communism. On the immediate, surface level of consciousness and 'politics', communism may indeed specifically concern the working class; it is the workers, the mass of exploited wage-earners, who will according to Marx bring about the communist revolution and establish communist society. Communism belongs to the proletariat and the struggle to achieve communism is the class struggle waged by the proletariat against the capitalists and their sundry hangers-on. But what does this really signify? The conflict between capitalists and workers does not *simply* reflect the profounder conflict between capital and labour; indeed, if our foregoing remarks have any sense at all, there *is* no such thing as a conflict between capital and labour, since in capitalism there is no 'labour' as such, conceived *independently* of capital. In capitalism, there is only capital, all-embracing and all-pervading. Therefore, rightly understood, the conflict between workers and capitalists can only express the 'contradiction' within or *of* capital, i.e. the self-contradiction of capital. But then it would also seem to follow that communism *proceeds* from capital, it is the completion of capital, its dialectical conclusion, and it does not proceed from labour at all. Communism is not the victory of 'labour' over capital, it is not the emancipation or liberation of 'labour', it does not mean in the least that capital is now destroyed, annihilated, devoured by 'labour'. On the very contrary, the emancipation of the *workers* means the final triumph of 'capital', and in this ultimate triumph capital is *re-born*, assumes a different appearance and is given a new name, viz. communism. However, in so far as communism is 'conscious mastery' over nature, if it is the 'association of producers', if it is the flowering of 'free, universal individuality' and the satisfaction of 'manysided needs and pleasures', it is that which capital *tended to be* from its very first historical emergence. In communism capital *as capital* is completely dissolved, it ceases to be a 'relation' dividing producers, but this dissolution is not a disappearance; rather it is further, total permeation of all productive relationships and general consciousness. Producers in communism are not 'capitalist workers' (which would mean carrying on the present antagonism), but the humanized self-consciousness of capital, the 'monster' now shedding its withered skin and revealing for the first time its authentic, human character.

There are three further definitional characteristics of communism in Marx, which, although troublesome and unsatisfactory if considered from an abstract, dualistic viewpoint, become more

Fusion

meaningful when seen in the light of Marx's fully developed, fused dialectical stance. The first concerns Marx's initially puzzling statement in the *Eighteenth Brumaire* that the future is 'content' and as yet has 'no name'. (We noted this statement, and registered our bafflement over it, in Chapter 1.) Now we can see, however, that in a very profound sense Marx's statement is correct and fully warranted by his theory, or understanding, of capitalism. The future *could* have no name, no form, and the term 'communism' is only a label of convenience, suggestive and inspiratory (and appropriate for agitational and propaganda purposes), but still too restrictive in its connotations. Communism as a definite form of social organization, etc. has still a distinctly utopian, visionary flavour, and at this highest point Marx's thinking is anything but utopian. Communism for Marx must then in the strictest sense signify *nothing*, confronting the *being* of capitalism, and it is capitalism that *becomes*, unfolds its own essential nature. The future, 'communism', is that which is foreshadowed by capital, the light of which capital is the shadow, the storm of which capital is the first breeze, the day of which capital is the dawn. There is no transcendent teleology in the transformation of capitalism into communism, but only the simple, visible and immanent process of 'potential' becoming 'actual', or capitalism attaining to the level of its own *truth*. What is significant here is Marx's very sharp and emphatic distinction (as we noted earlier) between the present (capitalism-communism in unity) and the historical past; although inevitably there are linguistic parallels and analogies employed in the effort to intimate the nature of the present, the *point* of the present age, its *differentia*, is that it is unique and has no essential resemblance to past, Oriental, Hellenic or Judaic, formations and ideals. Communism is only the present unfolding, and it is not the resuscitation of any past forms, not the realization of age-old dreams, not a wished-for fulfilment, not a substantive end, not a concrete goal which anyone can or should set out to 'achieve'. It achieves itself, through us, both in the objective and subjective senses, as active producers-consumers and as 'critics' of capital.

Thus (secondly) the essential quality of the future is 'freedom', in the most authentic, pregnant sense of 'freedom' possible: it is open, undeterminable, unknowable, self-determining. It is infinity in the 'true' sense (as Hegel formulated this difficult but highly relevant notion in the *Science of Logic*) of showing the self-transcendence of the finite: we are leaving behind, destroying 'capital' but the true meaning of this destruction is not starting something anew, turning a new page, radically changing direction, but *confirming* the finite as infinity, eliminating not *it* but only its 'finitude'. Freedom, in the hallowed phrase, is the 'transfiguration of necessity': it lies then in the recognition of the absolute necessity of capital, as the real, existing world, but its recognition in terms of *its own* infinity, its own freedom, the existing world as *moving*. So then, thirdly, we can perhaps make more satisfactory sense of Marx's earlier understanding of communism as simply the 'means', the external institutional framework (abolition of private property, rational organization of production, etc.) which is expected to provide the 'conditions' for the realization of freedom. We noted that in the earlier texts there is some ambiguity attaching to Marx's meaning, whether communism is only a 'means' or a substantive end, or both, and we argued that it is incoherent to look upon communism as external means only. However, this is so only from a dualistic point of view, if the nature of the 'content', the substance, is simply assumed and imagined to be totally *different* from the existing. But if we come now to the recognition that the 'content' of communism is nothing but the further unfolding of the content of capitalism, then communist 'organization' not only becomes meaningful but is now properly defined as 'means' *only*, viz. something that is contingent, hypothetical, a matter of mere instrumentality, almost a tentative suggestion. There is nothing sacrosanct about any institutional arrangements, including those usually understood as 'communist organization'. The content is what counts, the means are secondary: it *looks* now as though the freeing of the potential of capitalism is best achieved by communist transformation, but the emphasis is on *freezing*, not on the methods adopted; the latter, unlike the essential content, can change. Therefore, in the last resort and from this highest vantage-point, we can once again, and now fully, glean the *problem* of Marx's 'communism', and appreciate why, though on the one hand unhesitatingly professing to be a communist, on the other he always showed himself reluctant to use the term with the near-religious aura and idealistic certainty characterizing so many of his radical contemporaries, employed the word 'communism' only sparingly and clearly preferring its adjectival to its substantive form, and looking upon himself as a 'revolutionary' or 'critic' or 'scientist' instead.[52] It makes sense: to be a 'communist' in Marx's fully matured, perfectly fused dialectical understanding means no more, and no less, than to be a *very profound* 'capitalist'.

Fusion

So where do we go from here? In this chapter a very deliberate attempt was made to present an out-and-out 'Hegelian' Marxism, and this perhaps required a certain degree of interpretive licence, not to say hyperbole. I would like to maintain, however, that this is an 'Hegelian' Marxism in a more authentic, more satisfactory sense than what usually goes by this designation, and also that it is a possible, nay plausible, reading of the philosophical assumptions of Marx's science of political economy and borne out especially by the theme, the statements and the general flavour of the *Grundrisse*. I am not in any sense pretending, however, that it is the *unambiguous* message of Marx's mature theoretical work, nor that there are not numerous arguments and definitions, in the *Grundrisse* itself as well as in *Capital* and in various texts from Marx's last period (to be commented on in the following chapter), that would clearly contradict the foregoing interpretation. There is, undoubtedly, an Hegelian, dialectical theme in Marx's mature understanding of the relationship between capitalism and communism, but this does not mean that this is the *only* theme and that Marx in this period becomes an 'Hegelian', nothing else. The problems, tensions, internal conflicts of communism remain there in Marx's thought, all the time. In this elevated Hegelian perspective Marx's far-reaching gaze is simultaneously an intent taking in, recognition of the immediate surroundings, surface and depth mutually mediating, interpenetrating each other; however, it is in the nature of this perspective that it can be held on to only with difficulty, it is prone to become disunited, its two constituents falling apart. In concluding this chapter, then, it seems to me that two questions will require some attention. Firstly, if the Hegelian theme in the mature Marx is taken seriously, and regarded as the highest peak of Marx's intellectual achievement (as I have done), what does this exactly signify for Marx's thought in general and Marx's concept of communism in particular? And secondly, noting the continuing (or resurfacing) dualism of Marx's thought and concentrating on its non-Hegelian features and particularly on the non-dialectical (in the above sense) understanding of communism, what exactly does *this* signify for Marx's thought? Our discussion of this second question will then naturally lead us to the subject matter of the ensuing chapter.

As regards the first point then: the dialectical unity of capitalism and communism in Marx is Marx's highest *intellectual* achievement, but it is at the same time a *pyrrhic* victory which raises serious doubts concerning the rationale and 'relevance' (in the practical, political sense) of what has subsequently been termed 'Marxism' and which includes not only the theories and actions of Marx's 'communist' followers, but also Marx's own work as publicist and committed fighter in the cause of communism, i.e. his involvement in the organization of the International and in workers' parties. To be an 'Hegelian' in this full sense is a mixed blessing; it elicits genuine accolade unreservedly bestowed on a thinker of the first rank, but at the same time it elevates that thinker too high above the hurly-burly of political controversy, into the august, stern, lonesome ivory-tower of the *philosopher*. To the extent that the dialectical unity of capital and communism is asserted, or implied, by Marx, to that extent Marxism becomes politically irrelevant and inconsequential, a source of inspiration perhaps but hardly a constructive doctrine or a programme or distinct line of 'criticism' even. If the dialectical path is followed out consistently, the result is the reduction of communism to a pure *standpoint*, the 'genuine resolution' of the contradictions of the existing world in thought only, without any positive message, and communism *qua* the determinate negation of capitalism, and even more so as the historical successor to capitalism, completely vanishes from view. You cannot have a vision of something that is *not*, you cannot build or prepare for something that has no reality and therefore no possible conceptual representation either. Communism as the highest vantage-point of reality, i.e. of capitalism, thus presents only its *pure* negation but not its concrete negation, and as pure negation it becomes indistinguishable from affirmation. This is the high, but inescapable, price one has to pay for being able to assert that communism is *reality* and that it is *necessarily* entailed in capitalist development. If it is seriously maintained that capitalism 'inexorably' proceeds to its own downfall and transcendence, and if it is at least half-seriously intimated that the *quality* of communism is already subliminally present in capitalism in its existing shape, then to be a 'communist' may mean – literally – anything. The field is entirely open. Communism then *may* mean violent revolution, political subversion, open civil war, proletarian organization, sabotage, strikes, barricades, red flags, etc., but it may also mean opting out, doing one's own thing, passive resistance, quietism, co-operation with the state, tactical compromises, etc. And why not actual, positive *support* for the existing capitalist system? If its *development* can only hasten its *demise*? Who is the better communist, the militant trade union leader who actually *retards* the full development and flowering of capitalism, or the private entrepreneur and owner of capital who, by his frantic efforts to maximize his own profits, only accelerates the undermining of his own social position?[53] The answer to these questions is by no means as straightforward as it might appear at first, and this basic ambiguity of the Marxist position (this being only the reverse side of its, at this point, genuinely philosophical and dialectical character) goes at least some little distance towards explaining the continuing strategic as well as tactical dilemma of Marxist movements and individuals, whether in power or in opposition: to subvert capitalist regimes or foster 'peaceful co-existence', to develop socialist markets or emphasize 'moral incentives', to be patriotic or internationalist, to work for 'popular fronts' or infiltrate bourgeois parties or go into splendid isolation waiting for the clock to strike, or start insurrections, etc., etc. Everything may help eventually, but nothing in particular is *necessarily* the right attitude or policy. This is not, really, the problem of determinism versus freedom, but rather the problem of *complete* freedom, of being totally assured of the future but not being able to *distinguish* its features as they evolve and take shape out of the present. The gods now *are* the centre of the earth, but who exactly are the gods and where, after all, is the earth? Communism is now at last grasped as reality, but it is this very reality that completely devours, absorbs, eliminates communism from the scene. Marx's philosophical and scientific achievement is staggering, awe-inspiring, spectacular, but in the last resort it leaves for the 'communist' Marx nothing further to do.

Obviously Marx himself did not consider the situation in this light and believed, as his later writings and public roles amply prove, that as a revolutionary and a communist he had a great deal more to do indeed. And there is at least a strong suspicion that he would have reacted to interpretations of his thought like the one adumbrated above with disdain, incredulity and his accustomed polemical venom. The 'dialectical unity' of capitalism and communism – what utter nonsense! This presentation of his views at their highest scientific peak would most probably have appeared to him (and it would be *odd* if it did not appear so for the most devoutly committed among his latter-day followers) as malicious, confused, petty bourgeois obscurantism, pointless metaphysical speculation, sheer mysticism. Communism may very well in some interesting ways *grow out* of capitalism, building on the 'material conditions' produced by the latter, but it still does not follow that capitalism and communism are 'essentially' the same. Communism is *absolutely* different from capitalism, it is the concrete negation of capitalism, an entirely *new* society which we can perfectly comprehend now and for which the organized proletariat, representing the conscious power of labour, is at present fighting. Communism is the future, capitalism is the past, communism is desirable and capitalism is execrable, communism signifies the true birth of humanity *in contrast* to capitalism which represents alienation, exploitation, misery, the rule of this hideous 'monster' over the producers. There is no need to belabour the point now: this truculent, fighting, committed side of Marx is there in the *Grundrisse*, not to mention *Capital* and various other texts from the 1870s. The question that has to be asked here, however, is this: is the continuing assertion of the *difference* of communism in the light of Marx's dialectical standpoint (with its implications fully drawn out) to be considered an *advantage* for Marx, something that renders his thought more coherent, more credible? I would like to suggest that our answer to this question should be in the *negative* (though formulated with due caution).

It is true that this differential, fighting, committed standpoint makes for the continuing political *relevance* of Marx's doctrines, and it makes it at least initially meaningful for a Marxist to be a 'communist', in the usual sense, e.g. actively engaged in the struggle to 'overthrow' the capitalist system or 'construct' communist society. However, it seems to me to be possible to argue that this political relevance of Marx's communism can only be purchased at the expense of foregoing theoretical coherence and intellectual excellence. It marks a clear *descent* from Marx's dialectical vantagepoint. The situation here is the exact opposite of what we concluded was the ultimate fate of 'Hegelian' Marxism where the price of Marx's achievement turned out to be Marx's supreme irrelevance to the political struggles and divisions of this world. There Marx was kicked upstairs. Here Marx is hurled back into the arena, and let us not be mistaken about this being a *downward* process. This is not at all difficult to see, and we shall in any case have an opportunity to develop this stage of our argument more fully in the remaining part of this study. The point is, surely, that in so far as it is maintained that communism is essentially *different* from capitalism and that it is something that has to be fought for in *determinate* ways (i.e. to speculate in the stock-exchange is *not* to be construed as 'communism'), it must also be asserted that communism is not *real*, that it is still essentially a visionary object, something beyond the horizon. In other words, it means simply reasserting a *dualistic* standpoint, accepting that the *gap* between reality and the ideal still obstinately persists. And this at once brings back the nagging questions and ultimate doubts discernible in the innermost recesses of Marx's thought, but this time even more intensively: if communism is not in the present, not a proper object revealed to insight, if it is purely the future, the light sharply opposed to darkness, the gods *contrasted* to the world, then why should we believe in its coming, not to mention its imminence? What makes communism credible, reasonable, and for that matter desirable, if it is not *already* discernible in our present, existing world? Is utopia, the conjuring up of 'shadowless' images, still then necessary for being a communist? Or, to put it the other way round, if communism is somehow, 'materially', warranted by the secular development of capitalism, and it is the 'real movement' of the present, then why does it take so exasperatingly long to arrive, to come out into the open, to *show* its reality? And, finally, if we do discern certain features of existing society which 'tendentially' point towards communism, is this 'communism' of the *real* world the same thing as *ideal* communism, genuine 'human liberation'? Are the communism of insight and the communism of vision the same thing? We shall see in the next chapter that Marx's confident, and in some ways increasingly dogmatic, tone in the later texts can only partially hide his concern with these questions and that his final stand on communism is once again dualistic, i.e. showing his ultimate failure to prove that communism belongs to, develops out of, the real world.

5 Receding Vision

By now the underlying problem of communism in Marx's thought will have assumed a clearer meaning in our minds. This problem is essentially one of achieving the meaningful unity of vision and insight, presenting the 'word' as 'flesh', or establishing the reasonableness, credibility, reality of something that (as yet) exists only in thought, as an ideal. In previous chapters we have surveyed Marx's progression in his understanding of communism or the good society, through its developmental stages as 'genuine resolution' to 'real movement' and culminating in communism as dialectically united with its opposite, capitalism. Our conclusion in Chapter 4 was that this last, but in pure theoretical terms highest, formulation of communism presents Marx's thought with a choice: either the dialectical view is now followed out consistently to its ultimate consequences, in which case being a 'communist' in the practical, political sense becomes meaningless, an indistinct position: or, in order to save communism for politics, to make Marxism relevant in practice, the dialectical view has to be abandoned and in this case Marx is being faced once again with a world split in two, the reality of capitalism on one side and communism as pure vision on the other. Marx, in essence, chose the second alternative in the last phase of his working life, and attempted to deal with the consequences, admittedly with some success, but in the last resort his final position must still be interpreted as overall failure and *resignation* in the opposition between the world and the idea; at the close of Marx's life-work the gods were still not the centre of the earth.

This final stage in the development of Marx's thought, however, is still of great interest to us, not least because it is in some of the late texts, notably in *The Civil War in France* and *Critique of the Gotha Program*, that Marx comes again to write extensively and explicitly about 'communism' as such, his attention here almost matching the explicitness of the *Manuscripts*. And reading these texts makes us also more fully aware of a substantive connection between Marx's understanding of communism in 1844 and in 1875, and thus of a perfect closing of the circle: the dualism detectable in Marx's late work, once its outer layers are penetrated, is ultimately revealed as the original duality of 'genuine resolution' and 'crude communism', that is, 'genuine resolution' in the visionary, historical sense as the basic definitional quality of the good society, and 'crude communism' in the sense of being the 'communism' of the existing world, estrangement not transcended but merely generalized. What is of fascinating interest here, however, is the change in Marx's attitude and valuation, and hence while we must assert that there is an underlying conceptual unity of the *Manuscripts* with the later texts, we must at the same time be also mindful of the valuational, or ethical, *difference* separating them. To anticipate our discussion in ensuing pages: this change in Marx's valuation signifies his acceptance of the world, his positive appreciation now of what he rejected and condemned before, his advocacy of 'crude communism' as not only the necessary and foreseeable but also *desirable* form of the immediate future. Visionary communism or 'genuine resolution', though still steadfastly adhered to in speculative and rhetorical terms, *recedes* farther and farther over the horizon, into the mists of an inconsequential future; at the same time there is a clear emergence now of a 'realistic', down-to-earth, not to say pedestrian, understanding of communism, certainly credible but hardly 'ideal' in the perspective of Marx's overall design and original formulations. This is now almost purely a communism of *insight*, a state of affairs projected and anticipated on the basis of comprehending the real world, with clarity of detail and no shimmering vistas, seen through a transparent, uncoloured magnifying glass.

To put this in the context of our foregoing presentation: the *Grundrisse* theme highlights Marx's efforts to render communism credible by, as it were, up-valuing capitalism and presenting *it* as a sort of esoteric, potential communism: this is insight turning into vision. The alternative procedure, and this is what comes to light increasingly in the late texts, is to approximate communism to capitalism in terms of the latter's existing, *empirical* features, not the 'human essence' of capitalism but its mundane, heterogeneous, visible characteristics: this is vision turning into insight. That is, either the real world is depicted in ideal terms, or the ideal is itself translated into the recognizable elements and features of the existing world. As we have seen, the *Grundrisse* theme, magnificent though it is in its dialectical *tour de force*, leads ultimately to a dead end. The dominant theme of the volumes of *Capital*, of Marx's pamphlet on the Paris Commune of 1871, and of his critical notes on the programme of the German Social-Democratic Party, is on the contrary seemingly successful: it is, without the slightest doubt, meaningful to talk about a 'communism' which is *merely* a projection and generalization of capitalism, and nothing else; moreover, this mundane, heterogeneous, pedestrian communism not only presents us with a perfectly rational, intelligible *concept* but also testifies, in a roundabout way, to Marx's insight into the *real* (as distinguished from the wished-for and imaginary) movement of history in the modern epoch. Marx's mundane conclusion on communism in other words, or what we can also see as the conclusion of his 'grand' view, is by no means a fanciful reading of what is actually going on in the world. But this aspect, being incidental to the main purpose of our study, will be touched on in the last chapter.

The point to note here, of course, is that this seemingly (and to a certain extent genuinely) realistic shift in his position does not in the least solve Marx's basic problem. This problem, connecting the real and the ideal or uniting 'science' and 'revolution', is now merely transferred to another plane but not thereby eliminated. Whereas before, and if we discount the dazzling fiasco of Marx's dialectical soaring of the heights in the *Grundrisse*, Marx's problem was to effect a credible connection between capitalism and communism, his problem now is to establish a meaningful unity between two *kinds* or 'phases' of communism. On the one hand, it is perfectly feasible to look forward to a form of social organization, and corresponding consciousness, which merely *generalizes* existing productive relations, satisfies consumer demands, rationalizes the economic system, achieves some sort of fairness in the distribution of burdens and benefits, provides for more leisure time, extends educational facilities, carries on the struggle against nature more successfully, etc. – and there is no reason whatsoever why this form of society should not be called 'communism'. But on the other hand the more feasible this future outcome of capitalist development becomes, the more it is presented as the realization of existing secular tendencies, the more plausible and reasonable it appears from the present point of view, the more problematic it will be to see it *also* in terms of a cataclysmic, qualitative, dimensional *change* in human relations and consciousness, or as *the* 'good society'. This reasonable and pedestrian communism is anything *but* 'genuine resolution', it is anything *but* the definitive, once-for-all transcendence of social conflict, the decisive move from 'pre-history' to 'history', the final uncovering of the secret of human existence. It is nothing but *existing*, heterogeneous history carried forward. Why *should* it be anything else? What is really *essentially* different in it that could persuade us to see in it the fulfilment of human desires and aspirations? I do not think that Marx can come up with satisfactory answers to these questions and I shall argue later that his 'final solution' to the problem of communism, i.e. the splitting of communism into a 'lower' and a 'higher' phase, is less than fully convincing in this regard. We shall take a more detailed look at this problem, presented by the theme of *Critique of the Gotha Program*, in the last section of this chapter. Before we come to it, however, there are a few other problems to go into; the increasingly mundane, realistic Marxist stance on communism has many interesting facets, at least a few of which will deserve examination. We shall, accordingly, discuss the problem of 'nature' and 'labour' in Marx's mature thought, leading to Marx's observations concerning productive organization, and thereafter the problem of revolutionary transformation and violence; all these, of course, connect up with earlier themes and have already been touched on in previous chapters.

I made the remark in Chapter 4 that Marx's *Capital*, compared to the philosophical temper and stimulation of the *Grundrisse*, is a disappointing text in that it presents the fundamental issues in a too clear-cut, too rigid, too didactic and too one-sidedly committed manner. No one can deny its staggering qualities as a complete, comprehensive, rigorous treatise, and as the greatest monument to Marx's historical scholarship. However, in so far as its principal concerns and arguments assume the unproblematic character of communism, its value as a source for illuminating Marx's real position (i.e. the fundamental ambiguity or duality of this position) is considerably lessened. The main argument of *Capital is* thus rigidly unitary and one-sided, almost to the point of naivety: its great sophistication of scientific deductions and equations, and its enormously skilful, persuasive employment of historical detail, are matched by its surprisingly simple, untroubled ostensive viewpoint. Where the *Grundrisse* presents capitalism and communism in vital, dynamic, dialectical interaction, and we almost come to *feel* how and why the existing world turns inevitably into its seeming 'opposite', *Capital* sees the present bourgeois economic and social system and communism as two sharply and rigidly opposed entities. There is movement from one to the other, but the two antithetical entities themselves do not move. The dominant theme of *Capital* simply reasserts the earlier militant humanism of the *Holy Family* and similar texts, presenting communism as too obvious and reasonable a standpoint to need elaborate justification. We have already had occasion to note this, in a slightly different context in Chapter 1, and hence there is little point in going into detail now. It is in *Capital* that Marx emphasizes the 'topsy-turvy' irrationality of capitalism, its successful 'bewitchment' of consciousness, to which the basic, transparent rationality of 'human' production stands in the sharpest contrast. The 'transparent and rational form' of human relations, which is to be achieved in communism, is the archimedean, methodological anchor on which rests the whole elaborate structure of Marx's critique of political economy, and the anchor itself here must of course be assumed to be firm and solid. In fact, the dominant theme of *Capital* carries on *one* particular strand in the earlier-composed materialist conception of history, i.e. Marx here once again argues from the concealed transcendental position of 'men' who 'enter into definitive productive relations' and who therefore can in time comprehend these relations and achieve mastery over them – again, this point was afforded some attention in Chapter 3 (where we remarked on the unresolved tension between this transcendental and visionary humanist position and Marx's more genuinely immanentist, i.e. proper *historical* position), and thus we need not bother too much about it here. Suffice it to remark that this dualistic historical stance is effectively overcome in the *Grundrisse*, only to reappear in *Capital*.

But the interesting and highly relevant point to note here is that this dominant humanism (and corresponding dualism) of *Capital* is effectively counterbalanced by the peculiar realism of some of its subordinate and relatively less conspicuous themes. There are two things involved here, to be discussed in turn. In the first place, the position taken in *Capital* concerning external 'nature' and particularly the relationship between nature and human 'labour' is in striking contrast to Marx's position in the *Grundrisse*. The latter is a predominantly dialectical treatise, an unmistakable Hegelian text, the special excellence of which lies in its *grasp* of opposites in unity, in its registering the interpenetration of capitalism and communism on the profoundest level. Now another and hitherto unremarked aspect of this dialectical position is its implied *denigratory* view of external nature. In Hegel's system of philosophy, of course, nature as the 'Other' of Spirit is quite clearly relegated to a secondary, derived position, and completely 'overcome' in Spirit's recognizing itself in the whole of reality. Marx, to be sure, mercilessly exposes and ridicules this 'idealist' Hegelian stance, especially in his early writings. The point is, however, that this very *same* Hegelian 'idealism' also comes through (as it must) in Marx's own dialectically conceived and inspired texts, certainly in parts of the *Manuscripts* and most strikingly in the *Grundrisse*. The dialectical unity of capitalism-communism is the conceptual equivalent in Marx of the Hegelian 'Spirit', it is substance turned into subject, the *divine* superiority and centrality of the human species in the entire scheme of reality. Now of course Marx does not say, and it would be ridiculous to interpret him even as implying, that Spirit (i.e. the human species) is *prior* to nature, in time or in logical, conceptual terms. The independent reality of nature, and its priority over the human race in point of time, in secular history, are accepted and asserted by Marx without any equivocation. However, Marx's thought takes on a decidedly Hegelian direction when it comes to considering the *future* asignificance of nature *vis à vis* the human species. For Marx in the *Grundrisse* nature almost entirely loses its importance, not to mention its superiority; the victory of man over nature is *precisely* the essential quality which unites capitalism and communism into one dialectical whole. Capitalism-communism signifies the highest point reached in the development of the human race and therefore it must mean the relegation of nature into the background. And corresponding to this view of nature, in the Marxist dialectical texts (the *Manuscripts* and the *Grundrisse*) there is an elevated, almost spiritual conception of human 'labour' as 'species-activity', as free creation rather than toil and drudgery, as the expression of the divinity of man rather than the sign of his oppression and degradation. Labour here is almost the precise equivalent of the ceaseless creative 'activity' of the Hegelian Spirit, as Marx's *subject*, too, mankind in capitalism-communism, corresponds to the Hegelian subject.

As Marx sees it in the *Grundrisse*, the mythological, i.e. imaginary, domination of the forces of nature, characterizing classical thought, 'vanishes with the advent of real mastery'[1] over these forces. The 'rich individual' who emerges out of capitalism regards his labour 'no longer as labour, but as the full development of activity itself, in which natural necessity in its direct form has disappeared . . .'[2] 'For the first time [i.e. in bourgeois society], nature becomes purely an object for human-kind, purely a matter of utility; ceases to be recognized as a power for itself; and the theoretical discovery of its autonomous laws appears merely as a ruse so as to subjugate it under human needs...'[3] The wealth produced in modern capitalism, Marx argues further, is to be seen as 'the full development of human mastery over the forces of nature, those of so-called nature as well as of humanity's own nature'.[4] Again, as Marx insists, 'nature builds no machines, no locomotives, railways, electric telegraphs, self-acting mules, etc. These are products of human industry; natural material transformed into organs of the human will [*in Organe des menschlichen Willens*] over nature, or of human participation in nature. They are *organs of the human brain, created by the human hand*; the power of knowledge, objectified.'[5] The subjugation of nature, its being reduced to the 'organ of the human will', is the achievement of human brain-power directing human muscle-power, that is, human *labour*, and Marx in the *Grundrisse* (following closely the line of the *Manuscripts*) puts particular emphasis on the serious character of labour as the basic definitional quality of the human species. He draws a distinction, in refuting the views of Adam Smith, between the 'historic forms' of labour as slavery, drudgery, activity that is 'repulsive' and externally 'forced', on the one hand, and labour in its full future significance on the other. Labour *now* is 'repulsive', only because it 'has not yet created the subjective and objective conditions for itself' in which conditions it 'becomes attractive work, the individual's self-realization [*Selbstverwirklichung*]'. Marx immediately adds here, now hitting out to the Left as it were, that this 'in no way means that it becomes mere fun, mere amusement, as Fourier, with *grisette*-like naivety, conceives it. Really free working, e.g. composing, is at the same time precisely the most damned seriousness, the most intense exertion.'[6] And later he expands on the point: 'Labour cannot become play, as Fourier would like... Free time – which is both idle time and time for higher activity – has naturally transformed its possessor into a different subject, and he then enters into the direct production process as this different subject. This process is then both discipline, as regards the human being in the process of becoming; and, at the same time, practice, experimental science, materially creative and objectifying science, as regards the human being who has become, in whose head exists the accumulated knowledge of society.'[7] The point to note is that here Marx's perspective is a *unitary* one: in the future, in communism developing out of capitalism, there is going to be a new 'subject', the human being synthesizing in himself the attributes of capital (brain-power) and the sheer energy of labour, subjecting nature to his will, and whose labour is now neither toil nor play but the integrated, higher unity of both.

What a difference there is though, between this confident, glowing, soaring, unitary presentation in the *Grundrisse*, full of Hegelian *hubris* and dazzling dialectic, and the sober, sedate, serene, not to say sad, message coming out of *Capital*. Let us not misconstrue the point: as I have said earlier, it is impossible to separate these two texts *entirely*: there is a great deal of dialectical fire-display in *Capital*, too, and the *Grundrisse* itself hovers between a dialectical and a non-dialectical, dualistic stance. But still one can hardly miss the overall atmosphere and import of *Capital*, which are clearly indicative of a spirit of cosmic resignation and accommodation. In the smaller context of the struggle between capital and labour, the tone of Marx's *magnum opus* is full of confidence, optimism, even arrogance, but this is coupled in the larger context, concerning the ultimate *meaning* and *significance* of communism from the human point of view, with a decidedly unexciting, matter-of-fact, mundane perspective. The sharp dualism between the existing world of capital and communism is further reflected in a dualism *within* Marx's understanding of communism. There is a continuing, and at times quite bombastic, *lip-service* (it is no more than that, once we come fully to understand Marx's position) paid to the ideal of communism as 'genuine resolution' and fulfilment, as a real dimensional change in human affairs. In 1872, for example, and admittedly in the course of a public address, Marx still considers it fitting to refer to communism as the 'kingdom of heaven on earth [*Himmelreich auf Erden*]' which, unlike ancient Christians, the modern proletariat is to achieve through political struggle.[8] But alongside this there is the much more credible, substantive and 'insightful' message which clearly indicates the *this-worldly* character of future changes in social organization, the inescapable historicity of communism, its partaking of the *same* dimension as social formations hitherto.

In *Capital* Marx more or less completely acquiesces in the continuing – and indeed, *permanent* – superiority of nature over the human species. And correspondingly his earlier vision of 'labour' as integrated species-activity, as full and free individual self-realization, is all but completely overshadowed by a decidedly pessimistic view of labour as *eternal* toil and drudgery. Labour, as Marx says, 'as the creator of use-values, as useful labour, is a condition of human existence which is independent of all forms of society; it is an eternal natural necessity which mediates the metabolism between man and nature, and therefore human life itself'.[9] Now, and this might at first appear only as a subtle shift of emphasis but in truth it is revelatory of a deep-seated ambiguity within Marx's thought, 'man' is presented as a part or aspect of nature in the 'metabolism' of the labour process, rather than (which is suggested by the earlier view) nature as a part or aspect of man. In Marx's words: 'Labour is, first of all, a process between man and nature, a process by which man, through his own actions, mediates, regulates and controls the metabolism between himself and nature. He confronts the materials of nature as a force of nature ... he acts upon external nature and changes it, and in this way he simultaneously changes his own nature. He develops the potentialities slumbering within nature, and subjects the play of its forces to his own sovereign power.'[10] Although admittedly the closing terms in this last sentence suggest the continuing presence in Marx's thinking of the earlier idealistic stance (and of course it *is* present, residually, which is why we are calling attention to the fundamental ambiguity and duality of the Marxist position), at the same time the context clearly shows that this human 'sovereign power' ought not to be understood literally, in the strict sense, as 'sovereignty' *over* nature. It is a hyperbolic, symbolic, circumscribed kind of 'sovereignty', nothing else, a sphere of *relative* and *restricted* 'freedom' and 'mastery', very clearly predicated on the acceptance of the ultimate superiority of nature. As Marx's statement, only a few pages later, reveals the position: 'The labour process, as we have just presented it in its simple and abstract elements, is purposeful activity aimed at the production of use-values. It is an appropriation of what exists in nature for the requirements of man. It is the universal condition for the metabolic interaction between man and nature, the everlasting nature-imposed condition [*ewige Naturbedingung*] of human existence, and it is therefore independent of every form of that existence, or rather it is common to all forms of society in which human beings live.'[11] Can anything be more explicit than this? What *is* human 'sovereign power' under the 'everlasting nature-imposed condition of human existence'? Or, as Marx puts it in a letter, written in 1868: 'Natural laws cannot be abolished at all. What can change in historically different circumstances is only the *form* in which these laws assert themselves.'[12] How much room does this really leave for the human being to assert his mastery of nature?

Here we come upon the famous passage in the posthumous third volume of *Capital*, which perhaps more than anything else in the late texts demonstrates beyond any serious doubt Marx's final acceptance of an irreducible, irreparable *duality* in the world in which human beings now live and will continue to live in the future. It is an eloquent but also rather strange passage, appealing in its sobriety, serenity and realism, but at the same time infinitely damaging in the perspective of (what could reasonably be taken as) Marx's earlier communist vision. 'Just as', Marx argues here, 'the savage must wrestle with nature to satisfy his needs, to maintain and reproduce his life, so must civilized man, and he must do so in all forms of society and under all possible modes of production. This realm of natural necessity expands with his development, because his needs do too; but the productive forces to satisfy these expand at the same time. Freedom, in this sphere, can only consist in this, that socialized man, the associated producers, govern the human metabolism with nature in a rational way, bringing it under their collective control instead of being dominated by it as a blind power; accomplishing it with the least expenditure of energy and in conditions most worthy and appropriate for their human nature. But this always remains a realm of necessity [*Reich der Notwendigkeit*]. The true realm of freedom [*das wahre Reich der Freiheit*], the development of human powers as an end in itself, begins beyond it, though it can only flourish with this realm of necessity as its basis.'[13]

Very little gloss is needed here to sharpen the focus on this final, and surprisingly stark, denouement of Marx's understanding of communism. The position here revealed is almost jarring in its abstract, rigid, Kantian duality, and it is shot through by a spirit of noble, classical resignation. Gone are, it seems, Marx's somewhat heady expectations concerning the future definitive subjugation of nature, its being reduced to the 'organ' of human 'will'. Now nature reigns supreme and the proper 'realm of freedom' for human beings, instead of being all-encompassing, all-pervading, splendid in its unitary centrality and victorious in its dialectical resolution of opposites (as clearly suggested by the dominant themes of the *Manuscripts* and the *Grundrisse*), is unceremoniously shifted to the wings, to a sphere 'beyond'. There is no suggestion here, as in Engels' *Anti-Dühring*, that mankind will ever definitively 'leap'[14] into a realm of freedom; quite the contrary, for Marx we are and remain *rooted* to necessity. The realm of freedom is here a mysterious, inconsequential entity, almost a Kantian *Ding-an-sich*, and there is no Hegelian Spirit overcoming nature, subject remains ethereal subject, and substance remains hard, inexorable substance. The future is seen by Marx no longer in terms of the gradual contraction and elimination of 'natural necessity' and its replacement by the 'rich human need' of the 'social individual', but on the contrary in terms of the *expansion* of natural necessity, and this is only mitigated, made tolerable by the continuing expansion of 'productive forces'.[15] There is, clearly, an overall cosmic *compulsion* in this future, everlasting productive 'development', it is not a matter of free choice, 'sovereign' decision by 'socialized man', but on the very contrary producers *must* be 'associated' in order to further *carry on* the battle, but not to win it, which is wholly beyond expectation. Human 'species-activity', labour, is consequently split right through the middle, into eternal toil and struggle on the one hand, and the development of powers 'as an end in itself' on the other, with no apparent traffic between them. And while this 'true realm of freedom' is a secondary, inconsequential, dependent residue, the other 'freedom' which Marx says is to be found *in* the realm of necessity is quite clearly a mere superficial semblance, a make-believe, a kind of 'cunning of reason' which renders human toil and the struggle against nature less unbearable. Here freedom simply refers to the 'collective control' of production, to ensure that there is the 'least expenditure of energy', etc. In view of the overall, heavy substantiality of nature and its 'expanding' necessity, 'collective control' may well signify an *advantage*, but it could hardly be taken as 'freedom'; and if there is no freedom, properly speaking, *from* nature for the human species *as such*, this 'collective control' could signify even *less* freedom for the 'social individual' whose 'self-realization' or 'free development' communism was supposed to bring about in the first place.[16]

There are, it seems to me, two fundamental questions to be asked about communism at this point, in the light of this revealing dualism of Marx's position in *Capital*; and our ensuing discussion later in this chapter will hopefully shed further illumination on the problems raised. In the first instance, just what precisely is the ultimate human *significance* of communist transformation, if all it achieves is a more rational, more properly organized, more structured and more self-conscious way in which to confront the eternal might of nature? The answer, surely, is that this consideration bestows on communism *very little* significance indeed, or that it shows up communism as a system of society, set of human relationships, and form of human consciousness, which only provide some *relative* advantages over capitalism. Let us be clear about the point being made here: I would not, on the one hand, wish to belittle the importance of these secular advantages in principle, while on the other hand I am not in any way admitting that Marx is actually correct in arguing that even *these* advantages would come about once there is a 'collective control' of production, etc. On this latter point, let us for the moment just cautiously suggest that Marx is not *obviously* wrong, that it is not entirely *senseless* or *absurd* to expect improvements in the human relationship to nature (i.e. matters relating to the burden of toil, the expansion of productive capacity, distribution of benefits, etc.) if we have an 'association of producers'. However, Marx's argument is not *obviously* correct either, and the least one can say here is that his presentation of the issues is too simple, too one-sided and too optimistic; *given* that production belongs to a 'realm of necessity', there must inevitably be some problems attaching to 'collective control' and the 'association of producers', and on these Marx, alas, is largely silent. This is of course by no means a sensational or original point to make, and I shall leave it at that, since this issue, the reasonableness of communism as productive organization *only*, will come up again, in subsequent sections of this work.

Here we have to concentrate on the theoretically more fundamental issue, viz. that this Marxist conception of communism as social organization predicated upon and carrying forward a realm of natural necessity appears to present communism as a relatively *insignificant* affair, just a small alteration in the inter-human context, confined to social productive relationships. Even assuming that this communism is 'better', more rational, fairer, more productive than capitalism, its superiority is only relative, and relevant only in this quite narrowly conceived context. If natural necessity remains largely what it is now, then what is the *point* of communism, why is it *worth* the effort, the hardship, the sacrifice that its establishment will inevitably involve? What difference, to use this somewhat grandiloquent expression, does communism ultimately make to the 'human predicament'? It is tempting to answer here, on the basis of Marx's own statements in the pages of *Capital*, that in this larger, deeper, and humanly vastly more significant perspective communism makes no difference at all, it does not alter the human predicament in any essential way, its relevance is only on the surface, concerned with issues and problems that must be seen as possessing a second-rate importance only. Communism presented in this light has no cosmic or anthropological meaning, it is

Insight and Vision

decidedly un-eschatological. What then? It will have been noted, of course, that we are once again veering uncomfortably close to a notion of *indifferent* communism, encountered earlier in the context of our probing the meaning of Marx's 'materialist conception of history'. There, in Chapter 3, our argument was that 'indifferent communism' is in the last analysis an unsatisfactory, incoherent notion which must be resolved in either of two ways. We shall not rehearse the argument here once again, except to point out that the Marxist scenario in *Capital* is subject to precisely the same sort of criticism: the cosmically, anthropologically, eschatologically 'indifferent' communism of collective control in the face of expanding natural necessity must *also* be resolved in one of two possible ways, developed and given substantive meaning in either of two opposed directions. Either it is shown that this communism is really *qualitatively* different from capitalism, but this is highly problematic in the admitted presence of continuing natural necessity and can only be done if a perfect 'realm of freedom' (i.e., as earlier, a true, moral human nature) is simply *read back* into it. Or, and this is the only meaningful alternative to the above putative solution, it is admitted that communism which thus *shows* itself to be different, *claims* to present itself as qualitatively different from capitalism, is in truth merely capitalism *carried on* under a different label. Once again, therefore: communism is either 'genuine resolution' or it is 'crude communism', either estrangement transcended or estrangement generalized. We shall take this point up again in our commentary on Marx's *Critique of the Gotha Program*.

The second question to be asked in the light of Marx's final dualistic denouement in *Capital* is this: how *can* there be a 'realm of true freedom' at all, one which is 'beyond' the realm of natural necessity, i.e. beyond the realm of nature? Or, to pose the question more pointedly: why should Marx assume, as he evidently does, that natural necessity will not *continue* to intrude upon human freedom, that it will not continue materially, substantively, essentially to *define* human action, relationships and consciousness? One possible way to argue this is to intimate, as Marx does especially in the *Grundrisse*, that capitalism already shows the way in which the realm of nature is being partially (but relevantly) transcended, that capitalism already expresses, on its profoundest level, the true human realm of freedom. However, if this dialectical solution is discarded in favour of the more obvious one, viz. in terms of the customary Marxist stance which places the emphasis on the *differ-*

ence between capitalism and communism (a view which is predominant in the *majority* of Marx's texts, including *Capital*), then Marx is presented with a big, perhaps insoluble, problem. Let us present this problem in a simple, graphic way: the *badness*, heterogeneity, imperfection, inhumanity, alienation, oppression, exploitation, antagonism contained in the capitalist system, embodied in the bourgeois epoch, are ultimately ascribed to 'natural necessity' by Marx. There can be no mistake on this point, Marx's writings here are remarkably unambiguous (and I shall forego the opportunity to flood the argument with a string of verbatim quotes), i.e. on the *essential* nature of capitalism being *not* the outcome of conscious human design and action, being *not* dependent on the will and caprice of capitalists and others. Capitalism is the full reign of natural necessity. Blind nature, as it were, fully pervades the human realm, through the chaos and impersonality of the market, through the 'jungle' of competition, through the domination of man's 'animal' instincts, and the like. Now the point is that in *Capital* communism is not exempted from this *same* natural necessity which is said not only to continue but actually to 'expand', the only difference being that in communism we are supposed to be possessing 'knowledge' of natural necessity, and therefore this necessity is not 'blind' (or rather, what Marx really means, that *we* are no longer confronting nature 'blindly'). But this is not as straightforward as it might sound. How *can* knowledge make an important difference if it is admitted that natural necessity will *still* be there? How can we know *now* that there are no other ways in which 'blind nature' might not enter into our lives, actions, relationships, consciousness? Where does natural necessity end? It is quite obvious that Marx cannot, in principle, have any direct empirical evidence of a realm of freedom *beyond* the present (unless, of course, the present is already seen in terms of freedom), and in any case the argument would be logically unsound. Natural necessity *causes* capitalism – from this it cannot be argued that the elimination of capitalism also means the elimination, or even curtailing, of natural necessity. There is, on Marx's showing therefore, no such thing as a 'true realm of freedom' except in the imagination and except in a trivial, pedestrian sense (e.g. as 'leisure-time').

Now, if we may digress just for a brief moment, it appears today, in the closing decades of the twentieth century and in view of advances made after Marx's time, that Marx's view concerning the relationship between capitalism and natural necessity was perhaps too simple and restricted. It is not possible to equate the abolition of private ownership of the means of production with the 'mastery' of natural forces and a 'true realm of freedom'. The history of radical thought after Marx, including the evolution of Marxism itself, is really nothing but a series of adjustments in the face of fresh discoveries concerning the *extent* of the realm of natural necessity; this realm, to say the least, appears now much more formidable and extensive than Marx and his generation of radicals seem to have believed (e.g. radicals today must be concerned with unconscious motivation, the Oedipus complex, the authoritarian personality, anomie, 'psychic Thermidors', etc.). It could be said without too much exaggeration and without too obvious *Schadenfreude* that notwithstanding modern radical sophistication, the 'true realm of human freedom' is just as elusive today as it was in Marx's time; if anything, we are farther away now from seriously *believing* in it, let alone endeavouring to realize it. But this is not our main concern here. The point to note is that in Marx's late texts, notably in *Capital*, there are many – indirect – indications that Marx *himself* was becoming rather sceptical concerning the intelligibility and realizability of a realm of freedom beyond natural necessity. It is not only that in his dichotomous presentation of the future (as noted above) the realm of freedom is circumscribed to such an extent as to make it well-nigh wholly inconsequential, relegating it to a sphere beyond labour (i.e. man's 'species-activity'), almost smothering it under the heavy, substantial, eternally pressing weight of nature. What is also relevant here are Marx's numerous and as it were backhanded observations in *Capital* suggesting that some of the most characteristic *features* of capitalist productive organization will continue to operate under communism. It is, as we remarked earlier, the exact reversal of the *Grundrisse* theme: the latter elevates capitalism to the status of an esoteric communism, whereas now communism is itself lowered, demoted, desacralized to appear as a kind of refined, rational capitalism.

Of interest here is Marx's somewhat disingenuous and unconvincing attempt to separate in *Capital* the function of 'directing authority' in production and the 'control' exercised by capitalists under the existing system. 'All directly social or communal labour on a large scale requires,' Marx says, 'to a greater or lesser degree, a directing authority [*Direktion*], in order to secure the harmonious co-operation of the activities of individuals, and to perform the general functions that have their origin in the motion of the total productive organism, as distinguished from the motion of its separate organs.'[17] Significantly here Marx employs the analogy of an orchestra to indicate the necessity of this directing authority (like a conductor) in all forms of production. Marx goes on: 'The work of directing, superintending and adjusting becomes one of the functions of capital, from the moment that the labour under capital's control becomes co-operative.' And then: 'The control exercised by the capitalist is not only a special function arising from the nature of the social labour process, and peculiar to that process, but it is at the same time a function of the exploitation of a social labour process, and is consequently conditioned by the unavoidable antagonism between the exploiter and the raw material of his exploitation.'[18] The sophistry, intended or unintended, entailed in Marx's position is quite conspicuous. In the first instance and in point of strict logic it is clear that Marx cannot jump to a notion of *pure* 'directing authority' from the given existent of capitalist control. Granted that capitalist control is a function of 'exploitation' and *therefore* 'antagonistic', it still does not follow that antagonism is *only* a consequence of exploitation, or that exploitation is the characteristic feature of capitalism *only*. This case, of course, parallels the argument considered above: just as Marx cannot logically restrict the baneful influence of 'natural necessity' to the existing mode of production, he cannot thus exclude the features of exploitation and antagonism *arbitrarily* from the general notion of 'directing authority' either.

But logic apart, the significant thing surely is that Marx considers it essential to bring in, indeed to emphasize, the notion of a 'directing authority' in communism. He returns to this notion in the third volume of *Capital* where in fact the point is more explicitly stated, Marx insisting that 'in all labour where many individuals co-operate, the interconnection and unity of the process is necessarily represented in a governing will [*in einem Kommandierenden Willen*], and in functions that concern not the detailed work but rather the workplace and its activity as a whole, as with the conductor of an orchestra'.[19] Perhaps the analogy should not be taken too literally, but it is highly suggestive and what it does suggest is an extremely highly organized, highly complicated, elaborately 'orchestrated' social system where functions are differentiated and even more sharply defined than in capitalism. A directing or governing will inevitably implies the presence of *command* and *instruction* in the system, and where there is a command there must also be obedience. It is not possible meaningfully to distinguish, as

Engels would blandly suggest later in *Anti-Dühring*, between the 'administration of things' and the 'government of persons',[20] especially since people in Marx's terms, are *primarily* concerned with 'things', with production, with waging the eternal struggle against an ever-expanding realm of natural necessity. It is *through* things that men are 'governed', in capitalism certainly, as Marx argues (i.e. through the operation of 'impersonal' market-forces), but also, it seems, in communism. More organization, more administration, means more government.

And as Marx further intimates in *Capital*, the communist system of production must also be a more highly bureaucratized system than capitalism. Communism means planning and planning involves an increase in the volume of tertiary functions. Unlike capitalism where 'social rationality' appears only *post festum*, after the event, and thus incapable of preventing 'major disturbances', communist society which has eliminated 'money capital' can and indeed 'must reckon in advance how much labour, means of production and means of subsistence it can spend, without dislocation . . .'[21] Moreover: 'Book-keeping . . . as the supervision and the ideal recapitulation of the process, becomes ever more necessary the more the process takes place on a social scale and loses its purely individual character; it is thus more necessary in capitalist production than in the fragmented production of handicraftsmen and peasants, more necessary in communal production than in capitalist.'[22] And: '. . . even after the capitalist mode of production is abolished, though social production remains, the determination of value still prevails in the sense that the regulation of labour-time and the distribution of social labour among various production groups becomes more essential than ever, as well as the keeping of accounts of this'.[23] Communism, which as Marx says in the *Grundrisse*, relies and builds upon the 'discipline' of the capitalist mode of production, extends and generalizes this discipline. In the vast and comprehensive association of producers everybody must have a definite place and function, and give one's best in terms of the plan and in accordance with the 'governing will' of the association; the whole community is *geared* to production, it is *defined* in terms of the struggle to be waged against natural necessity, there is very little outside, only a tenuous 'realm of freedom'. Communism then cannot be entirely unlike a modern industrial plant; it is to be seen as a huge, extended, all-embracing *factory*, modelled on the capitalist factory. In a strangely revealing way Marx actually intimates this much in *Capital*. Critically commenting on the contradiction within capitalism of the highly organized division of labour in the factory and the anarchic 'animal kingdom' outside the factory, he remarks: 'It is very characteristic that the enthusiastic apologists of the factory system have nothing more damning to urge against a general organization of labour in society than that it would turn the whole of society into a factory.'[24] Is it not true though? Why does Marx not consider it important to refute this charge there and then, and repeat in *print* what he had jotted down earlier, in the manuscript called *The German Ideology*, about communism being the complete abolition of the division of labour?

The overall and final impression gained by our 'reading *Capital*' (to plagiarize a famous title), therefore, is that its implied view of communism, of the system of production and society which is expected to replace capitalism, is *disjunctive* and thus marred by a fundamental incoherence which can, however, be revealed by close analysis. Marx's mature position on communism is irreducibly dualistic, he operates now with two conceptions, not one, and these two conceptions, although often misleadingly presented as harmonious and smoothly dove-tailing, are really incompatible with each other. The most direct way in which this duality is manifested is in Marx's *abstract* juxtaposition of a realm of necessity and a realm of freedom, which are expected to co-exist in the future. Here, at least, matters are expressed clearly, without any tergiversation or verbal adornment: communism means struggle, and this means not only struggle against nature but struggle between the two realms of necessity and freedom as reflected *within* the human community. That is to say, and for this extended understanding of Marx's position we have to adduce the evidence provided by various passages in *Capital* concerning productive organization, communism is presented as association united by a governing will, an orchestra performing as it were to the critical audience of nature, attempting to woo it and to impress it. In *Capital* Marx still, though not so lavishly as in the 'revolutionary' middle period, paints a glorious picture of future society after the dethronement of capital, but this *rhetorical* communism has really nothing to do with the *substantial* idea that emerges out of his considerations concerning the realm of natural necessity, direction, organization, bookkeeping and the like. On the one hand, there is nothing in Marx's critical account of capitalism that would adequately demonstrate – logically or empirically – that the noted and humanly relevant

Insight and Vision

features of this system (i.e. oppression, exploitation, alienation, etc.) are truly and self-evidently *confined* to this system. And on the other hand, Marx's guarded but surprisingly dead-pan, matter-of-fact and revelatory statements about the *enduring* characteristics of productive organization after capitalism strongly suggest (let us not put it any more categorically than that just now) that these noted features of capitalism just *might* continue to exist in communism also. Communism *qua* the rational, 'human' organization of the struggle against natural necessity has still to demonstrate its *essential*, defining quality as lying conclusively, wholly, irrevocably beyond the whole world of capitalism, beyond domination and beyond estrangement. Rhetorical flourishes and illogical leaps in the argument clearly do not suffice. Communism, as Marx manfully insisted in his polemics with 'utopian' writers, cannot be defended, advocated, established on *credal* grounds alone. But here, in Marx's *Capital*, what is argued beyond credal premises (and logically unconnected with them) is a communism that has – at least – a *striking* resemblance to capitalism. There is not a new, brave world visibly (intelligibly) emerging out of the old, but a *bifurcated* new world, one side of which is bravely (but only rhetorically and in the last resort *unintelligibly*) new, while its other side is nothing but a *brave* expression of the old, known world. In so far, then, as Marx's substantial idea of communism is not clearly, unambiguously distinguished from all the important organizational features of the world of capitalism, it is reasonable to ask the question whether it is not to be seen *essentially* as merely an empirical variant on capitalism, i.e. 'crude communism' that merely *generalizes* 'estrangement'. At the moment I am simply posing this question, but I shall attempt later an answer – largely (as might be expected) in affirmative terms – based on my interpretation of Marx's position in *Critique of the Gotha Program*.

However, it will be necessary first, and at this very point, so as to remain consistent with our broad chronological presentation of Marx's thought, to take cognizance of Marx's comments concerning the Paris Commune in 1871. It is to be readily admitted that *prima facie*, and perhaps also in a more profound sense, Marx's views expressed in connection with this historical event appear to weaken the interpretation I have been placing in this chapter on the direction of his mature thought. Though only for a short period, the events in Paris in the spring of 1871, following on the humiliating defeat and destruction of the Bonapartist Empire, revived earlier expectations of a successful revolutionary departure in a major European state, hopefully generating enough momentum to carry on the work of 1848–49. The spirit of revolution was again being resuscitated and there was an air of anticipation; radical changes were expected to follow. The events associated with the rise and fall of the Paris Commune, however, differed from the mid-nineteenth century revolutionary upsurge in at least three relevant respects. Firstly, this time radical expectations (with good reason) were more concentrated on France. Secondly, now the radical – socialist, communist, anarchist – camp could look back to some decades of solid organization and political experience, was numerically stronger, and had in Paris at least a power base that gave reasonable grounds for optimism. Thirdly, although the Commune lasted only a very short time and did not succeed in igniting revolutionary sparks elsewhere, it actually did set up a type of government and represented a kind of society which seemed consistent with radical ideas. The revolution, in other words, seemed now for the very first time to actually *work*; it was now no longer just a dream, a yearning, a wished-for fulfilment, or an abortive attempt, a might-have-been, but a real historical *fact*. The Word was at least visibly becoming Flesh, even though momentarily, immaturely, imperfectly. The Commune for Marx, therefore, appeared in the first and most important instance as an empirical, historical *vindication* of his theories, proving the actual possibility, nay reality, of proletarian self-government and communism; his dominant tone writing publicly about the Commune is reminiscent of his self-confident, impatient, optimistic revolutionism of 1848.

However, the Commune is also a *problem* for Marx, and it is of interest to note the amount of reticence, ambiguity and uncertainty entering into the panegyric he composed on the occasion. It is not only that he, together with Engels, was suspicious of the motives and ability of the Jacobin and Blanquist leaders of the Commune (Marx's own followers being relegated to the background), or that he thought that the Commune made some important strategic mistakes in dealing with its enemies inside and outside, or even that (as revealed in his private correspondence) he had a somewhat disparaging view of French radicals, including his own followers, the French section of the International.[25] More relevantly here, we must note the problem presented by the Commune for Marx's *thought*, on a more rarefied intellectual level: its occurrence and its character went against the grain of at least some of Marx's mature views concerning the possibility and nature of revolutionary change. It is of course not just a simple matter of saying that in Marx's terms the Commune should not have taken place, or if it did take place it should not be accepted as the real thing, i.e. as *the* great proletarian communist revolution (although this admission is actually made by Marx subsequently).[26] It is rather the nebulous matter of deciding what the actual character of the Commune *was*. Marx in his *Civil War in France* (Address of the General Council of the International), it seems to me, has to reconcile two things: on the one hand, the utopian, idealistic vision of revolutionary change, which looks upon revolution as *itself* and *immediately* creating an ideal world, goodness, perfection incarnate (to some extent Marx himself shares this view in the 1840s), and on the other hand, the increasingly realistic, careful and historically oriented Marxist view, which hails and advocates revolutionary change but sees it only as a *means* to the creation of an ideal world, sees revolution and the actual overthrow of bourgeois rule as transition and preparation only, *not* to be seen as the realization of ultimate, communist aims. There is a radical rupture between these two conceptions, but Marx in his pamphlet seems to subscribe to them both, with some curious results.

The dominant tone and message of *Civil War in France* are clearly hagiographical, and this is not simply due to Marx's propagandistic purpose but beyond that also to its being a residual expression of his earlier revolutionism and idealism, corresponding to the rhetorical view of communism as expressed in *Capital* and other mature texts. This first picture is that of a *beautiful* revolution, the 'glorious working men's Revolution'[27] which, as Marx seems to suggest, inaugurated a new way of life for Parisians overnight and which is in the sharpest ethical contrast to the social and political character of the defunct Empire. The workers, among them the 'high-souled and chivalrous Flourens', were 'too generous conquerors'[28] of the city, the 'magnanimity of the armed working men' being 'so strangely at variance with the habits' of the 'Party of Order'.[29] In the Empire 'financial swindling celebrated cosmopolitan orgies; the misery of the masses was set off by a shameless display of gorgeous, meretricious and debased luxury'. The Commune was 'the direct antithesis' of the Empire.[30] It displayed, in its rise as well as in its bloody defeat, the 'self-sacrificing heroism' of the Parisian population, in their midst the 'real women of Paris', 'heroic, noble, and devoted, like the women of antiquity.' Marx's enthusiasm seems unbounded:

'Working, thinking, fighting, bleeding Paris – almost forgetful, in its incubation of a new society, of the cannibals at its gates – radiant in the enthusiasm of its historic initiative!'[31] The Commune, further, signified for Marx the 'positive form' of the republic to which the Paris proletariat had long been aspiring, a republic that 'was not only to supersede the monarchial form of class-rule, but class-rule itself'. Unmistakably for Marx, the political organization of the Commune was something *new*, it was properly democratic, egalitarian and participatory. It 'was to be a working, not a parliamentary body, executive and legislative at the same time'. Communal councillors were 'chosen by universal suffrage' and were, like the police, 'responsible and revocable' agents of the people; so also were magistrates and judges. The members of the Commune in their majority were 'naturally working men, or acknowledged representatives of the working class', and 'public service had to be done at *workmen's wages*'.[32] Further: 'While the merely repressive organs of the old governmental power were to be amputated, its legitimate functions were to be wrested from an authority usurping pre-eminence over society itself . . . universal suffrage was to serve the people, constituted in Communes, as individual suffrage serves every other employer . . .' 'The Communal Constitution would have restored to the social body all the forces hitherto absorbed by the State parasite feeding upon, and clogging the free movement of, society.'[33] 'Wonderful, indeed, was the change the Commune had wrought in Paris! No longer any trace of the meretricious Paris of the Second Empire.' 'No more corpses at the morgue, no nocturnal burglaries, scarcely any robberies; in fact, for the first time since the days of February, 1848, the streets of Paris were safe, and that without any police of any kind.'[34] There could scarcely be a more idyllic picture than this.

But, for Marx, the democracy and egalitarianism of the Commune were still not its most significant aspects. Its elevation of 'society' over the 'state parasite' really expressed its *proletarian* and incipiently *communist* character. The Commune's 'true secret', as Marx declares, 'was this. It was essentially a working-class government, the produce of the struggle of the producing against the appropriating class, the political form at last discovered under which to work out the economic emancipation of labour.' Here then, 'with labour emancipated, every man becomes a working man, and productive labour ceases to be a class attribute'.[35] The Commune 'was the first revolution in which the working class was openly acknowledged as the only class capable of social initiative . . .'.[36] That initiative included, significantly for Marx, the disestablishment of all churches and thus the breaking of the 'spiritual forces of repression', and the opening up of educational institutions; thus 'science itself' was 'freed from the fetters which class prejudice and governmental force had imposed upon it'.[37] There were also measures, specifically mentioned by Marx, designed to aid workers in their work, such as the abolition of nightwork for bakers and the prohibition of fines on workers imposed by the employers. Was then the Commune to be seen as the first decisive step towards communism, the visible advent of the great and only change forward envisioned in the Marxist texts? Marx's remarks in this pamphlet clearly suggest that this was so. He asserts, echoing the well-known peroration in the first volume of *Capital*, that 'the Commune intended to abolish that class property which makes the labour of the many the wealth of the few. It aimed at the expropriation of the expropriators.' But, he goes on rhetorically, this is 'impossible communism', according to bourgeois apologists, or is it? Even 'intelligent' members of the ruling class now 'perceive the impossibility of continuing the present system'. So then, he concludes: 'If co-operative production is not to remain a sham and a snare; if it is to supersede the capitalist system; if united co-operative societies are to regulate national production upon a common plan, thus making it under their own control, and putting an end to the constant anarchy and periodical convulsions which are the fatality of capitalist production – what else, gentlemen, would it be but communism, "possible" communism?'[38] In essence, therefore, the Commune for Marx was then the *real* thing.

There is, however, another picture of the Commune emerging out of Marx's ringing address, and this picture is rather different from the first one. It suggests, in direct contrast to Marx's hagiographical write-up, that the Commune was not only the beautiful revolution, but also the *ugly* revolution (like June 1848), an event which, whatever remote futuristic significance could be attributed to it from the outside, still belonged, qualitatively speaking, to the *existing* world. This second picture, we might say, is much more consistent with the realistic direction of Marx's mature thought, and we could also argue that, against appearances perhaps, it is inconsistent with Marx's first presentation in the same text of the 'glorious revolution' which had wrought 'wonderful changes' in Paris. The first, and cautious, give-away is contained in Marx's sober observation (again echoing many a statement encountered in his earlier texts) that the workers expected no 'miracles' from the Commune, had no 'ready-made utopias', and that in order to create that 'higher form to which present society is irresistibly tending by its own economic agencies, they will have to pass through long struggles, through a series of historic processes, transforming circumstances and men'.[39] This clearly means that neither human beings nor circumstances are qualitatively different *now*: on the surface, on the level of political and perhaps economic organization, things *appear* different, here there is a sharp break, a 'revolution', but down below in the substantive depths of society there is an unbroken *continuity*. And indeed, Marx does not stay with historical abstractions, but openly refers to the more unsavoury aspects of the Commune, to people and events that display its this-worldly character. In the first instance, and in what is obviously an understatement but nonetheless remarkable in the context, he admits that 'in every revolution there intrude, at the side of its true agents, men of a different stamp', such as those who have no insight into the movement, and others 'mere bawlers' who 'sneaked into the reputation of revolutionists of the first water'. Marx adds ruefully: 'After the 18th of March, some such men did also turn up, and in some cases contrived to play pre-eminent parts.'[40] Further, Marx argues: 'They are an unavoidable evil; with time they are shaken off; but time was not allowed to the Commune.'[41] One might want to question here Marx's rather less than well-founded optimism that evils of this sort are shaken off 'with time', and one might also observe, in parentheses as it were, the total inadequacy of Marx's half-hearted admissions to account for Communal repression and terror, the machinations of the dreaded Rigault and his associates in the Commune police, the summary executions and murders, etc. which, without doubt, played an essential part in making the streets of Paris 'safe' for the first time since February 1848. And at this point we might also note briefly, though this is only circumstantially relevant, that Marx's general description of the Commune, its 'heroism' and 'self-sacrifice', constitute at best only a half-truth; to a number of eye-witnesses the short-lived Commune was characterized more by the confusion, cowardice, immorality, internecine squabbles and incompetence of the leaders, and the perpetual drunkenness of the rank and file, than any kind of imputed 'glory'.[42]

However, the important point here is Marx's statement that evils of this kind are 'unavoidable' in a revolution. The revolution, in other words, is not in full control of its own life and direction; it does not (or not yet at any rate) signify any kind of 'mastery' over human affairs. It is still at least in this one respect reminiscent of the 'anarchy' and 'convulsions' of the old order. But Marx goes even further. It is not simply the case that the revolution, *good* in its essential quality but still too *weak* to purify itself from unwanted associates, is thus recognized as being heterogeneous; here the evil, though 'unavoidable', is still presented as something *extraneous* to the revolution itself. Marx also intimates, darkly but the point can hardly be mistaken, that the revolution is essentially destructive in nature, it does and must perform *evil* acts, though its actions are justified in terms of its 'historic mission'. A case in point is the incendiary activities of the defenders of the Commune, which Marx defends, in Machiavellian style and in tones similar to his hard remarks in 1848–49, by reference to the necessities of warfare. 'In war', he says, 'fire is an arm as legitimate as any other', arguing that this holds good particularly 'in the war of the enslaved against their enslavers, the only justifiable war in history . . .'[43] Further he adds: 'If the acts of the Paris working men were vandalism, it was the vandalism of defence in despair, not the vandalism of triumph, like that which the Christians perpetrated upon the really priceless art treasures of heathen antiquity; and even that vandalism has been justified by the historian [*vom Geschichtsschreiber gerechtfertigt*] as an unavoidable and comparatively trifling concomitant to the titanic struggle between a new society arising and an old one breaking down.'[44] Here what is noteworthy is Marx's evident intention to go further than justifying the destruction of buildings, etc. in Paris only in terms of 'defence in despair', which, one should think, might have been quite sufficient. Behind this partial and contingent justification of particular and contingent acts, Marx evidently feels the need for a transcendental justification of revolutionary violence and destruction *as such*. This too, the ugly face of revolution, is 'unavoidable' in the 'titanic struggle' between the new and the old. This destructiveness, according to Marx, is 'comparatively trifling'. 'Comparatively' to *what*? It is not enough to answer here, as Marx presumably would, that revolutionary violence, repression, vandalism, excesses, despair, etc. are 'trifling' in comparison with the long-term, systematic and generalized oppression and exploitation of the existing order, for the simple reason that these latter phenomena *themselves* can be denounced as 'evil' only in the perspective of a transcendental *good*, or an outlying *vision*. For the (Western)

Receding Vision

religious consciousness, this transcendental good is *not* in this world, in material or historical reality, but in heaven and in the righteous soul. For Marx and radical revolutionaries in general, the good that justifies evil and in terms of which destruction is 'comparatively trifling', resides essentially in this world, in historical reality.

Does it though? Marx's highly committed, glowing, rhetorical, even emotional pamphlet on the Paris Commune fails to show this. It should have become evident in our foregoing analysis that now Marx really writes about two separate things which can be presented as one and united only in his overall revolutionary communist perspective, in his fully integrated concept of communism which purports to hold his insight and his vision together. The vision or the end, communist society, is good, *therefore* we should see the heterogeneous present in terms of its *productive* capacity, not for what it *is* and *does*, but for what it leads to or creates. It is the 'historian', as Marx revealingly puts it in the statement quoted above, that justifies the actions of the new world in its titanic struggle with the old. The new world, the new *quality*, exists only in the perspective, the mind, the vision, the imagination of the 'historian'. Take this away, and what is left? The ugly revolution. Existence, as Marx's numerous and honest, though undertoned, admissions concerning the Commune make abundantly clear, does not *directly* bear out the revolutionary promise, it does not (as it ought to, in Marx's terms) *demonstrate* either the transcendental goodness or the historical possibility of the end. Marx's rhetorical phrases concern only qualities which he, *qua* 'historian', reads into existing reality, and as we have seen he is not entirely in one mind even on the extent of their application; the overall conclusion and message of *Civil War in France* is that the Commune is vindicated only in terms of its future significance. Thus, once the gloss is rubbed off, the two unrelated entities become visible on the surface. On one side the vision, the *idea*, translates into the vaunted qualities of this 'glorious revolution': its democratic egalitarianism, its heroic self-sacrifice, the 'wonders' it produced. On the other side the clear insight into *actual* history, the facts without transvaluation, make one mindful of existing, mundane qualities: excesses, mistakes, unavoidable evils, essentially *unchanged* men and circumstances. It therefore seems reasonable to argue that the duality of *Civil War in France* is in fact the same duality as has been discovered in *Capital*. In the latter Marx perorates about the 'expropriation of the expropriators' and holds out the promise of a new and qualitatively different society replacing capitalism. But what he actually *says* about the actual features of this new society, i.e. its continuing subordination to nature, its complex productive organization, its directing authority, etc., fails to show that this new world *is* qualitatively different from the old one. And in the former while Marx is obviously enthusiastic about those qualities of the Commune which to him indicate its progressive novelty, he at the same time recognizes that these qualities do not exhaustively, or even essentially, describe the character of the Commune, but that the character of the Commune is *heterogeneous*, it might well point towards the new world but it also *partakes* of the old. The humdrum world of natural necessity as well as the violent world of the ugly revolution express 'substance' only; they still do not make 'subject' come real.

Let us then turn to our final text, Marx's *Critique of the Gotha Program*, composed in 1875 but published posthumously in 1891. Marx's comments here on communism can, I think, be legitimately seen as his last testament, and quite apart from this as it were patrimonial significance, this relatively short piece is probably unique for the clarity and explicitness with which it tackles the problem of communism, and for the (seemingly) easy and straightforward solution to this problem offered in it. I do not think, however, that this solution – Marx's conclusion on the subject – stands up to close scrutiny. In any event, *Critique of the Gotha Program* is a depressing text, and its laudable clarity and directness are considerably marred by Marx's visibly increasing impatience with and intolerance of other views. One feels that, while Marx may well be justified in his intention to exorcise 'Lassallian' concepts causing confusion among German socialists, he could perhaps have shown more sympathy and understanding towards his comrades-in-arms; after all, here the polemic addresses people who are supposed to fight for the same objective, and not self-professed opponents and rivals, as in the celebrated Marxist quarrel with Proudhon, Bakunin and Dühring. Furthermore and quite interestingly, the tone of Marx's remarks goes some way towards suggesting that Marx was perhaps getting now a little bit tired of 'revolution' in the sense of upheaval, destruction, armed struggle; no doubt, the bitter hangover after the debacle of the Paris Commune contributed to this mood (see how contemptuously in the *Critique* Marx dismisses 'democratic litanies'), and so did Marx's age, while on the positive side, it seems, Marx was then getting more optimistic concerning the chances of the organized workers' movement in some countries gaining its objective peacefully, not without political struggle but without a cataclysm.[45] The *Critique*, whilst militant and uncompromising in tone, is remarkably moderate and circumspect, even conservative, in what it says concerning the *immediate* future, and it is noticeably free of any kind of visionary zeal or millenarianism. Indeed, Marx's sharp distinction here between the 'first' or lower and the 'higher' phases of communism already foreshadows in a curious way what was to become the distinctive political profile of the German Marxist movement, its separation of ultimate aims and short-term policy objectives, leading eventually to Vollmar's and Bernstein's revisionism. Bernstein's dictum that 'the movement is everything, the aim is nothing', is already here in an embryonic form. For Marx, too, the 'movement', i.e. the 'lower phase' of communism, is in effect *everything*, while the 'aim', communism in its higher phase, is *nothing*, it has no substance, no reality, no real relevance to or connection with the existing world; it is retained (one might guess) partly for rhetorical purposes and partly as an unconscious residue of Marx's earlier revolutionary expectations, just as rhetorical communism, 'transparent' and 'rational' production, 'free association', etc. often figure in the pages of Marx's *Capital*.

We are concerned here really with one short but extremely important section of the *Critique*, containing Marx's 'marginal notes' on Paragraph 3 of the Program of the German party, the subject being the emancipation of labour as an objective of the party. According to the Program, this objective demands 'the promotion of the instruments of labour to the common property of society and the co-operative regulation of the total labour with a fair distribution of the proceeds of labour'.[46] What can be so terribly wrong with this formulation, we might well ask, especially if you are a socialist or a 'communist'? (The close similarity of this article to Clause IV of the Labour Party Constitution will, of course, have been noted.) There is *plenty* wrong with it, Marx thinks, and while he attacks the *language* of the Program as being too timid, too moralistic, too heavily influenced by bourgeois ideology, at the same time he also lashes out against the *substance* of the Program as being – in effect – too starry-eyed, too forward-looking, too revolutionary! The 'proceeds of labour' are dismissed by Marx as a 'loose notion', while he suggests that the concept, 'fair distribution', does not adequately distinguish between existing bourgeois society and communist society, or in other words that moral categories like 'fairness' apply only within given modes of production. That is, distribution is already 'fair' now, in capitalist terms, and Marx points out that 'socialist sectarians' also have their varied (and presumably inconsequential) notions about fair distribution. However, it seems to me that one would miss the point of Marx's criticism if one were to concentrate only on modes of expression; the language of the Program is certainly 'loose' and would be untenable in the strict terms of historical materialism, but what Marx really objects to is the *substance* of the principle involved, as it becomes quite clear in the sequel. In other – and plain – words, Marx is *against* the idea that the 'proceeds of labour' should go undiminished to the labourers, and he is also *against* 'fair distribution', i.e. distribution on moral grounds, in communism. This might sound strange at first, but this is indeed the case. The 'proceeds of labour', Marx argues, must be defined as the 'total social product' of communist society, and from this product certain quantities must be deducted, before we come to any kind of distribution. He offers here an ominously full list of necessary deductions: for replacement of the means of production, for further expansion, and for reserve or insurance funds to provide against accidents, etc. And he asserts that these deductions are an 'economic necessity' and 'their magnitude is to be determined according to available means and forces, and partly by computation of probabilities, but they are in no way calculable by equity'.[47] The point could hardly be expressed in plainer terms: *first* comes necessity, defined presumably by the 'governing will' in communist society, and only then *'equity'*, if we reach equity at all. It is doubtful, to say the least. Marx then goes on to argue that even the remaining portion of the total social product, after the above necessary deductions, is not for immediate distribution among producers for purposes of individual consumption, but we still have to deduct: the general costs of administration (Marx hopefully, and inconsistently, adding that these would progressively diminish in communism), satisfaction of common needs, such as schools, health services, and funds for those unable to work.

Here we come to distribution proper, i.e. the considerably diminished social product left for individual consumption. What are the principles governing communist society in this regard, and what is specifically communist about them? Communism will differ from capitalism, Marx says, in that here 'producers do not exchange their products' and 'in contrast to capitalist society, individual labour no longer exists in an indirect fashion but directly as a component part of the total labour'. However, immediately Marx continues by intimating that this change, though fundamental in principle, in actual, palpable fact, from the *producers'* point of view, amounts to very little indeed. Here, in communism, 'the individual producer receives back from society – after the deductions have been made – exactly what he gives to it', i.e. a certain quantity of labour. The worker 'receives a certificate from society' and 'with this certificate he draws from the social stock of means of consumption as much as costs the same amount of labour. The same amount of labour which he has given to society in one form he receives back in another.' Where is the difference then from capitalism, as it might appear to the workers themselves? 'Content and form', Marx argues somewhat sophistically, 'are changed, because under the altered circumstances no one can give anything except his labour, and because, on the other hand, nothing can pass to the ownership of individuals except individual means of consumption.'[48] Fair enough: there are no *capitalists*, thus no individual exploitation, no inequality and power based on ownership, and therefore, according to Marx's definition, no 'capital' either. We *have* passed the great divide between 'pre-history' and 'history'. But even though we might have got over the watershed in point of (deep, esoteric, scientific) principle, we are still in the same old world as regards the surface, in appearance and perception. Workers here are still confronted by the united power of 'society', by something which may not *be* 'capital' but which very suspiciously *looks like* capital, certainly from the workers' point of view, even if not from the scientist's. Marx makes it absolutely clear that in communism 'obviously the same principle prevails as that which regulates the exchange of commodities, as far as this is exchange of equal values'. Hence, he goes further, '*equal right* here is still in principle – *bourgeois right*, although principle and practice are no longer at loggerheads . . .' This means that equal right 'is an unequal right for unequal labour'. There are no class differences, 'because everyone is only a worker like everyone else; but it tacitly recognizes unequal individual endowment and thus productive capacity as natural privileges'. In content, this is a right of inequality, like every right. There are here unequal individuals, and, Marx adds in parentheses, 'they would not be different individuals if they were not unequal', who must be measured by an equal standard, i.e. the value of labour. 'Thus,' Marx concludes, 'with an equal performance of labour, and hence an equal share in the social consumption fund, one will in fact receive more than another, one will be richer than another, and so on.'⁴⁹

Of course Marx understands very well, and makes no bones about it, that the 'communist' society thus described, egalitarian and efficiently organized though it might be in comparison with bourgeois society (which is, however, not *demonstrably* the case), is a very far cry from communism as an absolutely *desirable* form of society, as freedom, happiness and 'mastery' of nature, as the full satisfaction of individual needs and full individual development of capacities, as the *locale* of the 'rich social being', communism as 'genuine resolution'. This is communism that is only a *tiny step* away from capitalism, if that. 'What we have to deal with here', as Marx bluntly puts it, 'is a communist society, not as it has *developed* on its own foundations, but, on the contrary, just as it *emerges* from capitalist society; which is thus in every respect, economically, morally and intellectually, still stamped with the birth marks of the old society from whose womb it emerges.'⁵⁰ So the above described features, which Marx calls 'defects', 'are inevitable in the first phase [*in der ersten Phase*] of communist society as it is when it has emerged after prolonged birth pangs from capitalist society'.⁵¹ But this is of course not the end, not the final fulfilment. Marx does not forget to add his customary peroration: 'In a higher phase of communist society [*in einer höheren Phase der kommunistischen Gesellschaft*], after the enslaving subordination of the individual to the division of labour, and therewith also the antithesis between mental and physical labour, has vanished; after labour has become not only a means of life but life's prime want; after the productive forces have also increased with the all-round development of the individual, and all the springs of co-operative wealth flow more abundantly – only then can the narrow horizon of bourgeois right be crossed in its entirety and society inscribe on its banners: From each according to his ability, to each according to his needs!'⁵² *Here* we have then 'genuine resolution', Marx's ideal and vision retained and restated, in this singularly eloquent and succinct sentence. The *whole* of Marx *qua* 'communist' is encapsulated in this dramatic statement, the exalted view of human labour of the *Manuscripts* and the *Grundrisse*, abolition of the division of labour as envisioned in the *German Ideology*, the prospect of free individual development proclaimed in the *Communist Manifesto*, the abundant flow of wealth as anticipated in *Capital* and numerous other writings. The circle is finally closed, Marx's thought is fully consummated.

Receding Vision

But, needless to say, the *problem* of communism in Marx is still not eliminated; if anything, it looms much larger, much more disconcertingly, after a consideration of these passages from the *Critique*, than it has done ever before. The duality is now entirely out in the open, in its naked rawness, in its disjunctive heterogeneity, in its damning divergence and the incompatibility of its two basic elements. The first but perhaps not the most important point to note here is the brevity and relative *isolation* of the sentence Marx devotes to the 'higher phase' of communism in this context, in his critical discussion of communist principles. While he deliberately goes out of his way, in great and perhaps too superabundant detail, and with a jarring note of pedantic irritation, to *damp* the moralizing enthusiasm of his comrades, and to hold them back from unduly high hopes and utopian expectations, he appends this single sentence concerning the ultimate communist ideal almost as an afterthought, an inconsequential flourish, an empty rhetorical embellishment, so as to compensate for his bluntness, to provide an acceptable sugar-coating for his bitter and prosaic realism. Although heavy and concentrated in its content, this single statement is noticeably incongruous in the *context*, in tone as well as substance. Really, one feels, what Marx intends to convey in the *Critique* is his objections to communism, not his advocacy of it, and his summary reference to the 'higher phase' is not much more than his poetic justification for raising these objections.

The second, and somewhat more significant, point to note is that Marx's glowing characterization of the higher phase in this one sentence of the *Critique*, though definitely in line with numerous statements in other texts, at least in one crucial respect seems incongruous with his remarks in *Capital*, noted earlier in this chapter. This concerns the character of human 'labour' in communism. As we have seen, the *Critique* reiterates the dominant message of the *Manuscripts* and the *Grundrisse* in that it envisages the *integration* of human labour in communism, defines labour here as 'life's prime want', i.e. as 'species-activity', effort expended for its own sake, itself a form of fulfilment. But this message is already, and in unmistakable terms, contradicted in *Capital* (the first as well as the posthumous third volume) where Marx refers to labour as 'eternal nature-imposed necessity'.[53] These two views, I would submit, are incompatible with each other: communism is either the sublime *transcendence* of natural necessity or the grand *confirmation* of natural necessity, labour either the mark of human freedom or the

Insight and Vision

mark of human subjection, spontaneous creation or continuing struggle – but not both. Communism either signifies the *real* world, the existing world as we know it, with a little bit of cosmetic alteration added to it, or it signifies an *ideal* world – but not both.

The third and to my mind by far the most important point, however, has to do with the *relationship* between the lower and higher phases of communism, as formulated in the *Critique* only. It is not, after all, necessary to probe Marx's ulterior motives and hidden intentions (if we *could* determine them in the first place), nor to invoke the evidence of other texts, in order to note the underlying problem of communism as revealed here. The higher phase of communism presents us with an extremely attractive vision, but the point is surely that this vision has absolutely nothing to do with the lower phase, as described in the same text. There is *no* relationship between them, the two are merely juxtaposed, this time in *historical* terms (as distinguished from the *abstract* juxtaposition of freedom and necessity in *Capital*), but we are not offered any compelling reason to believe that there are essential links between them. Marx simply says that the higher phase of communism will be *different* from the lower phase, but their putative unity and connection lie only in their name; they are both *called* 'communism' but the identical label denotes diametrically opposed entities.[54] Indeed, in the *Critique* Marx does not even assert that the higher phase *will* arrive eventually; he presents us here only with an abstract possibility, far remote in the future and only contingently related to the communism which is immediate, intelligible and (presumably, though this is not spelt out here) necessary. There is not even a hypothetical connection between the two phases, in that Marx does not appear to be arguing (let alone demonstrating) that *if* there is a lower phase, *then* the higher phase will and must follow. In so far as communism is 'necessary' and the 'inevitable' outcome of the further development of capitalism (an aspect of Marx's doctrine which we discussed in the previous chapter), this can refer only to the lower phase. Here, I think, Marx's argument is cogent, insightful, compelling. Capitalism *must* develop, must expand, must play out its own tendency to grow, etc. and it is, to say the least, *reasonable* to project its future progression in the terms that Marx calls the lower phase of communism. But after that, it is literally anybody's guess. The relationship between capitalism and the lower phase of communism is close, tight, concrete, meaningful; here we *are* dealing with reality. The relationship between the lower and higher phases of communism is, by contrast, remote, tenuous, wispy, uncertain and in the last resort unintelligible; we are no longer dealing with any kind of reality but with the product of our fancy and wishful imagination. It is an altogether different realm, a projected world of perfection and fulfilment, a 'shadowless' picture which can be brought to earth, connected to reality, only by the doubtful links of rhetoric, vision, belief and emotion.

This reasoning, however, might seem unfair, and it *is* unfair as long as we confine ourselves to bare logic. The higher phase does not *have* to come out of the lower phase – this much, I think, can be established quite easily but it is hardly a telling argument or a conclusive refutation of Marx's case (which is not our intention here anyway). A Marxist counter-argument could here still be advanced that the higher phase is nevertheless a *likely* outcome of the lower phase, that given the characteristics of the lower phase it is sensible and rational to expect its development in the direction of the higher phase. This is a point that we have to consider seriously, for it is on this issue (I believe) that the coherence and intelligibility of Marx's concept of communism ultimately depends. For this argument to be acceptable, however, it is imperative to show that the *actual features* of the lower phase have at least a closer resemblance to the overall character of the higher phase than to the actual features of capitalism, or that there is something in the lower phase, an embryonic tendency perhaps, that unmistakably points *towards* the higher phase and at the same time *away* from existing society. Does Marx argue this though? No, he argues the exact opposite, namely that the lower phase closely resembles capitalism and that its actual features are in direct contrast to the character of the higher phase. This is obvious and the documentary evidence has already been provided: in the lower phase there is exchange, compulsion to work, differential earnings and distinction in terms of wealth. We are dealing here with the same *people* as we encountered in capitalism, and the producer has a very similar relationship to the means of production to that which he had under the capitalist system. Marx's oft-employed obstetric analogy brings the point out graphically: the lower phase is the infant offspring of capitalism, it has come into the world after prolonged birth pangs, and it bears the birth marks of its parent. The implications of the analogy (if we are to take it seriously at all) of course go against Marx's ostensive reasoning, actually militating against any rational expectation of the arrival of the higher phase: if these 'birth marks' are necessary with the infant, why should we believe that the growing child and adult will be able to discard them, shed them at will? Will the adult *want* thus to repudiate his parentage?

In the lower phase we have the same people and we have relationships which, from the point of view of individual producers, appear very similar to the relationships obtaining under capitalism. The lower phase, therefore, *objectively* regarded, is 'crude communism' or 'estrangement generalized'. In Marx's later terminology this must therefore mean that here the relationship of *capital* is generalized. Here we must again, though from a perspective directly opposed to the one employed in the previous chapter, reflect critically on Marx's sometimes too easy identification of 'capital' and 'capitalists'. In *one* sense, no doubt, capital is 'overthrown' in the lower phase or in crude communism. But this is a sense of capital which appears meaningful only from the higher and remote viewpoint of the scientist; it is a technical definition which indeed makes perfect and exhaustive sense *within* the Marxist science of political economy but which is too narrow, and too question-begging, to carry its significance to the very *foundations* of this same science. This restricted, technical sense of capital is not its most important sense, it does not touch on the essential *quality* of the relationship as actually experienced in *both* capitalism proper and in the lower phase of communism. Estrangement or *separation* of 'society' and the individual producer/consumer unites the two forms. In the *Manuscripts* Marx explicitly calls 'society' the 'universal capitalist' in crude communism. In the *Critique* the lower phase has society, separated from and confronting the producers and consumers, dispensing burdens and benefits according to the 'value' of labour. 'Society' here has its own mind, own will, own rationality, own interest: it is the *buyer* of labour-power and the *seller* of goods for consumption. If this is not 'capitalism' in the most pertinent, profoundest and classical Marxist sense, then I don't know what is.

Yet the lower phase is supposed to lie beyond capitalism, in terms of scientific principle as well as ethical judgment. It is interesting to note, as has been remarked earlier, that while Marx resorts, in his description of the lower phase, to the *objective* features of crude communism, i.e. here everybody is a 'worker' (note also his identical characterization of the Paris Commune), he is silent on the *subjective* features. While crude communism in the *Manuscripts* is denounced in no uncertain terms, and connected with the greed, envy, possessiveness and 'unnatural simplicity' of the poor and uneducated mass, the lower phase in the *Critique* is curiously empty of ethical value-judgment; if anything, Marx's terms suggest that the *subjective* character of the lower phase is qualitatively different from the subjective character of capitalism, that it is somehow morally more acceptable, 'better', to be approved rather than denounced. But this surely won't do. How can these aforementioned objective features be presented as necessary in the absence of these subjective features? It is not only that we have here the same people as in capitalism, and that in capitalism people *are* greedy, envious, possessive, self-regarding, uncultured, irresponsible, irrational, dehumanized (how could capitalism flourish otherwise, or how could it be *understood* otherwise?). The projected institutional framework of the lower phase as a whole itself suggests, including those features which are conspicuously different from capitalism (e.g. here everyone must work, property cannot buy labour, etc.), that these subjective traits *must* be there. Without envy, greed, possessiveness the lower phase of communism quite simply does not make sense; in the absence of these features not only is it unlikely to come into being but it is literally impossible. With people assumed to be socially oriented, unselfish, devoted, honest, rational, displaying their 'true moral human nature', the lower phase of communism is revealed as a self-contradiction. Hence, if Marx's presentation of the lower phase is to be endowed with any meaning, we must fill in the gaps left blank in the *Critique*, and draw out explicitly those assumptions about human beings and relationships that alone render such a scenario credible. The implications, I would argue, point unmistakably in this direction, back towards the concept of crude communism and its 'generalized' estrangement. Why must 'society' deduct from the social product funds for replacement, expansion, and the care of the sick? Because individual rationality and morality clearly do not suffice: individual producers would not do this voluntarily, spontaneously. Why must producers be compelled to work by economic pressure, i.e. remunerated strictly in terms of the 'value' of their labour? Because and only because they would not expend their energy otherwise, because labour for them is still toil and drudgery, because they are by their ('historical' but nevertheless enduring) nature indolent and self-regarding, consumers rather than producers, more 'animal' than properly human. Why will some producers be richer here than others? Because people value possessions, they are greedy and envious, they are still alienated from their human essence, their divine creative capacity. And so on.

Where is the big difference then? How and when and why do we pass through the celestial gate; can we ever erect the glorious banner of the higher phase? There is, to reiterate, nothing in Marx's actual description of the lower phase of communism to suggest that this point can or will ever be reached. The lower phase is in the real world, it is no more than rationalized capitalism, and the promised *big change*, Marx's vision, is shifted further and further away, into the unconnected historical distance. Yet Marx does indicate that, in spite of these *this-worldly* features of the lower phase, communism in this immediate form is still essentially, dimensionally different from capitalism. The lower phase has, it seems, a basic *moral* quality that for Marx differentiates it from the existing system. How does Marx manage to do this? The explanation, I think, is that he *reads back* the supposed moral quality of the higher phase into the lower phase. The lower phase is a hybrid construction, in part valid historical projection, in part philosophical retrojection: its actual characteristics, its details, its heterogeneity are revealed to Marx's insight, whereas its homogeneous, superior moral quality is transferred from Marx's vision. In other words, the Marxist vision of communism is brought in from above, from the outside, to effect an arbitrary transvaluation. Because you are occupying the vantage-point of the higher phase, of 'genuine resolution', you can look back and *see* this construction as the 'lower phase'. The visible, intelligible features of the construction display its mundane, historical, we might say immoral character, yet these very same features are endowed with a different and transcendental meaning, in the light of which they become at once moral and desirable. People in the lower phase are greedy, envious, possessive, self-regarding, unequal, irrational, yet in spite of this the lower phase as a whole is rational, united, progressive, humane. This is surely a circular argument, in terms of the *Critique* at least: the higher phase is to come after, and presupposes, the lower phase, yet at the same time the lower phase itself assumes the higher phase. The objective is or was, one can presume, to deduce or derive the higher phase as ultimate *result*, yet the higher phase is there at the very beginning as *departure*.

It will be noted that here we are in fact once again fast approaching the dilemma which, it was argued in the previous chapter, confronted Marx's *dialectical* trajectory, the line of reasoning which culminated in the recognition of the intrinsic conceptual unity of capitalism and communism. The implicit circularity of the *Critique* can only be resolved in terms of the *open* circularity of Marx's dialectical fusion of insight and vision, and then we are face to face with the same awkward questions. If the moral quality of the higher phase can be read back into the lower phase, then why can it not be read back further into capitalism? If *communist* greed, envy, possessiveness, inequality can thus be transvalued, then why not these *same* qualities as they appear in existing bourgeois society? If the infant is worthy of approval and nurture, then why not the parent? What is *really* wrong with the parent? *Where* is that elusive dividing line? Once again, the intended qualitative distinction between capitalism and communism disappears from view and all we see is the great, grey, bewildering mass: communism reaches into capitalism and vice versa, they are either both good or they are both bad. Estrangement is either there in both, or it is nowhere. If capitalism is lifted up into communism, then communism loses its *sense*. If communism is lowered into capitalism (as in Marx's *Critique*), then communism loses its *quality*. Taking the latter line means having to resign ourselves indefinitely to the domination of capital (call it 'society'), to the burden of estrangement, to relentless struggle, to toil and labour. Capital rules forever, we cannot see beyond it – is then Marx's ultimate message, properly understood. Communism as the 'higher phase' or as 'genuine resolution' or as the vision of the 'free association of moral human beings' is reduced once more to a *pure* standpoint, uplifting but historically, politically irrelevant. Farewell ye gods!

6 Heaven and Hellas

We must now pull the threads together and, however difficult and perilous such an undertaking may be, make at least an effort to state our conclusions in a somewhat bolder, more widely generalized and comprehensible manner. The result of our discussion in foregoing chapters, surveying the development of Marx's thought in terms of its central organizing concept, communism, is that at the end Marx *in his own terms* is not quite successful in solving the problem of communism. The problem of communism in Marx's thought is, as it were, the problem of life and consciousness in general (as it presents itself to the modern mind): the world, which is *here* and *now*, is imperfect and heterogeneous, constantly confronting me with puzzles, difficulties, disappointments, frustrations; I can certainly *deal* with it, in more or less adequate ways, but I cannot imagine it out of existence, cannot completely transvalue it or change it, cannot simply *identify* it with my notions of goodness and perfection. The real and the ideal are obviously closely related but they are not the same. Now it has been my contention in this study that Marx's thought – his great intellectual enterprise – is best interpreted as an endeavour to show the *reality* (reasonableness, historical warranty, imminence, esoteric presence) of communism. This does not mean, in Marx's case, that communism thereby ceases to be ideal, desirable, a visionary object; it remains that but in addition it also becomes an object of science, an emerging existent revealed to insight. Marx's overall endeavour is to fuse his vision and his insight, and this is achieved, as we argued in Chapter 4, in his conception of the dialectical unity of capitalism and communism. But this achievement, as it were, is only a momentary victory for Marx, and its gains cannot be consolidated: from this highest peak his thought again descends to the plane of a cosy dualism where the unity of the world and the idea is sometimes rhetorically asserted (though not, this time, dialectically *demonstrated*), sometimes explicitly denied. Overall, however, and excluding the dialectical climax to his thought, Marx's tendency is to *superimpose* his vision on his insight, endeavouring to redefine the results of his philosophical reflection and scientific investigations in ideal, visionary terms. This we have seen in such instances as the ideal definition of the proletariat as a 'non-class', the surreptitious transcendentalism of the materialist conception of history, the beautiful revolution, and the transvaluation of the 'first phase' of communism in the retrojective terms of the 'higher phase'. Right through his career as a writer, Marx emphatically and assertively affirms *this* world, but he tends to do this *as though* this world were another, ideal and visionary, world. It is this attempt that, in my view, fails in the last resort, and Marx's project is revealed as an unresolved dualism where the cracks are not filled but only pasted over with rhetoric. Vision and insight are fallen apart, what Marx's vision demands his insight cannot supply and what his insight validly reveals about the world goes against his vision.

But although our general conclusion concerning the central core of Marx's thought is thus critical, it is by no means argued in this study that Marx is altogether mistaken or confused either about the real, existing world or about the 'good society'. This is very far from being the case. It is Marx's *fusion* (whether achieved dialectically or attempted abstractly) that requires critical comment, but neither his insight nor his vision as such. Both, on the present interpretation, deserve full attention, and furthermore it can be argued – it *will* be argued, rudimentarily, in the closing part of this chapter – that the Marxist vision and the Marxist insight can be usefully, and in ways which might even be relevant to the actual political world, *co-ordinated*, as opposed to their being fused. First, however, it will be our task here to attempt to develop separately Marx's vision and Marx's insight, so as to yield us fully fledged themes or scenarios, which then can be further defined as particular expressions of larger, historical themes. There is, it might as well be admitted, a certain amount of imaginative and speculative construction in this developmental exercise, but (perhaps) the stimulus thus provided will outweigh the disadvantages occasioned by the overstepping of strict textual limits. It is, in any case, an open question as to when or where proper academic 'interpretation' should stop, and without wanting to digress into a discussion of methodology I may as well openly state my view, which is that the interpretation of academic texts (such as Marx's) ought not to have, in principle, any 'upper limit' at all. There is, undoubtedly, an absolute, hard, inevitable *beginning* or 'lower limit', viz. the texts. An interpreter must start from and must remain chiefly preoccupied with the texts he is studying. But it is only a part, and the least interesting part, of the job to clarify the 'meaning' of texts and to illuminate immediate 'contexts'. Over and above these tasks, an interpretation should also include a constructive characterization of the essential points revealed in analysis, and characterization in turn necessitates the *location* of these constructs in a suitable and more comprehensive intellectual whole. Only in this way is it possible to wrench the maximum amount of interest – information, illumination as well as inspiration – out of our texts. I must leave it to the reader to make his own judgment as to the manner in which and the extent to which this task is properly performed in these pages, but that it *is* the task that the present work should have carried out I have no doubt at all.

Marx's insight then, constructively developed, yields us what I have already described earlier as the *grand* theme. This signifies Marx's 'realistic' (in the colloquial, non-technical sense) attitude to the world, his attention properly focused on actual events and secular history, his understanding of communism as an *existential* phenomenon, a concern of actual, existing people and the fulfilment or satisfaction of worldly, secular aspirations. This is obviously not to say that Marx's insight, as opposed to his vision, is 'value-neutral'; there is no such animal in the universe of discourse we are considering here (and Marx didn't think that there was one either). Insight must also be expressive of a definite value-position, but the character of this value-position (as distinguished from the visionary stance) is that of approbation and confirmation: *this* is what is going on in the world and it is *good*. Communism understood in the grand idiom, therefore, connotes a resolutely this-worldly ethic, one which is based on objective knowledge, tied with inextricable conceptual links to the results of historical investigation, empirical observation and the 'scientific' conclusions drawn from these. Communism here then refers to the desirable, i.e. morally approved, aspects of the *real* world, to the world as movement, a future state of fulfilment which is as it were pushed forward by the past and is visibly, intelligibly emerging out of the actual historical present. It is because Marx, thinking in the grand manner, finds goodness in this moving world, that he tends to concentrate on *criticism*, on intellectual destruction (of fetishes, ideology, etc.), on the *negative* task of merely clearing away some of the obstacles facing the present, the world itself, retarding its progress. By contrast, a construction of the Marxist vision of communism yields us what I have been calling here the *sublime* theme. By this is meant Marx's 'idealistic' (again, in the general signification of this term) stance *vis à vis* the actual world, his half-hidden but nonetheless unmistakable *absolute* value-position, his moral disapprobation of the present. This is what is going on in the world, and it is *evil*. The sublime theme highlights Marx's revolutionary fervour, his wanting not to understand the world but 'to change it'. It also implies a constructive attitude, a definite and *selective* concern not only with the things that need changing and with destruction, but also with the things that will replace them. Communism conceived in the sublime idiom is expressive of a positive view of what is good and desirable, *independently* of the actual historical world. It is other-worldly, transcendental and, in opposition to the existentialism of the grand conception, it is *essentialist*, its departure being not the actual and diverse wishes and inclinations of existing human beings but the requirements of a true, universal, moral human nature. In terms of this idiom communism is not pushed forward by the past but on the contrary *it* pulls the present to its ultimate destination. Here then criticism is extended and is provided with a positive, substantive fulcrum.

So far, of course, we have not moved any great distance away from what has already and repeatedly been said about Marx's insight and vision in this book, and stated in these bare terms only, the two themes do not appear all that much different. The distinction between them may indeed appear too subtle, if not sophistical: the 'grand' and the 'sublime' seem complementary in the Marxist scheme of ideas, and, up to a point, they *are* of course complementary; no one would (or should) seriously want to assert that Marx was talking sheer nonsense all the time. But on further construction – through the drawing out of concealed implications and the disclosure of a certain elective affinity of ideas – the two themes will soon begin to display truly conflicting characters. Fully stated, they will be seen to embrace two entirely different, if not diametrically opposed, philosophies of history, society, politics, human values and satisfactions. Starting with the sublime perspective in Marx, we note first of all its transcendentalist, eschatological character: communism here is conceived as a state of being qualitatively, dimensionally different from past and present history. It constitutes a wholly new category, a novel plane of being and consciousness, defined in terms of its *difference* from the here and now. Present and past are heterogeneous, mundane, imperfect, essentially dark, in sharp contrast to this luminous, homogeneous, supra-historical future. Communism is the first and full humanization of mankind, the total revocation, transcendence of historical human estrangement. It creates a new, higher and morally perfect human being; there is now no conflict, no strife, no oppression, no domination, no important problem caused by ignorance or 'false consciousness'. The true needs of human beings are fully satisfied, people are now conscious and confident masters of nature, their own lives and their relationships. They are species-beings, many-sided 'rich social individuals' united in their essential activities and finding self-realization in acting out the character of the species, truly selfless, truly absorbed into their common defining humanity. This communism is the full realization of religion, a spiritual heaven; the vale of tears is transformed into the vale of joy, there is perfect concord and amity, infinite happiness. With full human rationality there is no longer any kind of 'determination' by the past, by historical forces; the continuous present determines itself. There is no politics, no government, separated offices of state or contending political parties; instead of class and class consciousness there is substantive, familial unity. The 'particular' character of human individuals is no longer a barrier to their elevation to species consciousness, but a direct means to it; now all understand and fully accept that the free development of each is the condition of universal species development. Human beings now engage their energies in actions which have a value in themselves, undertaken for their own sake; labour is no longer toil but artistic creation, life's prime want. In this communism there is no 'movement' which would disturb this blissful harmony; in so far as it has 'history', it is history sharply contrasted to what we recognize as such in the present world. For all serious intents and purposes, this is a *static* world, one which is lifted up from the vicissitudes of time. An *idyllic* picture of communism, a form of perfectly realized being, possessing moral finality, and characterized by the values of love and peace.

That all the above is contained in Marx's understanding of communism is scarcely deniable – and it will have been noted that my paraphrases and constructions come from the early as well as the mature texts. This idyllic picture, however, though present to the very end and manifested in Marx's rhetorical perorations in his hardest scientific treatises, is not always easily recognizable, for the simple and very relevant reason that it is accompanied by *another* picture, again to be gleaned from Marx's writings covering his entire intellectual career. This other picture, Marx's grand theme and the extension of his insight, presents communism as a thoroughly mundane, secular, historical entity. In this perspective communism appears not as an idyllic world, but as a thoroughly *exciting* world, a form of existence full of drama, dynamic turns and turbulence. Instead of transcendence here we have continuity with the present, instead of eschatological assurance there is constant dialectical restlessness, instead of moral perfection and finality here we encounter an infinite expanse of changes, particularities, the largest diversity. Communism here is the direct, conscious negation of religion, the resolute affirmation of this world, this heterogeneity, with all the hopes and desires but also the necessary frustrations and compromises that worldly existence entails. Communism is no heavenly nirvana but life writ large, pulsating, expanding, suffering, recovering, experiencing heady triumphs and crushing defeats. The operative ideals are not peace and love, but rather freedom, movement, change, assertiveness and above all struggle. The human relationship to nature continues unchanged, except that the eternal superiority of nature is now consciously recognized and heroically confronted. The unity of the species and the individual here means the enlargement, not the absorption, of the self and its identification as a fighting member with definite, absolute tasks; the struggle with nature must be waged and to be human means to be able and to want to partake. Association is demanded by a hostile universe which has to be contained, resisted, made use of, but which can never be conjured out of existence or humanly transvalued or reduced to irrelevance. Further, communism here is not seen as the transcendence of politics, but the most thoroughgoing *politicization* of human society; it is born not of lofty feelings but worldly demands, born of strife and bitterness, conceived in a spirit of anger and revenge, not forgiveness or world-weary renunciation. Communism is the destruction of bourgeois society and the ending of class exploitation, but it is also the continuation and further extension of the historical tasks that the bourgeois epoch and capitalism *began* performing but could not successfully bring to a conclusion. Communism is not the simple world of innocent, playful children, but the complex, infinitely organized world of hardened adults. There is no perfection but perfectibility, in the sense of unlimited expansion of undefinable directions. Human beings fight, work, live and die, and they thoroughly enjoy themselves; they have no 'true needs' which, once satisfied, will turn them into contented vegetables, but *ever-expanding* needs and wants;[1] they take full measure of all that life offers, accepting the consequences.

The sacred and profane images of communism stand opposed to each other, and *pace* glib words and assurances from Marx (or anybody else) they are not at all easy to reconcile and harmonize. It is the easiest thing in the world to *say* that the gods now dwell in the centre of the earth, that communism is both peace and freedom, idyll and excitement, the sublime transcendence of history and at the same time the grand carrying-on, expansion of history. Logic, experience, history and commonsense reflection all refute such impatient sleights of hand. The more fully expanded, the more the two scenarios are revealed in their *stark* disjunction. Sublime communism is cast in the image of the benign sage or scholar or prophet, the devoted lover of nature and mankind, young or old, with shining eyes and a clear, unwrinkled countenance. Grand communism has the face and figure of the *worker*, hard, wizened, bitter, determined, perspiring in effort and hardship but also in satisfaction. Communism solemnly worshipping at the altar of humanity and communism irreverently cursing at nature, communism with a faint sigh and communism with a resounding burp, communism having the fragrance of ambrosia and communism reeking of garlic and dripping. In terms of the well-known historical stereotypes, we might suggest that Marx's grand theme has a hard and flat *masculine* quality in that it highlights the virtues of assertion, struggle, conflict, competition, heroism and risk-taking. Communism in the sublime style, by contrast, has a soft and wavy *feminine* image, with its emphasis on love, peace, amicable union, sharing this with utopianism of all ages, conjuring up 'the golden age, the land flowing with milk and honey, the eternal feminine . . .'[2] Sublime communism has an air of the *country*, while grand communism expresses an unmistakably *city* atmosphere. Marx, of course, talks about the abolition of the distinction between town and country in communism, but this still leaves it open whether this expected new unity will have a predominantly urban or rural image – again, the two are by no means the same. In the country you find joy in hearing the birds sing and smelling hay and 'fishing in the afternoon'; the city is concentratedly human, it is life in the cobbled streets, in grime and closeness, in constant excitement, in many-sided human contact. This is where the *proletariat* is at home, whereas the country, with its 'unspoilt' idyllic romanticism, is home to declassé poets, contemplative scholars, nature-lovers – as well, of course, as to the bourgeoisie. Sublime communism is like a joyful, flower-bedecked procession, singing in unison and with celestial ecstasy; grand communism is like a noisy, boisterous, unruly carnival or bacchanalia where, as in Hegel's *Phenomenology of Spirit*, every guest is drunk. In the former we chant 'for he is a jolly good fellow', in the latter we shout 'the referee is a bastard'. And of course one could go on, almost *ad infinitum*, adding more and more, vividly contrasting, images to this short list. The contrasts might well seem exaggerated, but in fact very little has been added to what Marx and Engels are themselves asserting or intimating in various writings; the only thing we have done is to *separate* what in the Marxist texts are on the whole presented in a pleasingly *fused* shape. There the grand and sublime themes are not only intermeshed but, quite often, verbally identified, as though the two referred exactly to the same thing, 'communism', with no important problems involved whatsoever. Yet, as we have endeavoured to show in foregoing chapters, Marx also in some measure, and intermittently, shares the doubts and uncertainties which, when given full rein, result in this very same diverging pattern of antithetical images or idioms. Our concluding analytical separation of the two themes, in other words, could be said to have some justification in *latent* Marxist terms, too.

To show that there is an inner tension in Marx's concept of communism is one thing, to attempt to define the elements of this tense duality in exact terms and either to erect them into clear contrasting principles or assign them to various chunks within Marx's doctrine is quite another. Insight and vision, as we defined them in the first chapter, refer to approaches or optical directions, and even the two more generalized and ambitious notions we have elaborated in this chapter, the grand and the sublime themes in the Marxist understanding of communism, could not very well be sharpened into a pair of mutually exclusive and *logically* contradictory principles. Their contradiction, as shown above, is existential, not logical, and it can be revealed only by speculative construction. Marx has no two concepts of communism but *one* concept which is dualistic, thematically divided, and in so far as it is accepted (as I argue it should be) that communism is the central core of Marx's thought, it follows that there is only one 'Marxism', properly speaking (and not two, three or more), and it is, too, dualistic in essence, characterized by an inner tension, an underlying and ever-gnawing *problem*. In interpretation it is of course useful, even advisable, to note and fasten on to this problem, but any attempt to go further and abstract a pair of clearly, sharply opposed principles from Marx's thought is fraught with danger. It can be done, assuredly, and the result is often neat and attractive and at first glance valid, but this kind of well-meaning conceptual puritanism is bought at the price of distorting the texts and losing the particular flavour of Marx's doctrine. The conceptual opposites, commanding and stimulating at first in their analytical transparency, are revealed on closer examination to be little more than artificial labels hiding goods that do not fit the description placed on them. There is no 'philosophy' and 'myth' in Marx, though there is something that could well be described as 'philosophical myth' or 'mythical philosophy'; there is no clear principle of 'freedom' contrasted in Marx to a principle of 'determinism', though this abstract separation, too, looks good at first; in truth what can be presented as freedom is also deterministic (i.e. assuming a true human essence and moral determination) and what is described as determinism is also libertarian (i.e. issuing in what I called earlier 'indifferent' communism).[3] Marx's science of history and political economy is saturated with philosophical humanism, while his philosophical anthropology or 'concept of man' is heavily, determinedly historical and even materialistic. Marx's vision and Marx's insight are covering a terrain that is modulated and divided yet also continuous, resulting in a tension and a dualism that are noticeable and striking but which can never be neatly separated in cold analysis. Janus had two faces but he was one person.

We fare no better, it seems to me, if we attempt to locate the origins of Marx's dualism in the thought of his immediate predecessors or 'traditions of discourse' from which he adapted in the course of his intellectual development. That Marx's thought had a heterogeneous ancestry and that he himself was quite conscious of the need to integrate the various elements, derived from various sources, into his emerging unified doctrine, is of course entirely true and in fact the Number One commonplace in Marxist scholarship. That this kind of analysis into various different traditions and predecessors has some important, short-term elucidatory uses is also undeniable, e.g. understanding Marx's thought in terms of its constituent elements adapted from German idealist philosophy, French socialism and English political economy, or more observantly, noting the presence, in differing states of digestion, in Marx's thought of utopianism, anarchism, Jacobinism, millenarian thought, and the like; on a different level of exegesis, again, Marx's thought can usefully be analysed in terms of the influences coming from Hegel (first and foremost), Cieszkowski, Feuerbach, Hess,

Weitling, Engels, or Saint-Simon, Fourier, Owen, Cabet, Proudhon, Blanqui, or Smith, Ricardo, Hodgskin, Bray, etc., etc. But there are at least two very telling reasons why this kind of analysis would be inadequate for the purposes of the undertaking before us here. Firstly, immediate predecessors and traditions do shed a light on various determinate and (often) visible *chunks* of Marxist doctrine but not on the fundamental duality of Marx's *approach* which can be detected in *all* such observable chunks or ingredient elements. The duality of vision and insight in Marx's understanding of communism is to be found in his philosophical anthropology (Hegelian and Feuerbachian) as well as in his conception of history (Hegelian and Saint-Simonian), also in his theory of revolution (Blanquist) and likewise in his science of capital (Ricardian). The second reason is less obvious and consequently in need of greater emphasis here. Analysing Marx's thought with interpretive attention focused on these elements allegedly adapted by Marx from these immediate sources carries the inevitable danger of erecting these sources *themselves* into hard abstracts, unproblematic unitary wholes which then stand before us impervious to further analysis. To concentrate on the 'Hegelian' character of Marx's dialectic and notion of alienation, or the 'Feuerbachian' derivation of his concept of species-being, or the 'Ricardian' understanding in Marx of the fundamental laws of capitalist production, etc. means tacitly to *assume* that these and similar conceptual chunks, albeit possibly problematic in Marx, present no serious problems in Ricardo, Feuerbach and Hegel. And this would be a big, and in my opinion unhelpful and erroneous, assumption.

The fascinating thing to note is that we can never really, in an academically satisfying manner, stop at anything that is more than a 'convenient' point in this process of retrospective exegesis. Let us be clear and emphatic on this point: no perfect state of interpretive conclusion or 'rest' can be attained, however wide and far we are casting our net, either trying to unearth a number of lesser known (or perhaps hitherto entirely unknown) predecessors of Marx, or taking into our gaze a more comprehensive vista of contemporary discourse (e.g. Darwinian evolutionary theory), or delving further and further back into European intellectual history. Unity, clarity, simplicity will remain forever elusive: influences and derivations seem unproblematic only from a safe distance; on a closer look they all, and quite exasperatingly for the interpreter, take on the characteristics of the *explanandum* itself and become just as heterogeneous, untidy, unintegrated, full of holes, crevasses, unexpected pitfalls, internal tensions, dualisms. However, it could still I think be argued that *some* locational schema are better than others, and in this particular instance my argument would be that we can make (at least relatively) better sense of Marx's communism if we do not confine our attention to immediate predecessors and contemporary traditions but instead seek our concluding orientation in the *largest* appropriate canvas available, namely in the Western intellectual tradition as such, and with special attention focused on its own, chronologically distant but (as will be shown in a minute) conceptually alive, heterogeneous, dualistic origins.

There is one paramount consideration which justifies taking this audacious step and although I am quite convinced of the validity of the view expressed in it, here I can refer to it only in an extremely condensed, rudimentary form. This consideration is that *modern* social and political thought itself, the *broad* category under which Marxist doctrine is to be subsumed, is subject to the same *sort* of analytical-interpretive judgment as has been meted out to Marx in this study.[4] Obviously in one important sense Marx's understanding and concept of communism is unique: the insight and vision we have been talking about here, and the grand and sublime constructions of communism, belong to Marx's thought only. However, in another and right now more relevant sense it appears reasonable to argue that the peculiarly Marxist problem of communism is really a miniature reflection of the problem of the *good society* encountered in modern European thought, with special but by no means exclusive reference to its 'radical' component; indeed, it is this problem which in the deepest perspective *defines* modern thinking as such. From Renaissance and Reformation, to Enlightenment and Revolution, and through the incredible variety of searches for the good society, for peace, justice, happiness, prosperity, knowledge, progress, equality, freedom, brotherhood, human dignity and fulfilment, true democracy and true liberalism, modern thinking and movements are preoccupied in their sundry individual ways with the very same problem we have located in Marx: bringing, or attempting to bring, ideal and real together, presenting the gods in their dwelling place in the centre of the earth. Vision, the gods, the ideal of the good society, faith in human perfection, are inextricably tied up with insight, reason, the earth, the resolutely this-worldly, secular, science-oriented character of the mainstream in modern social and political speculation.[5] Modern thought concerns itself with this stimulating but also irritating duality of vision and insight, of the gods and the earth, but it cannot as such go beyond this concern to reach an ultimate and satisfactory conclusion, because modern thought *is* this duality.

To move towards a more adequate characterization of Marx's communism, therefore, it would appear advisable boldly to *skip* the modern age altogether, having grasped it as *one* and as being, in a manner of expression, 'Marx writ large', and to go back to the earliest known origins of our intellectual civilization, to those distant traditions which spawned over the centuries the exciting complex we recognize as the modern mind or spirit. What presents itself then as the finally most appropriate framework in which to explain the character and problem of communism in Marx is the original, primal duality of Western civilization, namely its *Hellenic* and *Judaeo-Christian* components.[6] Marx's communism is vision and insight brought together, it is the mutual interpenetration of the sublime and the grand themes, it is in the last analysis *Heaven* and *Hellas*. Now there is (obviously) nothing novel or original in taking this approach, and I would not even for a brief moment wish to take on the absurd pretence of having invented a brave new perspective on the problem and issues involved. Modernity in general, and Marxism in particular, have been treated by scores of eminent thinkers in terms of this very same historical duality, and even if I had the space or the erudition needed for the task there would be little point here in rehearsing these well-renowned, if not exactly platitudinous, arguments at any length. I shall therefore refer only to a few sources and in the briefest fashion possible. Where I would like to think though that the present study can at least make a plausible attempt at scoring (or let me put it even more circumspectly: nudging the giants of interpretative scholarship a little bit on their way, mapped out by themselves in the first instance) is on two counts. Firstly, the Hellenic-Judaic duality of Marx's thought is brought to bear here concentratedly on the problem of *communism* in Marx, and, having argued that communism is the central organizing concept of Marxist doctrine, in this concluding chapter the argument is rounded off by the contention that the *problem* of communism in Marx, i.e. its unresolved duality of insight and vision, is in fact *the* (equally 'unresolved') problem of the Hellenic and Judaic components of European civilization. Secondly, unlike the majority of interpretive endeavours in this field (those with which I am acquainted, at any rate), this study squarely argues that Marx's communism is dualistic and cannot be satisfactorily reduced *either* to vision *or* to insight; in this extended interpretive context this means to argue that Marx cannot be presented *either* as the greatest Jewish prophet of the modern age, the true Christ, the Deliverer and genuine upholder of Christian values – and nothing else, *or* as the first great social scientist of the modern age, the chief Enlightener, the true successor to Aristotle or Epicurus – and nothing else. It is customary for scholarly-minded critics of Marx to opt for the former line of unitary interpretation, while committed Marxist scholars, understandably, tend to go in for the latter. Both are right, up to a point, and both err in as much as they assert the unitariness, homogeneity of the subject of their interpretation. The point of Marx, of Marxist communism, is that it contains *both* components, in equal measure and mixed up in a truly fascinating kaleidoscope.

Crucial to an understanding of the difference between the Hellenic and Judaic traditions is their opposed attitude to history – and in Marx, as has already been indicated in earlier chapters, we can find both, joined up. As Bultmann described this difference: 'From Judaism comes the messianic belief depicted in advance by the Old Testament prophets – eschatology, that is, the doctrine of the last things, belief in the end of the world . . . This view sees history as a great drama, the end of which, according to both Jewish and primitive Christian conviction, is near at hand.'[7] To this we see opposed the Hellenic view: 'Historical movement is conceived of in the Greek world simply as cosmic movement, in which nothing new really happens in constantly new constellations, but always just the same. History here has no goal, and hence the Greek consideration of history is only interested in the past.' Bultmann goes on: 'In contrast to this, the *Jewish-Christian consideration of history* is orientated on the future, on the basis of which all the past is revealed as a unity, and as guided by a uniform plan of God.'[8] Or, as Eliade commented, in the context of the tragic pessimism of Greek philosophy and the myth of the eternal return, 'Judaism presents an innovation of the first importance. For Judaism, time has a beginning and will have an end. The idea of cyclic time is left behind. Yahweh no longer manifests himself in *cosmic time* (like the gods of other religions), but in a *historical time*, which is irreversible.'[9] And in the expression of Löwith: 'To the Greek thinkers a *philosophy* of history would have been a contradiction in terms. To them history was political history and, as such, the proper study of statesmen and historians. To the Jews and Christians, however, history was primarily a history of salvation and, as such, the proper concern of prophets, preachers, and teachers.'[10] Again, Collingwood argued that 'the Greek pursuit of the eternal was as eager as it was, precisely because the Greeks themselves had an unusually vivid sense of the temporal'.[11] For the Greeks 'thus history has a value, its teachings are useful for human life; simply because the rhythm of its changes is likely to repeat itself, similar antecedents leading to similar consequents'.[12] For the opposed tradition, as Collingwood sees it, history is the working out of God's purpose. 'Thus each human agent knows what he wants and pursues it, but he does not know why he wants it: the reason why he wants it is that God has caused him to want it in order to advance the process of realizing His purpose.'[13]

These accounts, of course, differ in many points of detail and emphasis but they do succeed in conjuring up a series of vivid contrasts which cannot help but stimulate students of the Marxist concept of communism. It is not too difficult, it seems to me (and not, as such, overly controversial), to detect in Marx's doctrine what these writers call the Judaeo-Christian tradition;[14] it is what I have called here Marx's 'vision' and of course it is dominant in most Marxist texts: human history is a unilinear process, a 'great drama' to be concluded in the near future, it is a story of salvation where agents' immediate and individual aspirations ('what the proletariat now wants') are secondary in importance to their supra-individual, transcendental determination ('what the proletariat is'), etc., etc. What is of much greater significance and interest to note, however, is that in addition to this Judaeo-Christian quality, and in hidden but nonetheless marked opposition to the modern secularized expression of this same messianic, prophetic, visionary, eschatological quality, we also find in Marx elements that are clearly derived from what these writers look upon as the Hellenic tradition. This, what I have called Marx's 'insight' in this study, is also present, though most often in a suppressed, subdued state, smothered under visionary rhetoric. For Marx history is not only a history of salvation, of the oppressed rising in ultimate victory over evil, but also *political* history, the story of *power*, of worldly excellence and leadership which marks out the succession of ruling groups in society, in a morally indifferent fashion. Furthermore, history has 'no goal' for Marx either, since it is self-determining: communism has no finality, no ideal to be realized, it is simply the present fully liberated, real movement, it means living human life to the full, with open consequences. Yahweh for Marx, to use Eliade's idiom, is also in 'cosmic time' as well as being in historical time, in as much as communism is seen as a *standpoint*, 'genuine resolution' understood as a set of philosophical principles and not as defining qualities. And lastly, as we could see especially in the previous chapter, Marx also shares the 'tragic pessimism' of the Greeks in relation to the everlasting 'realm of necessity', the cosmic framework which defines the limits of his 'optimistic' Judaeo-Christian vision. Löwith, therefore, goes wrong in my opinion and overshoots his mark, in asserting that Marx 'was a Jew of Old Testament stature' and that 'it is the old Jewish messianism and prophetism . . . and Jewish insistence on absolute righteousness which explain the idealistic basis of Marx's materialism'.[15] In Löwith's view, 'historical materialism is essentially, though secretly, a history of fulfilment and salvation in terms of social economy'.[16] Profound, though, as this observation is, it presents us with a severely truncated Marx only, and what is missing is Marx's insight, his great sense of reality. In a similarly one-sided manner, Eliade argues that 'Marx takes over and continues one of the great eschatological myths of the Asiatico-Mediterranean world – the redeeming role of the Just (the "chosen", the "anointed", the "innocent", the "messenger"; in our day, the proletariat), whose sufferings are destined to change the ontological status of the world'.[17] Again, it is not to be denied that Marx's thought does contain some elements of this eschatological myth, nor that this myth is an essential part of Marx's vision, but it would be a sorry travesty to adopt an interpretation of Marx couched in these terms only; it could only be done by disregarding the full evidence of the texts and it would result in a serious impoverishment of our understanding.[18]

Apart from this contrasting attitude to history to be found in the Judaic and Hellenic traditions, there are also a number of *substantive* views and images detectable in each, which connect up in a striking fashion with the sublime and grand themes of communism in Marx's thought. A brief reference to a few of these will be sufficient here. It is quite clear, for example, that the notions of 'alienation' and 'fetishism', connoting the deep immorality of present mundane existence, have their ultimate origin in Judaism, and they would make little sense in Hellenic thought (although the latter, certainly from the Stoics onwards, carries a certain amount of oriental influence). Consider, for example: 'Cursed be the man that maketh a graven and molten thing, the abomination of the Lord, the work of the hands of artificers, and shall put it in a secret place . . .' (Deuteronomy 27:15). Or 'Their land also is full of idols: they have adored the work of their own hands, which their own fingers have made' (Isaiah 2:28). Here we also find the image of perfect peace at the end of history: The Lord 'shall judge the Gentiles, and rebuke many people: and they shall turn their swords into ploughshares, and their spears into sickles; nation shall not lift up sword against nation, neither shall they be exercised any more to war' (Isaiah 2:4). Here there is transcendence of the present: 'For behold I create new heavens, and a new earth: and the former things shall not be in remembrance, and they shall not come upon the heart' (Isaiah 65:17). 'And I beheld a new heaven and a new earth; for the first heaven and the first earth were departed, and the sea is no more' (Apocalypse 21:1). Also the elevation of the lowly: 'And thy people shall be all just, they shall inherit the land for ever, the branch of my planting, the work of my hand to glorify me. The least shall become a thousand, and a little one a most strong nation: I the Lord will suddenly do this thing in its time' (Isaiah 60:21,22). 'To evangelize the poor he hath sent me, to proclaim to the captives release, and sight to the blind: to set the oppressed at liberty, to proclaim the acceptable year of the Lord' (Luke 4:17–19). 'Blessed are ye poor, for yours is the kingdom of God. Blessed are ye that hunger now, for ye shall have your fill. Blessed are ye that weep now, for ye shall laugh' (Luke 6:20–28). And: 'Thou wilt hear the desire of the needy. Thou wild strengthen their heart, thou wilt incline thine ear, So as to vindicate the fatherless and the oppressed, That earthly man may terrify no more' (Psalms, 9b, IV. 16–18). And so on. The sublime vision of communism, with its promise of a dimensional change in human consciousness and human relations, its expectation of fulfilment and happiness, its moral finality, its 'new earth', is already here, pristinely and poetically expressed in ancient texts that have ever since inspired the radical imagination, not excluding the most secular and seemingly worldly-oriented modern radical thinkers.

This is not, however, all that there is to Marx's communism; alternating and vying with its sublime visionary quality there is also its *genuinely* worldly orientation, its *grand* resignation to an ongoing, essentially changeless plane of human existence. For example, we find this worldly spirit, connoting human heroism but also the tragic quality of human life, in the famous myth of Prometheus the Titan who certainly acted as one chief source of inspiration for Marx throughout his life, starting from his bold inscription in the doctoral dissertation, quoting from Aeschylus.[19] In the legend Prometheus, having created man from earth and water, climbed the heavens with the aid of the goddess Athena and lit his torch at the chariot of the sun, bringing fire down to earth in order to benefit the human race and make them superior to other animals. Prometheus is harshly punished by Zeus and his liver is preyed on daily by an eagle, until he is rescued by Heracles. He then invents useful arts for the benefit of the human race, e.g. medicine and the domestication of animals. But, the point is, humans even then *remain* human and vulnerable, and Prometheus thus becomes a symbol not of human divinity and the great triumph against the gods (i.e. nature), but of continuing and defiant human struggle in the face of heavy odds. Not the divinity, but the dignity of man. In the words of a well-known historian of classical myths, 'this state of torment might have been brought to an end at any time by Prometheus, if he had been willing to submit to his oppressor . . . But that he disdained to do. He has therefore become the symbol of magnanimous endurance and unmerited suffering, and strength of will resisting oppression.'[20] And as another writer has expressed it: 'The darkness of Prometheus signifies precisely the deficiency of one who needs fire in order to achieve a more perfect form of being. In obtaining this higher form of being for man, Prometheus shows himself to be man's double, an eternal image of man's basically imperfect form of being.'[21] And: 'Thus it was Prometheus who made human existence *human*: man remained vulnerable, suffering, mortal like the animals, but he did not remain submissive like the animals. Liberated, he was still chained and punished; this was the existence to which Prometheus raised man.'[22] Thus Promethean defiance, suffering and struggle can then also be seen as the symbolic expression of communist society existing in an ever-expanding realm of natural necessity, organizing and regimenting itself for the task of struggle, born of strife and mutual enmity, peopled by humans whose character was fashioned in the present world and who are brutal rather than divine, whose selfishness must be catered for by a system of rewards and punishments, who produce for their needs under the direction of a governing will, a robust and tumultuous kind of communism, a society whose *only* important distinguishing mark from the present is its total *clarity* about the magnitude of the tasks eternally confronting the human race: humans can, with difficulty, danger and effort, learn some of the arts of the gods but they will never become gods themselves. Here still, as for Polybius, 'the only method of learning how to bear with dignity the vicissitudes of Fortune is to be reminded of the disasters suffered by others'.[23]

Besides the Promethean myth and perhaps even more relevantly, the classical Hellenic experience of social and political organization, and the ideals connected thereto, can also serve as a stimulating model for the construction of Marxist communism in the grand style. Here we have *political* consciousness, as contrasted to the *religious*, *legal* and *moralistic* attitude characterizing the Judaeo-Christian tradition. The Greek world is centred on the *city*, this is where Socrates conversed with his friends, whereas Jesus preached in the countryside, 'outside the real limits of Hellenistic civilization'.[24] There is, furthermore, a radical difference in the understanding of freedom as the supreme political good between the two traditions. Both Jew and Greek, as an historian has put it, 'desired political freedom; but, to the Greek, freedom was an end, expressed in the free self-governing community, making its own laws and worshipping what gods it pleased, while to the Jew it was a means, preventing interference with his devotion to a Law divinely given and unalterable by man, and to a God beside Whom there could be no other object of worship'.[25] The distinction drawn by the young Hegel between the Judaeo-Christian and the Hellenic worlds, though exaggerated and historically suspect, is also and especially apt for an appreciation of the differences between sublime and grand communism. The students of Socrates, as Hegel argued, 'were masters in their own right'. 'Moreover, who was a fisherman remained a fisherman, no one was compelled to leave his house and household...' By contrast, the teaching of Jesus concerned isolated individuals who had no interest for the state. When a disciple asked him, 'Master, what shall I do, in order to become perfect?', the answer was to sell his goods and distribute them among the poor. Whereas 'the friends of Socrates had developed their capacities in many directions, had been infused by the republican spirit which bestows more autonomy on every individual and makes it impossible for one with a good mind to become entirely dependent on another person...'[26] Hegel builds this distinction up to yield two contrasting types of groupings which he calls here the 'positive' and the 'philosophical' sect. 'To a sect which looks upon moral rules as positive commands belong peculiarities which are wholly foreign to a philosophical sect.' These positive rules 'are appropriate, permitted and purposeful in the context of a small group of co-religionists, but ... as soon as this group expands its faith and indeed becomes a state, [they] will in part no longer remain appropriate or, in another sense, will become actually unjust and oppressive'.[27] Whether or not this statement is fair to Socrates and Jesus, and to Greeks and Jews in general, it surely says something relevant and interesting about Marxist communism, about its unresolved duality of moral perfection and moral self-determination, religious and political quality, substantive character as a way of life and formal character as a set of relationships, its uniformity and its diversity, its intended transcendence of the present world and its simultaneous affirmation of it, communism as sublime peace and communism as grand tumult.

Both the self-justificatory rhetoric and the reality of ancient Hellenic politics and especially Greek 'democracy', the latter revealed by its contemporary and modern critics, yield us interesting pictures, and they *are* relevant to Marx's rhetoric as well as his understressed – and insightful – description of the *reality* of communism. Periclean Athens, this being the most obvious model, appears at first glance in very attractive colours indeed, with a high resemblance to Hegel's 'philosophical sect' and to Marx's communism as freedom and earthly human happiness. The picture we gain from the Funeral Oration of Pericles is one of a free *political* community, based on formal ties of law and allowing particular diversity. It is not, as such, a society of religious devotion, of substantive unity or of social equality; individuals find their own satisfaction in their own way. The laws here 'afford equal justice to all in their private differences . . .', 'class considerations not being allowed to interfere with merit; nor again does poverty bar the way . . .' 'The freedom which we enjoy in our government extends also to our ordinary life . . . we do not feel called upon to be angry with our neighbour for doing what he likes . . .', '. . . at Athens we live exactly as we please . . .' 'But all this ease in our private relations does not make us lawless as citizens. Against this fear is our chief safeguard, teaching us to obey the magistrates and the laws . . .'[28] If you take away the institution of slavery and other features connected with the ethnicity of Hellenic politics, this is also a veritable picture of modern proletarian democracy, of communism in the 'first phase', ordinary people irrespective of their individual inequalities being left to run their own lives, under the laws (governing will). But of course this is far from being an *adequate* picture or a *fair* picture, either of tumultuous Athens or of tumultuous Paris. *Implied* here is a society of open and generalized conflict, a world of movement and excitement and also a world of quarrelsome individual relations, the permanent possibility of oppression and injustice. As a modern writer has expressed it, with reference to Hegel's aforementioned Hellenic ideal (but with indirect relevance also to Marxist communism): 'Greece stands for a society in which there is no subjectivity and hence no representation. It stands for a society which contains conflict and injustice, but which is substantially free, and hence the conflict and injustice are transparent and intelligible.'[29] Is this not meaningful in a more contemporary context? Or consider the verdict of Thucydides on Periclean democracy: '... what was nominally a democracy became in [Pericles'] hands government by the first citizen. With his successors it was different. More on a level with one another, and each grasping at supremacy, they ended by committing even the conduct of state affairs to the whims of the multitude. This ... produced a host of blunders.'[30] Xenophon the Orator, also called the 'Old Oligarch', said this about democratic Athens: 'They celebrate more festivals than any other Greek city, during which there is even less possibility of transacting public business; they handle more public and private lawsuits and judicial investigations than the whole of the rest of mankind.'[31] For Polybius, 'not only does the whole spectacle of their disunity and bickering appear disgraceful' but 'the situation is positively dangerous for all those who are taking part in the same voyage'.[32] Again, in the words of a modern writer, concerning Athens: 'If corruption is a recurrent theme, power – its concentration, justification, exercise, effects and control – is nothing short of an obsession, palpable in contemporary thinking at all levels.'[33] And lastly let us take note of Brutus, founder of the Roman Republic (another powerful source of inspiration for modern radicalism), who according to the account of Livy did well not to give too much freedom to the populace who were then 'a rabble of vagrants, mostly runaways and refugees'. If they had had complete freedom of action, they would 'have set sail on the stormy sea of democratic politics, swayed by the gusts of popular eloquence and quarrelling for power with the governing class of a city which did not even belong to them, before any real sense of community had had time to grow. That sense – the only true patriotism – comes slowly and springs from the heart: it is founded upon respect for the family and love of the soil. Premature "liberty" of this kind would have been a disaster: we should have been torn to pieces by petty squabbles before we had ever reached political maturity ...'[34]

These are of course only scattered and random remarks brought in merely to provide additional illustration for our main concluding argument concerning the nature and the significance of the duality to be found in Marx's thought. Seemingly we may have moved a considerable distance away from Marx's highly complex notion of communism, but I would nevertheless contend that these historical illustrations do assist us in gaining the appropriate perspective for a judgment of this notion. Concerning the sublime theme in Marx's communism, or communism in the guise of heaven, our conclusion is straightforward: *this* communism is impossible. I shall not take any further trouble in attempting rationally to 'refute' it, as not only is the evidence of logic, common sense, history and political experience overwhelming, but here we also have the weighty arguments of Marx himself on our side, Marx who mercilessly ridiculed and dismissed utopian reveries and dreaming of any kind, and who would undoubtedly have repudiated this present 'sublime' construction of his own views, had he been *starkly* confronted with it. But he was not: in his own doctrines, as we can judge by reading and reflecting on the texts, communism in the guise of heaven was indeed present but *disguised* as earth, the sublime heavenly vision transplanted on to the plane of secular history. And, to reiterate, this sublime vision is not merely an adolescent stage in Marx's intellectual development but it is there right through to the end, surviving in Marx's rhetoric, in his heady perorations interlacing the sober texts on political economy, and also in *substantive* presentations, like the 'higher phase' of communism in *Critique of the Gotha Program*. Marx imposes his vision on his insight, he attempts to fuse the two in a visionary manner, reads absolutes into secular and (at first glance) morally indifferent events and processes. The picture he presents us of a society whose basic defining quality is 'genuine resolution' and/or where the free development of each is the condition of the free development of all is a very nice, very appealing, very attractive picture indeed, but alas it is nothing else than a picture. It is vision, imagination, artistic creation, inspiration, without a body. Nothing like this has ever existed on an appropriate scale in history, ancient or modern, Western or non-Western (of course there have been, are, and in all probability will be, 'positive sects', in the Hegelian sense, who preach and practice communism as a *religion*), and there is absolutely no reason to think that in future it will be any different. We are not gods and we dwell on earth – the rest is sheer fantasy. We can 'see' shining stars, picturesque clouds, the colourful rainbow in the distance, but what we *have* is craggy surfaces, shapeless pebbles and the fallen feathers of birds. However, the important point to make about Marx in our conclusion is not thus to pronounce critically on his vision of communism. The point is to criticize him for allowing his vision to obscure his insight, even though partially.

And here we come to the really difficult part of our undertaking, or that aspect of the Marxist doctrine where no straightforward judgment offers itself for use by the academic interpreter. The point concerns Marx's *insight* and what in this concluding chapter I have built up as the 'grand theme' in Marx's communism, or communism as Hellas. There are three remarks to be made, in an ascending order of difficulty and controversy. Firstly, as opposed to communism in the sublime style, grand communism is certainly *possible*. There is nothing utopian, nothing other-worldly about it. History furnishes numerous examples of societies organized for production under a governing will, egalitarian and meritocratic, even though in the past there were no instances displaying *all* the features contained in or connoted by the Marxist scenario. Primitive tribes may have been communistic without being rationally organized or meritocratic, ancient Sparta was regimented and (relatively) egalitarian without being organized for production, the Jesuits in Paraguay maintained a communistic organization without its being meritocratic, the modern Napoleonic and Bismarckian Empires (as Engels noted) were efficiently organized units, to some extent even socialistic in form but with an unemancipated working class, and so on; or we may note the reality of modern revolutions, notably 1792 and 1871 in Paris, which too displayed at least some of the requisite features. But of course there is no need to go back to the past for illustrations, as in this one (absolutely crucial) respect, it seems to me, we can and indeed ought to recognize the validity of Marx's *insight* or the *bare* terms of his science of political economy, divested of visionary embellishments: that is, communism is possible only in the modern age and it *assumes* conditions created by modern industry and capitalism. Marx's insight in this skeletal formulation simply means the recognition that there is a certain *direction* in modern industrial development and that capitalism, if it is to move in any way (and move it must), can only move in the direction of communism, though *not* communism as depicted in visionary terms but communism as a projection of existing, intelligible tendencies, communism in the *grand* style. It is not, as was made clear in the first chapter, part of our undertaking here to pronounce upon modern secular developments *after* Marx's time; our concern is here with Marx's texts only. But it would be overly pedantic, if not downright ridiculous and hypocritical, not to note at this point certain tendencies and developments, secular as well as ideological, in the modern age, since to me it is well-nigh incontrovertible that these in a large measure actually bear out Marx's projections or the validity of his insight. The lower phase of communism *exists*, it is a part or aspect of our socio-political reality in the modern world. Lest there be any misunderstanding: I am talking about a part of reality or a real tendency present in self-confessedly 'Marxist' regimes but by no means exclusive to them, while on the other hand concrete systems of society and regimes, Marxist or otherwise, have a *lot more* to them than this real tendency. I am not, in other words, in the business of knocking any particular government, country or movement as such.

Secondly then, it is as well to be clear about the actual moral character or quality of communism in this grand style, not as it would appear from an abstract moral point of view but as it is explicitly suggested by the terms of Marx's own doctrine. Hellas is essentially, irreducibly ambiguous; totally, unashamedly human, it has divine and diabolical strains woven into it, it thrills, excites, liberates, intoxicates but, in the last resort and left to itself, it is *terrible* reality. Why must this be so? I believe the answer lies in Marx's considerations themselves, in his actual terms and in the interpretive construction of his insight. Grand or Hellenic communism, as we made it clear earlier, is a construction of Marx's 'lower phase' and the latter, in turn, is the *objective* equivalent of 'crude communism' as described in Marx's *Manuscripts*. Crude communism is a system of generalized estrangement, the domination of undesirable moral qualities and forms of consciousness (e.g. greed, envy), the degradation of the human person (i.e. prostitution) and universal conflict, enmity. In Marx's later terminology this would be expressed as the continuation of the rule of *capital*, now not as a set of determinate relationships but as a haunting spiritual presence, not with one recognizable body but as a poisonous atmosphere pervading all relationships. This is no fairy-tale: as we could see in the previous chapter, the 'lower phase' has the terrible 'birth marks' of capitalism, it is *defined* in terms of qualities and relationships which are *exactly* like capitalist ones, with the exception of formal private ownership. But note here again that for Marx crude communism is not just like estrangement under capitalism, it is not just the extension of estrangement, but it is a *regression*, it is, morally speaking, *worse* than capitalism. Why *this* must be so is only inadequately spelt out in the *Manuscripts*, while obviously the *Critique of the Gotha Program* obscures the whole issue, presenting the 'first phase' as a clear, if only slight, moral improvement on capitalism. But, it seems to me, the important point about crude communism representing moral regression compared to capitalism proper is not its being connected to the 'unnatural simplicity' of workers. The point about it is that it is *only* capitalism, *only* estrangement, with all the historical stops and restraints pulled out. It is the pure spirit of capitalism under formally different and new institutions, a spirit that is now triumphantly roaming the land and no longer encumbered with the deadweight of tradition, it is open and naked and terrifying in its pervasiveness and arrogance. Scruples, religion, conscience, charity, family affection, the impartiality of the law, all the *hypocritical* and 'superstructural' paraphernalia are gone with the wind or withering away, swept aside by the great communist revolution, and only the bare essence of capitalism remains, its spirit. Yes, it is really an exciting and dynamic and merry world, like Athens and like Rome and like Paris, it is supercharged with materialism and greed and sex, envy and competitiveness and it is also, alas, dominated by power, corruption, suspicion, conflict, oppression.[35] It is the highest material civilization and technology, it is supremely 'rational' in dealing with nature but at the same time it is also a *brutalized* world. No one, as we put the point rhetorically earlier in this book, would really like to go to heaven, in so far as heaven is pictured as being *totally* different from the earth. But some of us at least (and some of the time) *would* like to enter Hellas. This is the price we have to pay.

Third and last, it seems to me that Marx's doctrine, taking insight and vision together, should then be construed as a *warning* about communism as well as being its advocacy. Marx's insight reveals the direction of capitalist development towards a form of society which is externally, organizationally (to some extent) different from capitalism but which still displays the humanly significant features of capitalism. Marx's vision is superimposed on this insight and presents the real in ideal terms. This attempt at conceptual identification is that which makes the communism of the real world more terrifying, more monstrous than it otherwise would be: that which is enduring and historically indefinite is thereby presented as a mere 'transition' which 'necessarily' leads to its overcoming. In this way we are *powerless* to tackle the reality of Hellas. Marx wants his vision to accomplish too much, to serve not only as the explanation of the world but to *be* the world. But this vision might also be employed in a different, if less ambitious way, a way which is ostensibly scorned by Marx but for which there are openings in the Marxist texts themselves. Marx, I believe, is essentially correct in arguing that 'communism is the riddle of history solved', but this contains a valid reference only to the over-arching, universal *principles* of morality and human conduct, to a superior philosophical vantage-point, but not to actual history as such. Communism in this sense, as indeed the 'genuine resolution' of the conflict among human beings and between humanity and nature, is the highest accolade of wisdom and goodness, it is among the fullest, most explicit formulations of moral truths we have encountered in history, it contains perhaps the only valid principles of good *government*. This is the point to grasp: there is no imminent change in human nature and consciousness, there is no transcendence of mundane reality, there is no impending disappearance or dissolution of law, state, power, inequality, structures and complexities, but there is the ever-present *problem* of good government, of dealing with human beings as they are: here Hellenic wisdom has to redeem Hellenic reality. That is to say, while fusion is a naive and dangerous fallacy, *infusion* might hold more promises: the vision of communism should not obscure the communism revealed by insight but instead should itself be brought to act as a check on it. Communism of the spirit over communism of the flesh. The task is to stem the tide, not to swell it, to contain and minimize the baneful effects of general estrangement and not to confound it by pretending that it doesn't exist or that it is only a passing phenomenon, not to proclaim the supersession of moral rules but to reassert morality, age-old but still valid and especially relevant in an age of chaos and turmoil, in the period of a *definitely* declining capitalism and equally definitely approaching communism, but communism of a very worldly, very scarred, conspicuously pedestrian character.

These are of course no more than vague hints, but further construction and speculation would be wholly beyond the confines of this book, already burdened as it is with sweeping pronouncements, particularly in this last chapter. Perhaps one closing remark should be added, which is that in spite of the uplifting quality and moral potential of the Marxist vision and in spite of the penetrating acumen contained in the Marxist insight, it is highly doubtful if Marx's doctrine of communism is really capable of development in the desirable moral direction, as mapped out above – and still meaningfully to be called 'Marxism'. Marx's thought is too heavily involved with the forlorn endeavour to fuse insight and vision to be able to extricate itself in the real world and demonstrate its overall coherence. Without God there is no religion, without communism (vision and insight fused together) there is no Marxism. You cannot have your God and eat it, you cannot entertain communism as *both* historical reality and the fulfilment of ideals. This is why, notwithstanding its intellectual excellence and epoch-making inspirational force, Marx's thought is obstinately confronted by communism as its chief *problem*.

Notes

Abbreviations

Karl Marx – Frederick Engels, *Collected Works*, 20 vols., London, Lawrence and Wishart, 1975 ff. (continuing). — *MECW*

Karl Marx – Friedrich Engels, *Werke*, 41 Bde, Berlin, Dietz Verlag, 1956 ff. — *MEW*

Karl Marx and Frederick Engels, *Selected Works in One Volume*, London, Lawrence and Wishart, 1980. — *MESW*

Marx – Engels, *Selected Correspondence*, Moscow, Progress Publishers, 1975. — *MESC*

Karl Marx, *Grundrisse der Kritik der politischen Ökonomie (Rohentwurf)*, Berlin, Dietz Verlag, 1953. — *GRU*

Karl Marx, *Grundrisse: Foundations of the Critique of Political Economy (Rough Draft)*, trans. by Martin Nicolaus, Harmondsworth, Penguin Books, 1973. — *Grundrisse*

Karl Marx, *Capital: a Critique of Political Economy*, 3 vols., trans. by Ben Fowkes, Harmondsworth, Penguin Books, 1976. — *Capital*

Karl Marx, *Theories of Surplus-Value*, 3 vols., trans. by Emile Burns, Moscow, Progress Publishers, 1969. — *TSV*

1 Communism and Marx's Thought

1. A.W. Wood, *Karl Marx*, London, Routledge and Kegan Paul, 1981, p.53.
2. ibid., p.54.
3. T.P. Burke, L. Crocker and L.H. Legters, eds., *Marxism and the Good Society*, Cambridge, C.U.P., 1981, p.4.

Notes

4. R.T. De George, 'A good society and the good society', ibid., p.11.
5. ibid., p.13.
6. Milan Kangrga, 'The Meaning of Marx's Philosophy', in M. Markovic and G. Petrovic, eds., *Praxis: Yugoslav Essays in the Philosophy and Methodology of the Social Sciences*, Dordrecht, Reidel, 1979, p.55.
7. *MECW*, 4, p.281.
8. *MECW*, 11, p.531.
9. *Grundrisse*, p.197.
10. ibid., p.460.
11. ibid., p.461.
12. ibid., p.515.
13. ibid., p.540.
14. *TSV*, 3, p.514.
15. *Capital*, 3, p.969.
16. ibid., p.368.
17. *TSV*, 3, p.259.
18. *Capital*, 3, p.911.
19. *TSV*, 3, p.429.
20. *MECW*, 6, p.497.
21. *Capital*, 1, p.171.
22. ibid., p.172.
23. ibid.
24. ibid., p.173.
25. ibid., p.99.
26. *MECW*, 6, p.144.
27. *MECW*, 10, p.127.
28. *MECW*, 3, p.227.
29. *MECW*, 11, p.106.
30. *MECW*, 14, p.656.
31. *TSV*, 3, p.498.
32. *MECW*, 6, p.178.
33. *MESC*, p.318.
34. *MESW*, p.181.
35. ibid., p.182.
36. *MECW*, 5, p.36.
37. ibid., p.37.
38. *MECW*, 6, p.166.
39. *MECW*, 5, p.89.
40. ibid., p.5.

2 Full Vision

1. *MECW*, 1, p.18.
2. ibid., p.423.
3. ibid., p.137.
4. *MECW*, 3, p.137.
5. *MECW*, 1, p.191.
6. ibid., p.155.
7. ibid., p.119.
8. ibid., p.192; *MEW*, 1, p.94.
9. ibid., p.193.
10. ibid., p.306.
11. ibid., p.265.
12. ibid., p.162; *MEW*, 1, p.58.
13. ibid., p.230.
14. ibid., p.256.
15. ibid., p.231.
16. ibid., p.235.
17. ibid., p.236.
18. ibid., p.301.
19. ibid., p.62.
20. ibid., p.73.
21. ibid., p.153.
22. ibid., p.163.
23. ibid., p.257.
24. ibid., p.309.
25. ibid., p.312.
26. ibid., p.363.
27. *MECW*, 3, p.29.
28. ibid., p.30.
29. ibid., p.31.
30. ibid.
31. ibid., p.159.
32. ibid., p.162.
33. ibid., p.163.
34. ibid., p.164.
35. ibid., p.167.
36. ibid., p.168.
37. ibid., p.117.
38. ibid., p.58.

39. ibid., p.204.
40. ibid., p.137.
41. ibid., p.198.
42. ibid., p.142.
43. ibid., p.144.
44. ibid., p.180.
45. ibid., p.181.
46. ibid., p.183.
47. ibid., p.186; *MEW*, 1, p.390.
48. ibid., p.187.
49. *MECW*, 1, p.220.
50. ibid., p.393.
51. ibid., p.394.
52. *MECW*, 3, p.143; *MEW*, 1, p.344.
53. ibid., p.279.
54. ibid., p.275.
55. ibid., p.274.
56. ibid., p.284.
57. ibid., p.307.
58. Engels' observations are shrewd, unromantic but not unsympathetic, and he goes as far as possible to reconcile these two extremes, workers who 'are deprived of all enjoyments except that of sexual indulgence and drunkenness' (*MECW*, 4, p.396) and who are yet 'far more humane in ordinary life than the bourgeois' (ibid., p.420). The bourgeoisie charge the worker with 'drunkenness, sexual irregularities, brutality, and disregard for the rights of property' (ibid., p.421), and not unjustly, Engels concedes, such conduct in his view following 'with relentless logic, with inevitable necessity out of the position of a class left to itself, with no means of making fitting use of its freedom' (ibid., p.423).
59. A few snippets, (obviously) cited out of context, but indicative of Marx's problem: '... this throng of people is made up of generations of stunted, short-lived and rapidly replaced human beings ...' (*Capital*, 1, p.380), '... manufacture ... converts the worker into a crippled monstrosity ...' (ibid., p.481), 'the worker ... now sells wife and child. He has become a slave-dealer ... working-class parents have assumed characteristics that are truly revolting and thoroughly like slave-dealing' (ibid., p.519 and n.), 'A great proportion of [printing workers] cannot read, and they are, as a rule, utter

savages and very extraordinary creatures . . . They become recruits for crime. Attempts to procure them employment elsewhere come to grief owing to their ignorance and brutality, their mental and bodily degradation' (ibid., p.615), 'The cleanly weeded land and the unclean human weeds of Lincolnshire are pole and counterpole of capitalist production' (ibid., p.853).

60. '. . . it is perverse stupidity to declare in one breath that the working classes are starved, degraded, and left in ignorance by a system which heaps victuals, education and refinement on the capitalist, and to assume in the next that the capitalist is a narrow, sordid scoundrel, and the working-man a high-minded, enlightened, magnanimous philanthropist . . .' G.B. Shaw, 'The Illusions of Socialism', (1896) *Shavian Tracts*, no. 4, The Shaw Society, London, 1956, p.14.
61. *MECW*, 3, p.313.
62. ibid., p.294.
63. ibid., p.295.
64. ibid., p.296.
65. ibid., p.297.
66. ibid., p.296.
67. ibid., p.299.
68. ibid., p.300.
69. ibid., p.302.
70. ibid., p.304.
71. ibid.
72. cf. J. van der Hoeven, *Karl Marx: the Roots of his Thought*, Assen/Amsterdam, Van Gorcum, 1976, pp.81–83.
73. *MECW*, 3, p.306.
74. ibid., p.342.
75. cf. '. . . it is knowledge, by which Marx means theoretical knowledge, that is the consummation of the whole historical process. Thus, Marx's debt to Hegel surfaces once again; for Hegel, also, the final consummation of history was the self-consciousness of a knowing mind' (van der Hoeven, op.cit., p.81). cf. also: 'This is pure Hegel, the reconcilation of "ought" and "is". It is also poetry and religion, albeit secularized and hidden in "scientific" terminology' (L.P. Wessell, Jr., *Karl Marx, Romantic Irony and the Proletariat*, Baton Rouge, Louisiana State University Press, 1979, p.145).
76. *MECW*, 3, p.297.
77. ibid., p.313.

3 Strengthening Insight

1. *MECW*, 5, p.49; *MEW*, 3, p.35.
2. *MECW*, 4, p.7.
3. ibid., p.85.
4. ibid., p.84; *MEW*, 2, p.89.
5. ibid., p.37; *MEW*, 2, p.38.
6. ibid.; *MEW*, 2, p.38.
7. cf. 'What basis has Marx for his belief that the consciousness of material need will have led, at the end of the revolutionary struggle, to a mass-scale perception of what is practically necessary, and hence to the success of the revolution? This trust can ultimately be explained only by Marx's tacit enfolding of the proletariat in the all too capacious cloak of the World Spirit, which *must* think and all at once realize what is reasonable . . .' (A. Wellmer, *Critical Theory of Society*, trans. by J. Cumming, New York, Herder and Herder, 1971, p.57).
8. *MECW*, 5, p.52.
9. ibid., p.53; *MEW*, 3, p.70 (N.B. in *MEW* this section is at the end of Part I).
10. ibid., p.88.
11. *MECW*, 6, p.212.
12. cf. 'The members of the redemptive class are, to be sure, positive entities, but only *qua* their finitude, *qua* their concrete interests. They become representatives of the whole society, not under the form of positivity, but under negativity' (Wessell, op. cit., p.191).
13. As correctly noted in a recent work, Marx could scarcely have equated the standpoint of communism with the 'proletarian point of view' as such, since for Marx the opinions as well as the experiences of workers are 'by definition confined to the surface of society', and 'as Marx himself says, many of the proletarian "yearnings" are really bourgeois in nature' (B. Parekh, *Marx's Theory of Ideology*, London, Croom Helm, 1981, p.174).
14. *MECW*, 4, p.113.
15. ibid., p.116.
16. *MECW*, 5, p.75.
17. ibid., p.292; *MEW*, 3, p.273.
18. ibid., p.379.
19. ibid., p.417; *MEW*, 3, p.402.

20. *MECW*, 6, p.144.
21. ibid., p.177.
22. *MECW*, 10, p.337.
23. cf. 'In *The German Ideology* communism is not understood as the definitive "solution to the riddle of history", the realization of the "species man", rather this conception, which reappears in degraded form in the theories of the "true socialists", is sharply criticized' (J. Zelenj, *The Logic of Marx*, trans. by T. Carver, Oxford, Blackwell, 1980, p.131). This is, of course, no more (but no less either) than a half-truth.
24. *MECW*, 5, p.31.
25. ibid., p.35; *MEW*, 3, p.25.
26. ibid., p.36.
27. ibid., p.37.
28. ibid., p.42.
29. For the 'Preface', see *MESW*, pp.180–84; see also Marx to P.A. Annenkov, 28 Dec. 1846, *MESC*, p.30.
30. *MECW*, 5, p.4.
31. *MECW*, 6, p.192. cf. also: 'Our desires and pleasures spring from society; we measure them, therefore, by society and not by the objects which serve for their satisfaction. Because they are of a social nature, they are of a relative nature' (*MECW*, 9, p.216).
32. cf. 'At first sight, it is true, this materialistic reduction of ideals to historical necessities very closely resembles an abandoning of ideals. But one only has to remember in which direction, according to Marx, the laws imposed by "material necessities" lead to the development of history, and one immediately realizes that, far from giving up his revolutionary ideals, Marx believes he has succeeded in preserving them by incorporating them into actual history' (N. Lobkowicz, *Theory and Practice: History of a Concept from Aristotle to Marx*, Notre Dame, University of Notre Dame Press, 1967, p.408).
33. cf. 'The difference between the present upheaval and all earlier ones lies in the very fact that man has at last found out the secret of this process of historical upheaval . . .' (*MECW*, 10, p.244).
34. It has been rightly emphasized recently that in terms of Marx's 'Old Testament' eschatology human practice reflecting human purposes is 'perhaps free to err in the short run' but must ultimately 'conform to divine or historical law' (M. Wolfson, *Marx: Economist, Philosopher, Jew: Steps in the Development*

of a Doctrine, London, Macmillan, 1982, p.196). A.W. Gouldner, however, is of the opinion that 'critical Marxism' and 'critique' 'require a value grounding for choice and for the criticism of what is, *but they do not actually have one*' (*The Two Marxisms: Contradictions and Anomalies in the Development of Theory*, London, Macmillan, 1980, p.55). The influence of Gouldner's extremely stimulating and masterly *opus* on this study is gratefully acknowledged here; I have, however, been led to conclusions considerably at variance with his.

35. *MECW*, 5, p.47; *MEW*, 3, p.33.
36. ibid., p.81.
37. ibid., p.256 n. (From a passage crossed out in the MS), *MEW*, 3, p.239.
38. *MECW*, 6, p.499.
39. ibid., p.506; *MEW*, 4, p.482.
40. It is probably true that Marx's scenario and actual examples in this passage were adapted from the utopian writer, Fourier. Shlomo Avineri, however, has rightly observed the *real* difference between Fourier and Marx: 'Fourier's is a regimented system, meticulously worked out in its details, totalitarian in its aspects. Marx's vision is, on the contrary, that of free human activity. Because of historical reasons one tends to identify the utopians with voluntarism and Marxism with a regulated society: it is, however, the other way round' ('Marx's vision of future society and the problem of utopianism', *Dissent*, 20, Summer, 1973, p.327).
41. cf. '. . . is there a human need for total fusion of particular motives with the common good? If so, is this need biological or cultural? What is the empirical evidence for its existence? Either the professedly scientific critique dogmatically assumes what it ought empirically to prove, or it surreptitiously relies on the philosophical critique set forth in *The Economic-Philosophic Manuscripts*' (S. Moore, *Marx on the Choice between Socialism and Communism*, Cambridge, Mass., Harvard University Press, 1980, p.24).
42. *MECW*, 4, p.130.
43. ibid., p.131; *MEW*, 2, p.138.
44. *MECW*, 5, p.438; *MEW*, 3, p.424.
45. *MECW*, 6, p.41.
46. ibid., p.45.
47. ibid., p.403.

48. ibid., p.132.
49. ibid., p.211.
50. ibid., p.212.
51. ibid., p.231.
52. ibid., p.333.
53. ibid., p.47.
54. ibid., p.56; *MEW*, 4, p.22.
55. *MECW*, 7, p.149.
56. *MECW*, 12, p.169.
57. *MECW*, 7, p.147.
58. ibid., p.152.
59. *MECW*, 9, p.453.
60. *MECW*, 10, p.282.
61. *MECW*, 12, p.446.
62. *MECW*, 10, p.281.
63. ibid., p.287; *MEW*, 7, p.254.

4 Fusion

1. *Grundrisse*, p.278.
2. *Capital*, 1, p.92.
3. ibid., p.929; *MEW*, 23, p.791.
4. ibid., p.103.
5. *MESC*, p.225.
6. *Capital*, 1, p.103; *MEW*, 23, p.28.
7. As correctly stated in a recent work: 'The concept of a science of history does not include the notion that historical events are predictable. In so far as Marx and Engels are concerned, the only predictable event is the final outcome: communism' (J.P. Miranda, *Marx against the Marxists: the Christian Humanism of Karl Marx*, trans. by J. Drury, London, SCM Press, 1980, p.82).
8. *MECW*, 6, p.494; *MEW*, 4, p.472.
9. As Gouldner rightly notes, scientific Marxism also returns to Hegel, 'to restore its sense of a comprehensive order' (Gouldner, op.cit., p.77). And: 'Hegel's objective idealism . . . postulates the very depersonalized structures and determinism

that Marx *retained* even while rejecting Hegel's idealism' (ibid., p.93).
10. *MECW*, 6, p.487.
11. ibid., p.489.
12. *MECW*, 13, p.58.
13. *Grundrisse*, pp.409–10; *GRU*, p.313.
14. ibid., p.161.
15. ibid., pp.487–88.
16. ibid., p.105.
17. ibid., p.162.
18. ibid., p.163.
19. ibid., p.325; *GRU*, p.231.
20. ibid., p.409.
21. ibid., p.540; *GRU*, p.438.
22. ibid., p.542.
23. ibid., p.244.
24. ibid., p.245.
25. ibid., p.287.
26. ibid., p.289.
27. ibid., p.325.
28. *Capital*, 3, p.567.
29. ibid., p.568; *MEW*, 25, p.453.
30. ibid., p.569; *MEW*, 25, p.454.
31. *MECW*, 6, p.487.
32. Again, as Gouldner rightly notes, the bourgeoisie for Marx is the 'paradigm of revolution *en permanence*' (Gouldner, op.cit., p.385).
33. *MECW*, 6, p.166.
34. *Grundrisse*, p.420.
35. ibid., p.421; *GRU*, p.324.
36. ibid., p.515.
37. ibid., p.541; *GRU*, p.440.
38. ibid., p.749.
39. *TSV*, 3, p.267.
40. *Grundrisse*, pp.831–32; *GRU*, p.716.
41. ibid., p.303; *TSV*, 3, p.296.
42. *Grundrisse*, p.258; *GRU*, p.169.
43. ibid., p.278.
44. ibid., p.271; *GRU*, p.183.
45. ibid., p.272.
46. ibid., p.361.

47. ibid., p.454.
48. ibid., p.461.
49. ibid., p.470; *GRU*, p.374.
50. ibid., p.706.
51. ibid., p.496; *GRU*, p.396.
52. It may be of some interest to note here that in Engels' famous speech at Marx's graveside in Highgate Cemetery (17 March 1883), where Marx is extolled as a 'man of science' and 'before all else a revolutionist' whose 'real mission' was the 'overthrow of capitalist society' and the 'liberation of the modern proletariat' (*MESW*, pp. 429–30), the terms, 'communism' and 'communist' do not occur at all.
53. There is a witty, and poignant, passage in a Circular Letter addressed by Marx and Engels to associates in Germany, with some relevance to the point made here: 'There I must really praise the "Communist" Miguel, who proves his unshakeable belief in the inevitable overthrow of capitalist society in the course of the next few hundred years by swindling for all he's worth, contributing his honest best to the crash of 1837 and so *really* doing something to bring about the collapse of the existing order' (*MESC*, pp.304–5).

5 Receding Vision

1. *Grundrisse*, p.110.
2. ibid., p.325.
3. ibid., p.410.
4. ibid., p.488.
5. ibid., p.706; *GRU*, p.594.
6. ibid., p.611; *GRU*, p.505.
7. ibid., p.712.
8. *MEW*, 18, p.160.
9. *Capital*, 1, p.133.
10. ibid., p.283.
11. ibid., p.290; *MEW*, 23, p.198.
12. *MESC*, p.196.
13. *Capital*, 3, p.959; *MEW*, 25, p.828.
14. *MEW*, 20, p.264. As was remarked in our Preface, a discussion of Engels' independent works is not part of this study, the exclusion being justified in terms of simplicity and

Notes

interpretive propriety; it in no way implies *as such* a denigratory view of Engels' works. However, at this point it may be appropriate to note briefly that the *visionary* element in Engels is more conspicuous and less successfully integrated with *insight* than in Marx; this could, I think, be quite easily documented by reference to Engels' earliest writings as well as to his later texts, such as *Anti-Dühring, The Origin of the Family*, 'On Authority', etc.
15. cf. 'the distinction between higher leisure activity and toilsome industrial labour suggests a resignation from the vision of the *EPM* [i.e. *Manuscripts*], in which communism achieves the true resolution of the conflict between freedom and necessity' (J.L. Loewenstein, *Marx against Marxism*, trans. by H. Drost, London, Routledge and Kegan Paul, 1980, p.87).
16. cf. Wellmer, op.cit., p.117.
17. *Capital*, 1, p.448; *MEW*, 23, p.350.
18. ibid., p.449.
19. *Capital*, 3, p.507; *MEW*, 25, p.397.
20. *MEW*, 20, p.262.
21. *Capital*, 2, p.390.
22. ibid., p.212.
23. *Capital*, 3, p.991.
24. *Capital*, 1, p.477.
25. *MEW*, 32, p.579.
26. From a letter, dated 22 February 1881: 'Perhaps you will refer me to the Paris Commune; but apart from the fact that this was merely the rising of a city under exceptional conditions, the majority of the Commune was by no means socialist, nor could it be' (*MESC*, p.318).
27. *MESW*, p.280.
28. ibid., p.283.
29. ibid., p.282.
30. ibid., p.287.
31. ibid., p.296.
32. ibid., p.287.
33. ibid., p.289.
34. ibid., p.296.
35. ibid., p.290.
36. ibid., p.291.
37. ibid., p.288.
38. ibid., p.291.

39. ibid.
40. ibid., p.295; cf. also *MESC*, p.249.
41. ibid., p.296.
42. Marx in his correspondence in 1871 consistently refers to the overall 'decency' of the Commune, matching his dominant tone in *Civil War in France*, and writes to Liebknecht for example: 'You must not believe a word of all the stuff you get to see in the papers about the internal events in Paris. It is all lies and deception. Never has the vileness of the bourgeois newspaper hacks displayed itself more splendidly' (*MESC*, p.246). For a rounded and more plausible picture, however, see for example A. Horne, *The Fall of Paris: the Siege and the Commune 1870–1871*, Harmondsworth, Penguin Books, 1981, esp. pp.384–428.
43. *MESW*, p.303.
44. ibid., p.304; *MEW*, 17, p.359.
45. *MEW*, 18, p.160.
46. *MESW*, p.317.
47. ibid., p.318.
48. ibid., p.319.
49. ibid., p.320.
50. ibid., p.319.
51. ibid., p.320; *MEW*, 19, p.21.
52. ibid., p.321; *MEW*, 19, p.21. N.B. Marx himself does not use the term 'lower phase' in the text. It is adopted here as a permissible paraphrase in order to highlight the contrast to the 'higher phase'.
53. cf. Loewenstein, op.cit., p.89.
54. In later Marxist parlance the term 'communism' is confined to denote Marx's higher phase, whereas the lower phase is called 'socialism'. We register essential agreement with Moore's conclusion: 'Marx adopted communism as a goal, on moral and philosophical grounds, before he adopted the approach of historical materialism and scientific socialism. For nearly forty years he fought the socialist alternative . . . Yet the principles of historical materialism and scientific socialism, applied to the present in order to predict the future, do not point beyond a socialist society. After the *Manifesto*, and to a greater degree after *Capital*, communism became for Marx a goal he was unwilling to abandon but unable to defend' (Moore, op.cit., p.89).

6 Heaven and Hellas

1. cf. P. Springborg, *The Problem of Human Needs and the Critique of Civilization*, London, Allen and Unwin, 1981, ch. 6 ff.
2. E. Bloch, *On Karl Marx*, New York, Herder and Herder, 1971, p.36.
3. See p.80 and ch. 3, n. 34.
4. As Gouldner notes, the tension in Marxism 'is part of the deep structure of Western thought that it shares' (Gouldner, op.cit., p.37).
5. 'Faith' and 'reason' are already united in early modern radical thought, including the perspective of radical Christians after the Reformation who sought, quite seriously, to establish the Kingdom of God on earth. See, for example, Engels' account of Thomas Münzer and the Anabaptists (*MECW*, 10, pp.421–22), or C. Hill, *The World Turned Upside Down: Radical Ideas During the English Revolution*, Harmondsworth, Penguin Books, 1975, ff.
6. This exercise itself, needless to say, is quite un-Marxian in spirit (in spite of the fact that latter-day Marxists show an increasing interest in this kind of patrimonial research). Marx and Engels heaped ridicule on the Israelite 'millennium' (*MECW*, 5, p.388) and on attempts to counterpose antiquity to Christianity, in the manner of 'German philosophers'. According to Marx and Engels, 'all these counterposings and historical constructions are of very little use' (ibid., p.144). Yes, if you can show that there is such a thing as the 'revolutionization of practice', etc.
7. R. Bultmann, *Essays Philosophical and Theological*, trans. by C.G. Greig, London, SCM Press, 1955, p.266.
8. ibid., p.267.
9. M. Eliade, *The Sacred and the Profane: the Nature of Religion*, trans. by W.R. Trask, New York, Harper and Row, 1959, p.110.
10. K. Löwith, *Meaning in History*, Chicago, University of Chicago Press, 1949, p.4.
11. R.G. Collingwood, *The Idea of History*, Oxford, O.U.P., 1948, p.22.
12. ibid., p.23.

13. ibid., p.48.
14. The term 'Judaeo-Christian' is a somewhat misleading simplification and those (like the present author) who claim no specialist acquaintance with theology have to heed Wolfson's warning: 'We should see that Judaism is not Christianity; the term "Judaeo-Christian" misleads more than it reveals by its frequent abuse as a means of dissolving Judaism into the dominant Christian culture' (Wolfson, op.cit., p.2). It is, of course, a matter of context, perspective and definition, and later Wolfson himself concedes: 'It is, of course, true that Old Testament conceptions had been embodied in the Evangelical religion in which Marx had been educated, and certainly the notion of history as the instrumentality of the Absolute was a leading Hegelian thesis, to which Marx acknowledged his indebtedness' (ibid., p.196). cf. also n.5. above.
15. Löwith, op.cit., p.44.
16. ibid., p.45.
17. Eliade, op.cit., p.206.
18. A few more examples: 'Having falsified Marx's message, Marxism addresses a materialistic message to addressees who do not exist and who therefore do not respond' (Miranda, op.cit., p.29). *Which* message? *Don't* they respond? 'It is not difficult to discern in Marx's later work – with its demand for righteousness, its stern judgment of existing society, its vision of a battle between Good and Evil, its hope of an absolute end to historical processes as we now know them – a return to the traditions of the Hebrew prophets' (S.S. Prawer, *Karl Marx and World Literature*, Oxford, O.U.P., 1978, p.287). Righteousness? Absolute end? ' "Marxist materialism" has indeed a theological telos. Only it is not God who is divine but *man*. Marxist man will transform himself into an "untroubled god" ' (Wessell, op.cit., p.100). Untroubled? 'Despite his intention, Marx had reached for the Jewish paradigm, and cast himself in the role of prophet' (Wolfson, op.cit. p.196). Prophet? Is that all? '. . . not only in its origin but in its very structure, Marx's philosophy has a profoundly theological character' (A. van Leeuwen, *Critique of Heaven*, London, Lutterworth Press, 1972, p.24). In its 'structure'? Which one? And now the other side. An eminent classical scholar compares Marx to Thucydides and sees Aristotle as a 'seminal influence' on Marx, as both started 'from the empirically

demonstrable premise' of social class (G.E.M. de Ste Croix, *The Class Struggle in the Ancient Greek World*, London, Duckworth, 1981, p.27, pp.55–6, p.74). A.W. Wood's emphasis on the historical, existential character of Marx's communism is a welcome corrective to the theological reading: '... it is a caricature both of Marx's conception of humanity and his vision of communist society to suppose that he either predicts or desires a static society in which all sources of human discontent have been done away with' (Wood, op.cit., p.26). The point is, of course, that neither the theological nor the historical story is an *exclusive* one.
19. *MECW*, 1, p.31. Marx, who had a very extensive knowledge of and absorbing interest in antiquity, had several other 'heroes' besides Prometheus, such as Epicurus, already noted, and Spartacus the slave leader whom Marx described in a letter to Engels as 'the most splendid fellow in the whole of ancient history' (*MESC*, p.115).
20. T. Bullfinch, *Myths of Greece and Rome* (1855), Harmondsworth, Penguin Books, 1981, p.42.
21. C. Kerenyi, *Prometheus: Archetypal Image of Human Existence*, trans. by R. Manheim, New York, Pantheon Books, 1963, p.78.
22. ibid., p.89.
23. Polybius, *The Rise of the Roman Empire*, trans. by I. Scott-Kilvert, Harmondsworth, Penguin Books, 1979, p.41.
24. De Ste Croix, op.cit., p.430.
25. W.W. Tarn, *Hellenistic Civilization*, London, Edward Arnold, 1952, p.226.
26. G.W.F. Hegel, *Werke*, Frankfurt a.M., Suhrkamp, 1971, Bd 1, p.52.
27. ibid., p.124.
28. Thucydides, *History of the Peloponnesian War*, trans. by R. Crawley, London, Dent, n.d. pp.121–23.
29. G. Rose, *Hegel Contra Sociology*, London, Athlone Press, 1981, p.125.
30. Thucydides, op.cit., p.142.
31. *Aristotle and Xenophon on Democracy and Oligarchy*, trans. and ed. by J.M. Moore, London, Chatto and Windus, 1975, p.45.
32. Polybius, op.cit., p.339.
33. J.K. Davies, *Democracy and Classical Greece*, Hassocks,

Harvester Press, 1978, p.116.
34. Livy, *The Early History of Rome* (Bks I–V, *The History of Rome from Its Foundations*), trans. by A. de Selincourt, Harmondsworth, Penguin Books, 1960, p.105.
35. In some ways this scenario resembles Gouldner's evocation of Marx's 'nightmare'; our construction is not so dramatic but perhaps it lies closer to the texts, i.e. to Marx's 'waking state'. For Marx in the 'nightmare', Gouldner suggests, 'socialism does not mean that the proletariat becomes the ruling class, but that the state becomes the dominant force . . . and its bureaucracy the new ruling class . . .' (Gouldner, op.cit., p.382). As readers of the *Manuscripts* will appreciate, however, there is no contradiction whatever between the proletariat becoming the ruling class and the state becoming the dominant force.

Index of Names

Index of Names

Althusser, L. 69, 94
Aristotle 29, 98, 174, 202n
Augustine, St 111
Avineri, S. 195n

Bakunin, M. 15, 150
Bernstein, E. 151
Blanc, L. 16, 92
Blanqui, L.A. 171
Bray, J.F. 15, 16, 67, 171
Bultmann, R. 174
Burke, E. 111

Cabet, E. 45, 171
Cieszkowski, A. von 170
Collingwood, R.G. 175
Croix, G.E.M. de Ste 203n

Darwin, C. 89
De George, R.T. 2, 3, 10
Dezamy, T. 45
Dühring, E. 150

Eastman, M. 6
Eliade, M. 174, 176
Engels, F. 2, 12, 17, 48, 60, 61, 62, 63, 66, 67, 72, 77, 78, 79, 89, 99, 106, 133, 140, 143, 169, 171, 183, 191n, 196n, 198n, 198n, 201n, 203n
Epicurus 29, 174, 203n

Feuerbach, L.A. 42, 46, 94, 170, 171

Fichte, J.G. 26, 29, 42
Fourier, C. 15, 130, 171, 195n

Goethe, J.W. 29
Gouldner, A.W. 195n, 196n, 197n, 204n

Hegel, G.W.F. 17, 23, 29, 34, 36, 38, 42, 43, 46, 47, 55, 89, 94, 95, 98, 110, 111, 115, 117, 128, 169, 170, 171, 179, 180, 181, 192n, 196n
Hess, M. 15, 52, 170
Hobbes, T. 111
Hodgskin, T. 15, 171
Hoeven, J. van der 192n

Jefferson, T. 36

Kant, I. 26, 28, 29, 42

Laplace, P.S. de 115
Lassalle, F. 15, 92
Leeuwen, A. van 202n
Lenin, V.I. 94
Liebknecht, W. 200n
List, F. 10
Livy 181
Lobkowicz, N. 194n
Loewenstein, J.L. 199n
Löwith, K. 174, 176
Lucretius 107

Index of Names

Mill, J.   17
Miranda, J.P.   196n, 202n
Moore, S.   195n
Morris, W.   15

Owen, R.   15, 171

Paine, T.   36
Parekh, B.   193n
Plato   111
Polybius   178, 181
Prawer, S.S.   202n
Proudhon, P-J.   15, 66, 69, 92, 150, 171

Ricardo, D.   12, 92, 171
Rousseau, J-J.   26, 30, 31, 36, 42, 111
Ruge, A.   45

Saint-Simon, H. de   15, 171

Schiller, F.   29
Shaw, G.B.   49, 192n
Smith, A.   130, 171
Spinoza, B. de   29
Stirner, M.   66, 67, 72

Thucydides   181, 202n

Vollmar, G. von   151

Weitling, W.   15, 45, 171
Wellmer, A.   193n
Wessell, L.P., Jr.   192n, 193n, 202n
Wolfson, M.   194n 202n
Wood, A.W.   1, 203n

Xenophon the Orator   181

Zelenj, J.   194n